The Far Right in the Balkans

MANCHESTER
1824

Manchester University Press

The Far Right in the Balkans

Věra Stojarová

Manchester University Press

Published by Manchester University Press
Altrincham Street, Manchester M1 7JA, UK
www.manchesteruniversitypress.co.uk

British Library Cataloguing-in-Publication Data is available

ISBN 978 1 5261 1702 1 *paperback*
ISBN 978 0 7190 8973 2 *hardback*

First published by Manchester University Press in hardback 2014

This edition first published 2017

The publisher has no responsibility for the persistence or accuracy of URLs for any external or third-party internet websites referred to in this book, and does not guarantee that any content on such websites is, or will remain, accurate or appropriate.

Printed by Lightning Source

Contents

Figures and tables

Figures

Tables

Acknowledgements

This text has been undertaken as part of the Research Project 'Transformation of political and social pluralism in modern Europe II' (MUNI/A/800/2011). An Andrew Mellon Fellowship undertaken at IWM in Wien in autumn 2009 also made possible realization of the text. I would like to thank Daniel Bochsler, Natalia Chirienco, Jakub Šedo, Embassy of Czech Republic in Tirana, Blendi Kajsiu, Goran Čular, Cas Mudde, Lubomír Kopeček, Miroslav Mareš, Institut für die Wissenschaften vom Menschen in Wien, János Mátyás Kovács, Andreea Maierean, Lisa Bjurwald, Kondrad Adenauer Stiftung in Macedonia, and all reviewers at Manchester University Press for their help in looking for sources or critical comments. Last but not least, I would like to thank Gafur and others who took care of Malý and Velký Myšur while I was writing this book.

Abbreviations

AN	National Alliance (*Alleanza nazionale*)
ANA	Albanian National Army
ANS	Action Front of National Socialists (*Aktionsfront Nationale Sozialisten*)
	Ataka National Union Attack (*Natsionalen Sayuz Ataka*)
BDF	Bulgarian Democratic Forum (*Bulgarski Demokraticheski Forum*)
BDSS	Bosniak Democratic Party of Sandžak (*Bošnjačka demokratska stranka Sandžaka*)
BiH	Bosnia and Herzegovina
BK	National Front (*Balli Kombëtar*)
BKDP	Bulgarian Christian Democratic Party (*Bulgarska Khristian Demokraticheska Partija*)
BNF	Bulgarian National Front (*Bulgarski Natsionalen Front*)
BNP	British National Party
BNPP	Bulgarian National Patriotic Party (*Bălgarska Natsionalna-Patriotichna Partiya*)
BNRP	Bulgarian National Radical Party (*Bulgarska National Radikalna Partija*)
BNS	Bulgarian National Union (*Bulgarski natsionalen sujuz*)
BZÖ	Alliance for the Future of Austria (*Bündnis Zukunft Ősterreich*)
CD	Centredemocrats (*Centrumdemokraten*)
CNSAS	National Commission for the Securitate Archives
CP'86	Centreparty 86 (*Centrumpartij'86*)
CSU	Christian Social Union (*Christlich-Soziale Union*)
DF	Danish People's Party (*Dansk Folkeparti*)
DN	National Democracy (*Democracia Nacional*)
DPA/PDSh	Democratic Party of the Albanians (*Demokratska Partija na Albancite/Partia Demokratike Shqiptarëve*)
DPS	Democratic Party of Socialist (*Demokratska Stranka Socijalista*)
DPS	Movement for Rights and Freedoms (*Dvizhenie za Prava i Svobodi/Hak ve Özgürlükler Hareketi*)
DSHV	Democratic Union of Croats in Vojvodina (*Demokratski Savez Hrvata u Vojvodini*)

DSS	Democratic Party of Serbia (*Demokratska Stranka Srbije*)
DUI/BDI	Democratic Union for Integration (*Demokratska Unija za Integracija/Bashkimi Demokratik për Integrim*)
DVT	Warriors of Tangra Movement (*Dvizhenie Voini na Tangra*)
DVU	German People's Union (*Deutsche Volksunion*)
ENF	European National Front
EPP	European People's Party
EPP–ED	European People's Party–European Democrats
EU	European Union
FAP	Free German Workers' Party (*Freiheitliche Deutsche Arbeiterpartei*)
FBKSH	Albanian Front of National Unification (*Fronti Për Bashkim Kombëtar Shqiptar*)
FI	Forward Italy (*Forza Italia*)
FIDESZ-MPS	Fidesz–Hungarian Civic Union (*Fidesz–Magyar Polgári Szövetség*)
FN	New Force (*Forza nuova*)
FPCD	Christian Democrat Popular Front (*Frontul Popular Creştin şi Democrat*)
FPÖ	Freedom Party of Austria (*Freiheitliche Partei Österreichs*)
FrP	Progress Party (*Fremskrittspartiet*)
GERB	Citizens for the European Development of Bulgaria (*Grazhdani za evropeysko razvitie na Balgariya*)
HB	Croatian Bloc (*Hrvatski blok*)
HB	People Unity (*Herri Batasuna*)
HČSP	Croatian Pure Party of the Right (*Hrvatska Čista Stranka Prava*)
HDZ	Croatian Democratic Union (*Hrvatska demokratska zajednica*)
HIP	Croatian True Revival (*Hrvatski Istinski Preporod*)
HNS	Croatian People's Party (*Hrvatska Narodna Stranka*)
HOS	Croatian Defence Forces (*Hrvatske Obrambene Snage*)
HPB	Croatian Right-Wing Brotherhood (*Hrvatsko Pravaško Bratstvo*)
HP–HPP	Croatian Right–Croatian Right-Wing Movement (*Hrvatski Pravaši–Hrvatski Pravaški Pokret*)
HSLS	Croatian Social Liberal Party (*Hrvatska socijalno liberalna stranka*)
HSP	Croatian Party of the Right (*Hrvatska Stranka Prava*)
HSP-1861	Croatian Party of the Right 1861 (*Hrvatska Stranka Prava-1861*)
HSS	Croatian Peasant Party (*Hrvatska seljačka stranka*)
HSU	Croatian Party of Pensioners (*Hrvatska stranka umirovljenika*)
HZDS	Movement for a Democratic Slovakia (*Hnutie za Demokratické Slovensko*)
ICTY	International Criminal Tribunal for the former Yugoslavia
IDS	Istrian Democratic Assembly (*Istarski demokratski sabor*)
ITP	International Third Position
	Jobbik Movement for a Better Hungary

KKCMTSH	National Liberation Front of Albanians (*Komitetit Kombëtar për Clirimin dhe Mbrojtjen e Tokave Shqiptare*)
KLA	Kosovo Liberation Army (*Ushtria Çlirimtare e Kosovës* or *UÇK*)
KPN-SN	Confederation for an Independent Poland (*Konfederacja Polski Niepodleglej*)
LDK	Democratic League of Kosovo (*Lidhja Demokratike e Kosovës*)
LDP	Liberal Democratic Party (*Liberalno demokratska partija*)
LDPR	Liberal Democratic Party of Russia (*Liberalno-Demokraticheskaye Partiya Rossii*)
LN	Northern League (*Lega Nord*)
LPR	League of Polish Families (*Liga Polskich Rodzin*)
LS	Liberal Party (*Liberalna stranka*)
LSI	Socialist Movement for Integration (*Lëvizja Socialiste për Intigrim*)
MAN	National Alliance (*Movimento de Acção Nacional*)
MEP	Member of the European Parliament
MER	Ecological Movement of Romania (*Miscarea Ecologista din Romania*)
MP	Member of the Parliament
NATO	North Atlantic Treaty Organization
ND	New Right (*Noua Dreaptă*)
NDH	Independent State of Croatia (*Nezavisna Država Hrvatska*)
NDSO	National Movement for the Salvation of the Fatherland (*Natsionalno Dvizhenie za Spasenie na Otechestvoto*)
NDSV	National Movement of Simeon II (*Nacionalno Dviženie Simeon II*)
NLA	National Liberation Army (*Ushtria Çlirimtare Kombëtare*)
NOP	Polish National Rebirth (*Narodowe Odrozenie Polski*)
NPD	National Democratic Party of Germany (*Nationaldemokratische Partei Deutschlands*)
NS	New Serbia (*Nova Srbija*)
NSD	New Serbian Democracy (*Nova Srpska Demokratija*)
ODS	Civic Democratic Party (*Občanská demokratická strana*)
ONR	National-Radical Camp (*Obóz Narodowo-Radikalny*)
PBDSh	Party for Democratic Action (*Partia për bashkimin demokratik të shqiptareve*)
PBKSh	Albanian National Unity Party (*Partia Bashkesia Kombetare Shqiptare*)
PD	Democratic Party (*Partidul Democrat*)
PD-L	Democratic Liberal Party (*Partidul Democrat-Liberal*)
PDSh	Democratic Party of Albania (*Partia Demokratike e Shqipërisë*)
PiS	Law and Justice (*Prawo i Spraviedliwość*)
PLL	Legality Movement Party (*Partia Lëvizja e Legalitetit*)
PNG–CD	New Generation Party–Christian Democratic (*Partidul Noua Generaţie–Creştin Democrat*)

PNŢCD	Christian-Democratic National Peasants' Party (*Partidul Naţional Ţărănesc Creştin Democrat*)
PR	Conservative Party (*Partidul Conservator*)
PRM	Greater Romania Party (*Partidul România Mare*)
PRSh	Albanian Republican Party (*Partia Republikane Shqiptarë*)
PSD	Social Democratic Party (*Partidul Social Demokrat*)
PSSh	Socialist Party of Albania (*Partia Socialiste e Shqipërisë*)
PUK	Party of National Unity (*Parti Unitet Kombëtar*)
PUNR	Party of Romanian National Unity (*Partidul Unităţii Naţionale a Românilor*)
PUPS	Party of United Pensioners of Serbia (*Partija ujedinjenih penzionera Srbije*)
PVV	Party for Freedom (*Partij voor de Vrijheid*)
PWN-PSN	Polish National Union (*Polska Wspólnota Narodowa-Polskie Stronnictwo Narodowe*)
REP	Republican Party (*Republikaner*)
RSK	Republika Srpska Krajina
SAO	Serbian autonomous region (*Srpska autonomna oblast*)
SD	Sweden Democrats (*Sverigedemokraterna*)
SDA	Party of Democratic Action (*Stranka Demokratske Akcije*)
SDP	Social Democratic Party (*Socijaldemokratska partija Hrvatske*)
SDPS	Social Democratic Party of Serbia (*Socijaldemokratska partija Srbije*)
SDS	Democratic Forces (*Sayuz na Demokratichnite Sili*)
SDSM	Social Democratic Union of Macedonia (*Socijaldemokratski Sojuz na Makedonija*)
SDSS	Independent Democratic Serbian Party (*Samostalna demokratska Srpska stranka*)
SN	National Front 'Fatherland' (*Stronnictwo Narodowe 'Ojczyzna'*)
SNS	Slovak National Party (*Slovenská národná strana*)
SNS	Serbian National Party (*Srpska narodna stranka*)
SNS	Serbian Progressive Party (*Srpska Napredna Stranka*)
SPO	Serbian Renewal Movement (*Srpski pokret obnove*)
SPS	Socialist Party of Serbia (*Socialistička partija Srbije*)
SRS	Serbian Radical Party (*Srpska Radikalna Stranka*)
SRS CG	Serbian Radical Party of Dr. Vojislav Šešelj
SSJ	Party of Serbian Unity (*Stranka Srpskog Jedinstva*)
SVM	Union of Vojvodina Hungarians (*Savez vojvođanskih Mađara*)
SVP	Swiss People's Party (*Schweizerische Volkspartei*)
UÇÇ	Liberation Army of Çameria (*Ushtria Çlirimtare e Çamërisë*)
UÇPMB	Liberation Army of Preševo, Medveđa and Bujanovac (*Ushtria Çlirimtare e Preshevës, Medvegjës dhe Bujanocit*)
UDMR	Democratic Union of Hungarians in Romania (*Uniunea Democrată Maghiară din România*)
UNDP	United Nations Development Programme

VB	Flemish Interest (*Vlaams Belang*)
VMRO	Internal Macedonian Revolutionary Organization (*Vutreshno-Makedonska Revolusionna Organizatsija*)
VMRO–DPMNE	Internal Macedonian Revolutionary Organization–Democratic Party for Macedonian National Unity (*Vnatrešna Makedonska Revolucionerna Organizacija–Demokratska Partija za Makedonsko Nacionalno Edinstvoe*)
VMRO–NP	VMRO–People's Party (*Vnatrešna Makedonska Revolucionerna Organizacija–Narodna Partija*)
WB	World Bank
WE	Western Europe
YUL	Yugoslavian Left (*Yugoslovenska levica*)
ZchN	Christian National Union (*Zjednoczenie Chrześcijańsko-Narodowe*)

1

Introduction

In the 1990s, the Balkan Peninsula was awash in nationalism resulting from the outbreak of wars in Croatia, Bosnia and Herzegovina and Kosovo. The attempt to create governments for the independent states saw mainstream parties become agents of nationalism; on the basis, they would probably best be classed as parties of the political Far Right. Ethnic extremism was already firmly entrenched in the region because of an ongoing process of nation and state building. The ethnic extremist Croatian Defence Forces (*Hrvatske Obrambene Snage*, HOS) was created as the armed wing of the Croatian Party of the Right (*Hrvatska Stranka Prava*, HSP), while the ethnic extremist Kosovo Liberation Army (KLA; *Ushtria Çlirimtare e Kosovës* or *UÇK*) spun off several political parties in Kosovo. With declarations of independence by many entities and the gradual moderation and Europeanization of the political space came successive changes in the polities and politics of the region, tempered by the consolidation of power by old formations of the political Far Right and the emergence of new ones.

In Western Europe (WE), the Far Right underwent a rebirth of sorts in the 1990s; since that time, the vote percentage garnered by some of these parties has followed a sinusoidal pattern showing peaks followed by downturns. Western and Central and Eastern European (CEE) parties currently (2009–2011) in ascent include the Party for Freedom (*Partij voor de Vrijheid*, PVV), which came in second in European Parliament elections in the Netherlands in 2009, boosting its share of MPs from nine members to twenty-four members in the 2010 parliamentary elections and playing a key role in forming the government; the Freedom Party of Austria (*Freiheitliche Partei Österreichs*, FPÖ) and the Alliance for the Future of Austria (*Bündnis Zukunft Österreich*, BZÖ), who strengthened their positions in the 2008 elections with a gain of fifty-five seats total (out of 183); the Norwegian Progress Party (*Fremskrittspartiet*, FrP), which came in second in the 2009 elections, gaining three more seats than the party had in the previous race (41 out of 169); the Hungarian Movement for a Better Hungary (*Jobbik*), which placed third in the 2009 EP elections; the Swiss People's Party (*Schweizerische Volkspartei*, SVP), which won the elections in 2007 with 29% and repeated its victory in 2011 (though with decrease to 26.6%); and, most recently, the Sweden Democrats (*Sverige-demokraterna*, SD), who crossed the minimum threshold in September 2010 and entered Parliament for the first time. By contrast, electoral gain for the Danish People's Party (*Dansk Folkeparti*, DF) recently declined slightly to 12.3% in the 2011 parliamentary elections[1]; the British National Party (BNP) remains on the margins of the political spectrum, with no representation in parliament. Far Right parties have either been accepted and integrated into coalition governments or lent the coalition its legislative support (the Austrian FPÖ, Danish DF) or follow the German containment example and remain excluded from coalition governments at all levels (Belgium and the Flemish Interest (*Vlaams Belang*, VB[2]). As Mudde remarks, convincing ideological arguments may be made for the inclusion of 'extremists' ('democracy is for all'), while there may exist strategic reasons for excluding them (e.g. party competition) (Mudde in Eatwell and Mudde 2004:199).

Many scholars have examined the reasons for the gain in popularity by parties of the Far Right in both Western and Eastern Europe. A comprehensive answer is offered by Piero Ignazi: 'Post-industrial development enforced a change in value priority and belief systems and loosened the linkages between organized interests and political parties'. Ignazi follows up by noting this development initially radicalized political discourse and polarize the party system and then bringing about a partisan/electoral dealignment: 'Such radi-calisation and polarisation enlarged the political space and created room for new and more radical right-wing parties; de-alignment contributed to creating an unbounded and novel electoral constituency open to new electoral/partisan offers'. He comes to the conclusion that these two processes set in motion conditions for a party breakthrough into the system (Ignazi 2003:203). Ignazi detects a change in the priority of values, in which people who no longer know how to retain their jobs in a fast-changing, globalized world revise their value system, bringing about a 'silent counterrevolution'. The term encompasses the rise of Green and post-materialist parties under generational, ecological and societal change.

With the rise of Far Right parties in Western Europe and the fall of the Iron Curtain, researchers began to set their sights on the countries of the former Eastern Bloc. In so doing, significant questions arose: is the Far Right political family of Eastern Europe comparable to that of Western Europe? Is the same set of ideological roots present? Do the strategies and tactics used by the Far Right differ in Eastern Europe? Is there contact between Far Right parties in Western and Eastern Europe? Authors whose focus had been on Far Right parties in Western Europe have turned their attention to the countries of Central Europe. The first books dealing with the topic of CEE (e.g. Mudde 2005, Backes *et al.* 2009) were accompanied by a slew of articles. The journal *Osteuropa* organized entire special issues dedicated to the parties of the Far Right. To date, authors have either focused solely on the Far Right in CEE (e.g. Segert 2002, Mudde 2002b); attempted to compare movements, organizations and parties between Western and Eastern Europe (e.g. Beichelt and Minkenberg 2002a, 2002b, Butterwegge 2002, Weichsel 2002, Dočekalová 2006a, 2006b, Minkenberg *et al.* 2006); or presented case studies of Far Right parties (e.g. Grün 2002).

The Balkan region is one where the performance of Far Right parties deserves close monitoring. This is true not only because of the intense nationalism which engulfed the region, resulting in a 10-day war in Slovenia and subsequent conflicts in Croatia, Bosnia and Herzegovina, Kosovo, Macedonia and south-eastern Serbia. It also bears monitoring because of the EU promise that the doors in Brussels will open once the area is ready and the change that might bring to the Far Right party family in the region in the form of altered positions, new strategies and tactics, or the rise of new party formations. Because there is no existing literature dealing with the Far Right phenomenon in the Balkans, the purpose of this text will be to serve as an introduction for research into Far Right political parties in the region. Its aim will be to depict the chief issues and problems which surround research into the Far Right party family in the Western and Eastern Balkans[3]; the aim is neither to arrive at a new definition of the Far Right nor to rationalize the term *Far Right* itself.[4] Rather, the primary intent is to offer a picture of the Balkans as a whole. Because nation and state building have been delayed in Bosnia and Herzegovina, Kosovo and Moldova (with concomitant delays in the development and consolidation of their party systems), these countries have not been included in the analysis. The political parties in these systems continue to demonstrate strong nationalist features, while party systems remain blurred and unconsolidated. Finally, Greece was not included because of great cultural and political differences[5]; negative cases (see Mahoney and Goertz 2004) are presented, as well, to test outcomes. The text will therefore take as its focus the politics of the Far Right in Croatia, Serbia, Montenegro, Macedonia, Albania, Bulgaria and Romania.

Answers to the following questions, among others, are sought:

1. Are the Far Right parties of the Balkans ideologically different or similar to Far Right parties in WE?
2. What are the principal factors behind the Far Right party successes in the countries in question? How is the rightmost section of the political spectrum in the Balkans structured, and how does this impact on the success of the Far Right party family in these countries? Is there only a single party, or are several such parties present? Why? Does the existence of a strong Right-wing party marginalize parties of the Far Right? Why are parties of the Far Right more successful in some countries than others? Why have Far Right parties sprung up in some countries but not others?

3. Do social attitudes and values conform in general terms to those of Far Right constituencies in Western Europe and CEE?
4. Are the laws relating to banning parties because of hate speech, nationalist propaganda or revisionism very different in use and practice from those of Western Europe?
5. What sort of strategy and tactics are employed by Far Right parties?
6. What is the impact of party leadership and organizational structure?
7. Do the parties have their own paramilitary structures?
8. Do parties on the Far Right cooperate with each other, or rather do they exhibit mutual hostility?

The first section of the text is devoted to terminology and conceptualization; the next chapter provides a brief overview of the historical legacy. This is followed by a section describing the politics of the Far Right in the countries under discussion, with the aim of selecting parties for further analysis, and a chapter devoted to the ideology of the parties. Chapters 6 and 7 clarify the context surrounding the cases under analysis. Chapter 8 then focuses on the people who vote for parties of the Far Right, and it also deals with the implementation in law. The succeeding chapter investigates internal party factors: the strategy of parties on the Far Right, their organization and leadership, role of paramilitary organizations[6] and international collaboration between parties. In each chapter, the analysis itself is preceded by a comparison with the Western European context; also touched on are similarities to Central and Eastern Europe.

There were two dilemmas to be faced in writing this volume. The first is that party systems in some Balkan countries have not yet consolidated. This makes it highly difficult to differentiate parties on the Left from parties on the Right, since they are constantly emerging and vanishing. Which parties, then, should be included? Shall we include only those which define themselves as parties of the Far Right? Doing so would obviously skip over a great number of parties who choose to define themselves in some other way. Shall we include only relevant parties (coalition/blackmail potential) or include all parties which have at some point been represented in parliament? What should be the criteria, then, for choosing a party? Since party name and transnational federations are of little use, parties might generally be chosen in accordance with the following criteria (Mudde 2007:33):

1. Parties which are generally described as being on the Far Right (extreme Right, radical Right, Right-wing populism, etc.) in the academic literature
2. Parties with historical predecessors on the Far Right
3. Parties with allied parties in neighbouring countries
4. Parties which expressly label themselves as being on the Far Right or whose name so indicates

5. Parties which collaborate with Far Right parties in Europe
6. Parties exhibiting a Far Right ideology

Were we to adopt the criterion of historical predecessors being present, the new anti-immigrant and other parties would be left out. If we were to analyse parties allied to other parties in neighbouring countries, we would need to exclude the HSP, among others, which would never cooperate with what it views as the antagonist Serbian Radical Party (*Srpska Radikalna Stranka,* SRS). If we chose to work with parties which have expressly labelled themselves as being on the Far Right, we would not be able to treat National Union Attack (*Natsionalen Sayuz Ataka,* Ataka), which does not wish to be labelled 'Far Right' party. If we decided to include parties which collaborate with Far Right parties in Europe, we would have to face up to the fact that cooperation among Far Right parties is scarce. And last but not least, ideology: first off, there's disagreement among scholars as to what the core features of Far Right parties are – as Mudde paraphrases Klaus von Beyme: 'We seem to know *who* they are even though we do not exactly know *what* they are' (Mudde 2000b:7). In order to avoid further confusion, a decision was taken to select parties generally described as being on the Far Right in the academic literature.[7]

In order to be selected for inclusion in the text, the party must have contested at least one primary election, either alone or in coalition, and gained a minimum of one parliamentary seat. In order to provide a view of the overall context, other parties not fulfilling the conditions noted above (by failing to be represented in parliament or lying close to, but not actually in, the Far Right family of parties) will be included in Chapter 4 which surveys Far Right politics in the region as a whole. Examined will be party systems in the Balkan countries which have been selected starting in 2000 and continuing until the present (2010). The year 2000 was selected as a starting point for the analysis in view of the continual process of state building in the region in the 1990s and the existence of undemocratic regimes in both Croatia and Serbia, for whom the significant Far Right categories of *system* and *anti-system* are irrelevant. This is because moderate parties were in the opposition, striving to change the undemocratic system. The overall context, however, is also presented, so data from the 1990s may appear, as well.

The analysis of each country includes more than one party whenever applicable. For the purpose of the analysis, the following parties were selected according to the above-mentioned criteria: HSP, SRS, Serbian Radical Party of Dr. Vojislav Šešelj (SRS CG), Internal Macedonian Revolutionary Organization–People's Party (*Vnatrešna Makedonska Revolucionerna Organizacija–Narodna Partija,* VMRO–NP), National Front (*Balli Kombëtar,* BK), (*Vutreshno-Makedonska Revolusionna Organizatsija,* VMRO), Ataka and Greater Romania Party (*Partidul România Mare,* PRM). The parties are treated as a single unit; significant factions are noted only when it is relevant to do so. The chief focus is on political parties. In order to provide an overview, a brief chapter about organizations has been added, since some of these might overlap or be closely related to the parties.

An analysis of party documents has been undertaken, including party programmes, manifestoes and internal party texts, accompanied by an assessment of party policy. A questionnaire was also adapted from the most recent book by Cas Mudde (Mudde 2007), translated into all the relevant local languages and circulated.[8] Attempts have also been made by the author at personal contact with the parties in the Balkans, albeit with little success. Most parties do not wish to communicate with the public and remain closed off from the outside world. This makes information difficult to get at. Internal party documents were used for Chapters 5 and 9. Secondary literature was then used as a supplementary source.

When dealing with party ideology, a qualitative approach to text analysis was chosen, despite critics who oppose its use as being subjective and overly interpretive and who prefer the exact results offered by quantitative analysis. But although such a quantitative analysis may provide objective results, it offers no overall context, something which is essential to grasp the issue under consideration. The choice was then made to choose a form of qualitative text analysis with an initial list of potentially relevant characteristics and features. This list was constructed on the basis of the ideological features noted in the literature focusing on Far Right parties and movements.

In most cases, the book by Czech political scientist Šedo (2007) and the Adam Carr Archive served as sources for election results up to the present. Terminology in the text has been adopted on the basis of party documents and should not be interpreted as meaning that the author takes sides with any of the rival parties. The author does not alter the transcription of names; differences in transcription may occur in direct quotations (đ vs. dj; ç vs. č or q). The Latin form is used when the language uses both Latin and Cyrillic script, while an English transcription is used for the languages which use only Cyrillic (e.g. Živkov vs. Zhivkov).

Notes

1 Danmarks Statistik. Resultater Folketingsvalg, 15.8.2011. Available online at www. dst.dk/valg/Valg1204271/valgopg/valgopgHL.htm.
2 In 2004, the Vlaams Blok (Flemish Block) was outlawed by a decision of the Court of Cassation which found the party in violation of laws against racism. A new party, Vlaams Belang, was formed afterwards.
3 'Western Balkans' is a political term brought into being by the EU. It encompasses all of the countries of the former Yugoslavia, minus Slovenia plus Albania. The term Eastern Balkans relates to Bulgaria and Romania.

4 For terminology and overall conceptualization, see Chapter 2.

5 Greece had struck out on the path towards transition two decades earlier, and the impact of entry into the European Community (EC) on Greek politics has been significant.

6 I am aware that paramilitary structures are not part of the normal political milieu and that the paramilitary structures of Far Right parties are not common in WE, though they may take on importance within the Balkan area (since the strong link between paramilitary organizations and political parties was characteristic for the Balkans in the 1990s) and, more specifically, regarding Far Right parties which have kept their own paramilitary structures in Eastern Europe (e.g. the Movement for a better Hungary (Jobbik) and the Magyar Garda, the National Party and the National Guard in the Czech Republic, or the New Right (*Noua Dreaptă,* ND) preserving its links to the New Generation Party–Christian Democratic (*Partidul Noua Generaţie–Creştin Democrat* (PNG–CD) in Romania).

7 I am aware of the tautology this implies, that is, what made scholars start talking about these parties in the first place. Nevertheless, such a criterion is valid for political science research and has been used by political scientists including Mudde (2000a).

8 The outcome, however, was less than satisfactory: twenty-six party questionnaires were sent out but only one was filled in and returned. The questionnaire focuses on the self-definition of the party in terms of ideology and asks about party leaders and membership, as well as international contacts. The author would like to give special thanks to Cas Mudde for his consent to use the questionnaire translated into local languages from his latest book, *Populist Radical Right Parties in Europe.*

2

Terminology and conceptualization

Political science offers no comprehensive theory which takes in all the phenomena of the Far Right. A great amount of scholarship has focused on the Far Right, with no consensus as to terminology or how the Far Right is to be conceptualized. This chapter is meant as an introduction to the literature on the Far Right aimed at choosing the terms and conceptualization to be employed throughout the book.

Pavla Dočekalová has divided approaches to the study of the Far Right into five main subgroups: the historical approach, the theory of post-material values, the socioeconomic approach and modernization theory, political opportunity structures and the character and nature of the parties (Dočekalová 2006a, 2006b:262). The historical approach regards the Far Right as a revival of Fascist movements from the interwar era, while the theory of post-material values sees the rise of the Far Right as a silent revolution against so-called post-material values (multiculturalism, solidarity, protection of the environment, gender issues, etc.) which are increasingly pervasive due to advancing living standards. This latter approach is not really pertinent to the Balkan region – if it is discussed, this is only due to pressure being brought by the international community that forces these issues to the forefront, despite the considerably lower standard of living in the Balkans vis-à-vis Western Europe (WE).[1]

The socioeconomic approach and modernization theory are based upon the structure of society and consider Far Right politics to be the outcome of rapid social and cultural change in modern societies, which try to head off these changes (Minkenberg 2002:337 cited from Dočekalová 2006a, 2006b:263). The rapid changes which have taken place in the Balkans relate to the socioeconomic and political transformation which occurred after the fall of the communist regimes as well as the redrawing of national boundaries. Rising social inequality and a lack of certitude contribute to elevating the position of the Far Right. The study of political opportunity structures focuses on the political continuum and the behaviour of political parties on both the Left and the Right, while the nature of the parties emphasizes the organization and strategy being used to attract public attention.

Terminology

Problems of conceptualization arise right at the outset in attempting to distinguish *Left* from *Right*. The greatest challenge comes in dealing with Serbian political parties, where *Right* and *Left* cannot be distinguished in any simple way. Rather, the chief division lies between those who support the previous Milošević regime and those who do not; in second place as a marker of political sympathies is the extent of authoritarian or nationalist values. The line between economic positions remains fuzzy. In this context, the Serbian Socialist Party may not simply be branded socialist or leftist, due to its policies in the 1990s and its pronounced nationalism (see, e.g., Bochsler in Stojarová and Emerson 2010:102–104). The same obtains in Albania, as well, where the main dividing line is support for the previous regime vs. the will to change, something which later metamorphosed into a personality-driven division between the two chief political parties. Also problematic is the Greater Romania Party (*Partidul România Mare*, PRM), which is usually branded Far Right despite the fact that its main reference point is the Ceauşescu regime, with a Left-wing orientation that is national, not international, and which stresses national values and national identity (see, e.g., Gallagher 2003).

The Right and Left poles of the political spectrum are most usually defined in socioeconomic terms. But in our context, most parties which have been branded Far Right cannot be situated at the Right end of the spectrum, since they either simply do not focus on economic issues or their economic views contain a mixture of both Left-wing and Right-wing values. Political philosophy is not much help either; it would identify the Right as being opposed to modernity. Mudde's conceptualization uses the delineation of Norberto Bobbio and defines Right as the belief in a natural order with inequalities, while the Left is seen as regarding significant inequalities between people as artificial and wanting to overcome them via active state involvement (Mudde 2007:26).

Issues with the terms *Right* and *Left*, however, are not the only terminological conundrum. Terminology related to the Far Right party family remains vague, and scholars have not been able to agree on common terms. Political parties and organizations of this type are labelled radical Right (e.g. Ramet 1999, Minkenberg 2008), extreme Right (e.g. Mudde 2000a, Mareš 2009), Right-wing extremist (Roberts 1994, Merkl and Weinberg 1997, Arzheimer and Carter 2006, Vejvodová 2008), neo-Fascist (Mammone 2009), neo-Nazi (Becker 1993), neo-populist (e.g. Betz and Immerfall 1998), anti-immigrant (e.g. Fennema 1997), ultraright or Far Right (e.g. Mareš 2003; Kopeček 2007), New Right (Schanovsky 1997), populist (Frölich-Steffen and Rensmann 2005) or Right populist (*Rechtspopulismus*, Hartleb in Backes and Jesse 2006, Urbat 2007). Anglo-Saxon academicians prefer the term radical Right to the terms

Far Right and extreme Right and as Sabrina Ramet remarks 'just as radical right politics may be understood as a particular incarnation of organized intolerance (within the limits specified), so too fascism should be understood as a subset of radical right politics, and Nazism as a subset of fascism' (Ramet 1999:4). The easiest terms to depict (where one might find some consensus) are probably the terms Neo-Nazism and Neo-Fascism, which are used for parties and groups that explicitly express a desire to restore the Third Reich (in the case of Neo-Fascism, the Italian Social Republic) or declare their historical ideological roots to lie in National Socialism (Fascism) (Mudde 2000b:11–12).

The term *anti-immigrant parties* is also sometimes used to describe the Far Right party family from the perspective of opposition to migration. Fennema develops a typology of anti-immigrant parties that runs from the general and diffuse (protest parties as non-revolutionary anti-system parties) to the specific (racist parties as single issue) and ideologically articulate (extreme Right as consisting of revolutionary anti-system parties). The concepts overlap, though they do allow for differentiation between varying types of anti-immigrant parties in WE. Protest parties are primarily the product of political alienation, racist parties arise from misgivings over national immigration policy, and extreme Right parties represent a political tradition in reaction to the spirit of international capitalism (Fennema 1997). The lack of immigration to the Balkan countries allows us to exclude *anti-immigrant parties* as being not relevant to our context.

The German academic world distinguishes quite strictly between the *radical and extreme Right*. In the German tradition, radicalism is represented by the term *verfassungswidrig* (unconstitutional). Extremism, by contrast, is represented by *verfassungsfeindlich* (hostile towards the constitution). Extremist parties may therefore be banned, since they do not wish to abide by the constitution of the German state; radical parties are not banned (cf. Mudde 2000b:12, Schanovsky 1997:15).[2] The extremes are therefore considered to be the ends of a linear distance but may also be imagined equally well to lie at the circumference of a circle or the surface of a sphere. A midpoint may be established lying equidistant to the extremes under a one-, two- or three-dimensional conceptualization. The principle of equidistance is inherent in the picture of the midpoint and the extremes (Backes 2007:245). In a similar way, Betz and Immerfall define Right-wing extremism on the basis of two core traits: 'the fundamental rejection of the democratic rules of the game, of individual liberty, and of the principle of individual equality and equal rights for all members of the political community, and their replacement by an authoritarian system in which rights are based on ascribed characteristics, such as race, ethnicity, or religion; and the acceptance, if not propagation, of violence as a necessary means to achieve political goals both at home and in foreign policy'. The authors then talk about contemporary Right-wing parties which stress their commitment to representative democracy and the constitutional order, abandoning ideological baggage that might sound too extremist (Betz and Immerfall 1998:3).[3]

A term which is currently in fashion regarding the radical Right is *populism*. The entire concept behind populism has not yet been fully articulated, or, better to say, no common consensus has evolved around the concept (cf. Panizza 2005). Its meaning remains indistinct. For a long period, populism was seen to be the development of policy in a way which was 'close to the public', playing on the emotions, prejudices and fear of people for its own purposes and offering apparently straightforward, clear solutions (Klein-Schubert: Populismus in Diers. (Hrsg). Das Politiklexikon, Bonn 1997, cited from Thieme 2007:13). Ionescu and Gellner remark on the relationship between populism and democracy: 'Populism is certainly compatible with democracy, though this is often denied. Insofar as it ignores the need for institutions and pluralism; insofar as it dislikes factionalism; insofar as it distorts social mechanisms which seem to it specialized and bureaucratic, it appears to undervalue the importance, and even the rights, of minorities, and to depart from rule of law' (Ionescu and Gellner 1970:247). Basically, there are two main approaches to the conceptualization of populism as summed up by de Raadt *et al.* (2004): under the first, populism is considered to be political tactics or strategy; the second approach is to understand populism instead as an ideology. de Raadt *et al.* emphasize the importance of the second approach; they consider populism to be an ideology based on 'hostility' to representative democracy. Construing populism as a kind of political style or tactics means to admit that all political parties can behave in a populist manner 'sometimes' (Mudde 2002a, based on de Raadt *et al.* 1998). Populism functions more as 'ideology without a world view' – it activates a very rigid form with variable content – 'anti-status-quo ideology' (Hartleb in Backes and Jesse 2006:208).

Canovan (1999) uses the minimalist definition and describes populism as a kind of revolt against established structures (elites) in the name of the people.[4] What type of revolt depends upon the target. According to Canovan, the revolt is led not only against those in power but also against the values of those elites. Populism is characterized by a single authority, that is, the people; it depends on populist rhetoric which speaks of a 'united people' or just 'our people'. In describing the populist political style, Canovan speaks of a simple, direct style. Populists formulate issues very simply and their solutions are straightforward and understandable to 'everyone'. Canovan then employs the important notion of the 'populist mood', which encompasses the emotions and enthusiasm of populists, populist efforts to bring in not only people naturally interested in politics, but also those who are ordinarily uninvolved. The populist mood has a revivalist flavour and, of course, the important factor of a charismatic leader. Populists personalize leadership very strongly, and the leader is the channel of communication with public. Paul Taggart found other characteristics which are bundled with populism and created a concept based on these features: hostility towards representative politics, established structures, elites and their values; the heartland and the people; a lack of core values; a sense of extreme crisis; the apolitical nature of populist movements; the role of a charismatic leader; and a chameleonic character (Taggart 2004:66–71).

Some authors consider the phenomenon of populism so unique that they feel compelled to assign it to a new party family. Susanne Frölich-Steffen and Lars Rensmann draw a distinction between Right extremist parties and national–populist parties, seeing these as disparate party families differentiated as in Table 2.1.

Similarly, Mudde distinguishes populist radical Right family parties not recognized as such (Croatian Democratic Union (*Hrvatska Demokratska Zajednica,* HDZ)) from non-populist radical Right parties that are often perceived as populist radical Right (e.g. Movement for a Democratic Slovakia (*Hnutie za Demokratické Slovensko,* HZDS)), with most of the latter belonging to a separate, somewhat overlapping, party family, that of neoliberal populism (e.g. Forward Italy (*Forza Italia,* FI)). Some parties within the conservative (e.g. Fidesz–Hungarian Civic Union (*Fidesz–Magyar Polgári Szövetség,* FIDESZ-MPS)), Czech Civic Democratic Party (*Občanská Demokratická Strana,* ODS) and (ethno) regionalist families (e.g. Basque People Unity (Herri Batasuna, HB)) show striking similarities to the populist radical Right but are not part of the populist radical Right family in their core ideology.

Table 2.1 A comparison of extreme Right and national–populist parties (Frölich-Steffen and Rensmann 2005:10)

	Right extremist parties	*National–populist parties*
System position	Anti-system	Anti-establishment–antietatism
Political strategies (politics)	Distinction from the system	Differentiation within and from the system, adaptation to the system
Form of ideology	Comprehensive anti-pluralism	Flexible, anti-pluralist effects
Ideology (policy)	Nationalist, racist	Homogenous will of the people against the ones above and the ones from outside
Polity–vision	Dictatorship, authoritarianism	Presidential democracy, debilitation of liberal constitution
Form of organization	Authoritarian, without inner-party democracy	Top-down parties, movement and personal antiparties, small inter-party democracy

Mudde then reminds us that such classifications have only temporary validity, since political parties and ideologies sometimes change over time – a number of parties that originated as populist radical Right parties have since transformed themselves into mostly conservative parties (e.g. HDZ) (Mudde 2007:58–59). Williams recognizes three categories: *parties with a fascist legacy* (e.g. the National Democrats in Germany), *entrepreneurs* (parties which saw opportunities in the political party system of the mid- to late 1980s and aggressively sought strategies to position themselves to take advantage of openings, e.g. the National Front in France in 1982–1983) and *bandwagoners* (watching expectantly as entrepreneurs reinvented politics on the fringes of the Right wing and then adopting a similar style, similar platforms and strategies for attracting support, e.g. the People's Party in Switzerland in 1992) (Williams 2006:56).

Some authors use the term populism to describe the more moderate parties of the extreme Right (Betz 1994, Betz and Immerfall 1998), while others add the adjective populist to describe a certain political style used by Right-wing extremist parties (Frölich-Steffen and Rensmann 2005) or see populism in terms of ideology (Mudde 2007). Betz uses the term *radical Right-wing populism* or *neo-populist parties,* Frölich-Steffen–Rensmann use the term *populist* or *national–populist parties,* while Mudde uses the term *populist radical Right parties.* While Frölich-Steffen–Rensmann do not distinguish between parties such as FI, Lijst Pim Fortuyn or Freedom Party of Austria (*Freiheitliche Partei Österreichs*, FPÖ) and label them all populist, Mudde disagrees and would label the former liberal populist and the latter populist radical Right.

Besides the above-mentioned terms and concepts, the term Far Right has also been used interchangeably to represent party family. The Czech researcher Miroslav Mareš modified the concept presented by Richard Stöss and proposed the term Far Right (ultraright) for both extreme Right and radical Right formations.

In terms of the terminology used in this text, the author would agree at this point with Mudde and Mareš that differentiation between the extreme Right and radical Right is essential. *Extreme parties* are therefore treated in this text as those positioned at the Right end of the Right–Left axis,[5] while *radical Right parties* would be positioned more to the centre and not stand in opposition to the constitution.

A common term is needed for both categories due to the fact that political parties change over time and their positions, ideology and strategies are not rigid. The term *Far Right* will accordingly be used from this point on for Right extremist as well as Right radical parties. I am aware of the fact that spatial analogies are of no use and that 'Far Right' is not a perfect term. But to be honest, I do not know of any political scientist who has come up with anything better. The term 'Far Right' simply encompasses both the radical and extreme

Far Left			Far Right	
Left extremism	Left radicalism	Democratic centre	Right radicalism	Right extremism
	A constitutionally delineated spectrum characterized by democratic order			

Figure 2.1 Model of extremism (Mareš 2003:33, modified model from Stöss, R. (1999) *Rechtsextremismus im vereinten Deutschland*, Bonn: Fridrich Ebert Stiftung, p. 18)

Right, and it is necessary that it do so: the positions of the parties remain fluid and shift in ideological space over time. I cannot use the term *radical Right* (as in Ramet 1999 or Minkenberg 2008), since this excludes the extreme Right; conversely, I cannot use *extreme Right* (as in Mudde 2000a) as it excludes the radical Right. The term *Right-wing extremist* (as used by Arzheimer and Carter 2006) also focuses more on the extreme Right than the radical Right. *Neo-Fascist* (Mammone 2009) excludes all Far Right parties lacking neo-Fascist roots. *Neo-Nazi* (Becker 1993) once again excludes all parties which are not neo-Nazi. *Neo-populist* (e.g. Betz and Immerfall 1998), *populist* (Frölich-Steffen and Rensmann 2005) and *Right populist* (*Rechtspopulismus*, Hartleb in Backes and Jesse 2006, Urbat 2007) are also unsuitable: populism may be inherent in Far Right parties but it is not their distinguishing feature vis-à-vis other parties. *Anti-immigrant* (Fennema 1997) is unsuitable to describe countries which lack immigration but do possess Far Right parties. And *New Right* (Schanovsky 1997) says nothing about the party family. For these reasons, it seems to me that *Far Right* is the most appropriate term, encompassing, as it does, both the extreme and radical Right. The adjective 'populist' will not be used in conjunction with extremism or radicalism, since populism (in terms of strategy and ideology both) is a characteristic which might be shared with political parties of other families and, conversely, parties on the Far Right may not be populist in nature. Other terms (radical Right, extreme Right, new Right, etc.) may appear in the text in citing authors who operate using these terms (Figure 2.1).

Conceptualization

The terminological confusion we have noted also leads to conceptual uncertainty. As Mudde points out, in twenty-six definitions of Right-wing extremism in the literature, no less than fifty-eight different features are mentioned at least once. Characteristics appearing in one form or another include nationalism, xenophobia, law and order, welfare chauvinism, racism, anti-Semitism, external exclusivity, internal homogenization, traditional values, westernophobia, revisionism, conspiracy, anti-globalization, populist antiparty sentiments and charismatic leadership (e.g. Betz 1994, Ignazi 1995, 1996, 2003, Merkl and Weinberg 1997, Ramet 1999, Mudde 2002a). Only five features are mentioned, in one form or another, by at least half of the authors: nationalism, racism, xenophobia, anti-democracy and the strong state (Mudde 1996:206 cited from Mudde 2004). Piero Ignazi, for example, suggests Far Right parties should be located at the right end of the Left–Right continuum, should have ideological links with Fascist mythology and principles and should hold values, have policies and put focus on issues which involve rejection (and delegitimization) of the democratic system. Ignazi then distinguishes between two groups: old traditional parties and new post-industrial parties. The first group retains some ties to the Fascist tradition; the second takes in new parties which have broken with the Fascist heritage (Ignazi 2003:33–34). Ignazi's position has nevertheless been questioned by some authors who note that, for example, the FPÖ, which Ignazi places within the second group, does not seek to delegitimize the regime (Kopeček 2007:284–285).

Kitschelt distinguishes between Fascism, welfare chauvinism, anti-statist populism and the new radical Right (Kitschelt 1995:35), while Minkenberg introduces a fourfold typology combining various aspects of other typologies in the literature following the modernization-theoretical argument, in that ideological variants may be identified by the concept of nation and exclusionary criteria may be applied. All four variants strongly seek internal homogeneity within the nation via the primary 'we group' – rejecting difference and plurality – and a populist anti-establishment political style. Minkenberg does not explicitly state the main differences between the four groups but instead assigns German and Polish political parties to the categories in order to arrive at an overall picture. For CEE, he further distinguishes between Fascist–autocratic and nationalist–communist ideologies, depending on the radical Right's point of reference vis-à-vis interwar Fascist and Right-wing authoritarian regimes or nationalist–communist regimes as they evolved, for example, in Ceauşescu's Romania (Minkenberg 2008:16, 105) (Table 2.2).

Minkenberg does not explain the differences in the four models but only assigns various parties to them and continues by suggesting two further categories for CEE, leading one to wonder whether the categorization might need enlarging to accommodate other countries or regions. The *religious fundamentalist Right* category is also problematic, since Poland is a unique case and it would likely be difficult to find other representatives of this group in other European countries.[6] The categories to which some countries have been assigned under the typology would also seem to be controversial: Samoobrana is a populist but not rightist party (rather anarcho-syndicalist-agrarian). Christian

Table 2.2 Major actors of the radical Right: Germany and Poland
(since the 1980s) (Minkenberg 2008:17)

	Party/campaign organization	Social movement organization	Subcultural milieu
Extremist Right	NPD	ANS/FAP, NPD	Neo-Nazis
(Fascist–autocratic	DVU	NOP, ONR	Kamaradschaften
Right)		PWN-PSN	
Ethno-centrist Right	Republikaner	NPD/DVU	Skinheads
(xenophobic Right)	KPN-SN	PWN-PSN	
Populist Right	Samoobrona	Zwiazek Samoobrona	
Religious-fundamentalist Right	ZchN, LPR	Radio Maryja	

Abbreviations/translations: ANS, Aktionsfront Nationale Sozialisten (Action Front of National Socialists); DVU, Deutsche Volksunion (German People's Union); FAP, Freiheitliche Deutsche Arbeiterpartei (Free German Workers' Party); KPN-SN, Konfederacja Polski Niepodleglej (Confederation for an Independent Poland); LPR, Liga Polskich Rodzin (League of Polish Families); ONR, Obóz Narodowo-Radikalny (National-Radical Camp); NOP, Narodowe Odrozenie Polski (Polish National Rebirth); NPD, Nationaldemokratische Partei Deutschlands (National Democratic Party of Germany); PWN-PSN, Polska Wspólnota Narodowa-Polskie Stronnictwo Narodowe (Polish National Union); SN, Stronnictwo Narodowe 'Ojczyzna' (National Front 'Fatherland'); ZchN, Zjednoczenie Chrześcijańsko Narodowe (Christian National Union).

National Union (*Zjednoczenie Chrześcijańsko Narodowe*, ZchN) is perceived by some scholars as a party of the conservative Right.

What, then, forms the core of the Far Right political party family? Traditional values may probably be excluded, since these are characteristic of the conservative party family, as well. Caution must be shown with regard to the Balkans, where the conservative social discourse is opposed to same-sex marriage, euthanasia and abortion and where the protection of traditional values is on the programme of most political parties (Milardović *et al.* 2007:43–61). The anti-globalization typical of the Far Left does not seem to be a principal concern either. Charismatic leadership cuts across party family lines and does not seem to be a core value of the Far Right party family. Nor does anti-immigration policy seem to be a defining characteristic – the immigration issue may be salient for WE but it is not present in the Balkans. Probably the most developed conceptualization is that of the Belgian political scientist Cas Mudde. In his book *The Ideology of the Extreme Right*, he concludes that *extreme Right parties* share an ideological core of *nationalism, welfare chauvinism, law and order and xenophobia.* The main ideological distinction within this extreme Right family is then between the *ethnic* and *state nationalist* parties, in which the former subgroup combines an extreme Right core with an ethnic nationalist and ethno-pluralist outlook and the congruence of the state and ethnic community is brought about by both internal homogenization and external exclusivity. The state nationalist party subgroup is so named because it has a state nationalist outlook. This defines the group on the basis of a civic (more flexible) criterion, which accepts all people born within a particular country or who wish to be naturalized into the group. The congruence of state and nation is to be brought about exclusively via internal homogenization and, more concretely, by a choice between assimilation and repatriation. Mudde subsequently concludes that the Flemish Interest (*Vlaams Belang*, VB) and Dutch Centreparty 86 (*Centrumpartij*'86, CP'86) are ethnic extreme Right parties, the Dutch Centredemocrats (*Centrumdemokraten*, CD) is a state extreme Right party, and the German People's Union (*Deutsche Volksunion*, DVU) and Republican Party (*Republikaner*, REP) cannot be categorized in either of these two subgroups because of the vagueness of their programmes (Mudde 2000a:181–182).

But seven years later, Mudde revised his conceptualization, striving for a minimalist definition. He concluded that 'extreme Right' is not an appropriate label for the party family, suggesting rather 'populist radical Right'. Mudde argues that the radical Right is the primary term in the conceptualization and that populism was missing in the older terminology despite its importance. *The populist radical parties* are then defined as political parties with a core ideology that is a combination of *nativism, authoritarianism and populism*; nativism is defined as an ideology which holds that states should be inhabited exclusively by members of the native group ('the nation') and that non-native elements (persons and ideas) fundamentally threaten the homogeneity of the nation-state. Mudde draws on the American tradition of including a nativism – nativist dimension which embodies a combination of nationalism and xenophobia. He then defines authoritarianism as the belief in a strictly ordered society in which infringements on authority are to be severely punished. Authoritarianism includes law and order and 'punitive conventional moralism'. Mudde then defines populism as an ideological feature and not merely a political style. He draws chiefly on the conceptualization of Canovan and regards populism as a thin, centred ideology that sees society as being ultimately separated into two homogeneous, antagonistic groups, 'the pure people' vs. 'the corrupt elite', arguing that politics should be an expression of the *volonté générale* (general will) of the people. In the populist democracy, nothing is more important than the 'general will' of the people, not even human rights or constitutional guarantees (Mudde 2007:20–31).

The second concept of Cas Mudde somewhat revises the first, since nativism could encompass nationalism, welfare chauvinism and xenophobia, while law and order may be considered an authoritarianism feature – the punitive conventional moralism would, in this case, bundle the former concept together with the inclusion of populism in terms of ideology. Since populism may cut across party family lines (or at least might be typical for parties in opposition), we take the first concept to be more suitable for application. This brings us to an understanding of the Far Right as consisting of political parties whose core ideology combines nationalism, xenophobia, law and order and welfare chauvinism.

The core feature under all definitions seems to be nationalism. We should therefore define what nationalism is before proceeding with our analysis of ideology in party documents. Cas Mudde first delineates the border between nationalism and ethno-regionalism and claims 'regionalism is best limited to groups that call for more autonomy of a region within a larger state structure' while interpreting 'nationalism in a holistic way including both civic and ethnic elements' (Mudde 2007:17, 29). For purposes of this study, we take *nationalism* to be internal homogenization (by assimilation, genocide, expulsion, separatism) accompanied by external exclusivity (bringing all members of the nation within the territory of the state by means of territorial expansion, e.g. population transfer). In other words, nationalist parties are those parties which seek to create a monocultural state within ethnic borders.

Xenophobia usually is defined as feelings of fear, hate or hostility directed towards ethnic foreigners. *Law and order* refers to the quest for order and authority. A demand is also made for swift and sure punishment of those who break the rules. Solitary confinement must be served under harsh conditions; the ultimate penalty is capital punishment (Mudde 1995:213–217). *Welfare chauvinism* refers to the notion that money should be used for the interests of one's own ethnic group and that jobs should be taken only by fellow nationals. Any foreign element, including immigrants, asylum seekers and even the European Union (EU) are portrayed as taking much-needed money from one's own nationals. A corollary demand is that more money should be invested in upholding a decent level of welfare and employment for one's own people (Mudde 2000a:50).

Related terms include *ethnic (ethno-territorial) extremism* which, unlike ethno-regionalism, promotes separatism/irredentism, claims cultural and political exclusivity and uses violence to achieve its goals (Mareš 2001:1) and *ethno-centrism* which is seen in the German tradition as a specific form of xenophobia defined as holding one's own Volk or nation to be superior to all others (Mudde 1995:213). Another term related to the Far Right and very often defined vaguely is *racism*. It is usually defined as 'a belief that race is the primary determinant of human traits and capacities and that racial differences produce an inherent superiority of a particular race' (*Merriam-Webster's Online*

Dictionary); to simplify, racism is the idea that one's own race is superior and has the right to rule or dominate others. However, despite not defining the term itself, the United Nations Convention on the Elimination of All Forms of Racial Discrimination relates race to ethnicity and does not make any distinction between prosecution based on ethnicity and race: 'the term "racial discrimination " shall mean any distinction, exclusion, restriction or preference based on race, colour, descent, or national or ethnic origin which has the purpose of effect of nullifying or impairing the recognition, enjoyment or exercise, on equal footing, of human rights and fundamental freedoms in the political, economic, social, cultural or any other field of public life' (United Nations 1965). The UN reading will be used throughout the chapters which follow.

As we have seen, there is great disagreement regarding the terminology and conceptualization of the Far Right. Based on the above discussion, I have chosen to employ the term 'Far Right' and Cas Mudde's conceptualization (a combination of nationalism, xenophobia, law and order and a strong state) to be used throughout the book.

Notes

1 International pressure for the introduction of multiculturalism in the Balkans and the adoption of gender quotas for regional parliaments is well known – where International Community (IC) has been present (Bosnia and Herzegovina (BiH), Kosovo, Macedonia), countries can pride themselves on having the highest percentage of women in their parliamentary chambers. For more see, for example, Stojarová *et al.* (2007).
2 Schanovsky remarks that the difference is one of etymology as well as semantics: the adjective *extreme* was taken over from Latin to German in the seventeenth century (extreme, the end of a distance), while the word radical came in the eighteenth century from the French (going to the roots, substantially).
3 This approach has also been criticized. Roberts speaks of 'the lack of satisfactory operational indicators of extremism' resulting in difficulty establishing the dividing line between radicalism and extremism (Roberts 1994:466. For more discussion of the relativity of the term 'extremism', see, e.g., Carter 2005:14–22).
4 For further definitions of populism, see Canovan (1981:4) and Panizza (2005).
5 The problems inherent in applying the Right–Left axis must nevertheless be borne in mind – for example, as concerns Green parties or, even more pointedly, the party systems of the Balkans, where the Right–Left continuum is restricted in its ability to characterize regional party politics.
6 Some authors label LAOS in Greece as being part of the religious fundamentalist Right. The first country which comes to mind outside Europe is likely Israel.

3

Historical legacies of the Balkan Far Right

This chapter looks at the Second World War predecessors of current formations on the Far Right and presents the overall context which existed during the 1980s and 1990s in the former Yugoslavia at the height of nationalism. The historical chapter is essential in understanding the overall context of nationalism in the Balkans and the rise of the Far Right formations.

The Croatian Far Right

The historical legacies of the Croatian Far Right date back to the nineteenth century – the Croatian Party of the Right (*Hrvatska Stranka Prava*, HSP) was established in 1861 by Ante Starčević and Eugen Kvaternik when they first presented their ideas about the Croatian question, calling for self-determination for the Croatian nation. The party leader, Starčević, not only rejected the idea of the Habsburg Monarchy but also plans calling for the unification of all southern Slavs. Moreover, he did not recognize Serbs as forming a nation and called for the unification of all lands which had ever been in Croatian hands, relying first on French and then Russian assistance.

The party, or movement, followed a complex path of development, fragmenting into various directions and factions holding differing opinions on the further course of Croatian politics regarding both the Austro-Hungarian authorities and ethnic minorities in Croatia and lands claimed by the Croatian nationalists. In spite of this, the notions of Pravaši and Ante Starčević have served as the ideological basis for virtually all Far Right movements arising during the course of the twentieth century. A significant role was played by a staunchly nationalist faction led by Josip Frank at the start of the twentieth century, later becoming the Pure Party of the Right (*Čista Stranka Prava*).

The rise of Yugoslavia (the Kingdom of SHS), a state in which the dominant role was played by Serbian political elites, brought a new dimension to Croatian nationalism and Right-wing extremist ideology. Most supporters of the Party of the Right considered the new regime to be illegitimate during the 1920s, and a new generation led by the lawyer Ante Pavelić demanded the creation of an independent Croatian state inside borders also encompassing Bosnia and Herzegovina and Sandžak.

Pavelić's wing of the HSP, consisting of an organization founded in 1928 entitled the Croatian Home Defenders (*Hrvatski Domobran*), adopted the ideas of Starčević and Frank on constitutional issues, along with their tense anti-Serbian nationalism, but in conflict with their notions, the organization was anti-democratic, antiliberal and anti-Semitic. (Frank was himself Jewish, causing him to be ignored later in history.) Pavelić's movement made the dissolution of the Yugoslav state part of its platform from the 1920s, joining all other actors, both domestic and foreign, who sought the same goal. Pavelić's internal politics were oriented towards cooperation with Internal Macedonian Revolutionary Organization (*Vnatrešna Makedonska Revolucionerna Organizacija*, VMRO); well his foreign policy was initially oriented towards Fascist Italy, even though the Italians definitely had ambitions which impacted upon Croatian interests and territory.

After the royal dictatorship was announced and the HSP was banned, Pavelić and several others emigrated. It was in exile that, in 1930, he founded the Croatian Liberation Movement (*Ustaški Hrvatski Oslobodilački Pokret*, HOP), later renamed Ustaša–Croatian Revolution Organization (*Ustaša–Hrvatska Revolucionarna Organizacija*). The movement's platform rejected a liberal civil state in principle and declared the superiority of ethnic Croats over all minorities in Croatia. The movement's platform also stressed the importance of peasants, morals and Catholicism. During the 1930s, Ustaša activists were responsible for a number of terrorist attacks against the Yugoslav authorities, culminating in their participation in the assassination of Aleksandr Karadjordjević and the French Foreign Minister, Louis Barthou, in Marseille in 1934, an act they hoped would destabilize the Yugoslavian state and force its breakup (Trifković 1998:51).

After the bettering of relations between Italy and Yugoslavia in the second half of the 1930s, the activities of the Ustaša organization were neutralized. A break, however, came during the Second World War, with the German attack on Yugoslavia in spring of 1941. Ustaša adherents found themselves at the head of the puppet Independent Croatian state, which included Bosnia and Herzegovina and was a totalitarian state in which the Ustaša was the only political organization permitted to function. The Ustaša's organization and activities were adapted to follow the Italian and German models – Fascist and National Socialist movements. Ustaša adherents sometimes labelled themselves National Socialists and created their own armed forces, the Ustaša Army (*Ustaška Vojnica*), modelled after the German SS, and their own youth organization with obligatory membership for children and young people between 7 and 21 years of age. The Ustaša regime promoted the notion of a unified Croatian nation – Catholics and Muslims – with Bosnian Muslims considered to be an integral part of the Croatian ethnicity. There were wide-spread discriminatory measures, including genocide, taken against Serbs, who made up 30.5% of the country. A similar approach was followed against Jews and Romanies.

After the downfall of Germany and the end of the Independent Croatian state, Pavelić fled the country to Argentina, where in 1956, he founded the Croatian Liberation Movement (*Hrvatski Oslobodilački Pokret,* HOP). HOP put out several publications, originating in Argentina, Australia, Canada and the Federal Republic of Germany (FRG) which disseminated Ustaša propaganda among members of the Croatian diaspora. HOP became one of the largest and most influential of Croatian immigrant organizations, and after the breakup of the Socialist Federal Republic of Yugoslavia (SFRY), it moved its headquarters to Zagreb, where it was set up as a political party. It did poorly in the 1992 elections, however, and since that time has not taken any further part in elections. The organization was strengthened in 1995 with the arrival of a portion of the HSP youth, but it has not played a significant role in the Croatian environment and has split into two factions.

The HSP was rejuvenated in 1990, when several members of the radical nationalist Croatian Democratic Party left due to internal disagreements and set up a committee to prepare for the rejuvenation of HSP. At the party's first meeting, Dobroslav Paraga was chosen as leader, a man who had the reputation of being a fighter for human rights, based upon his past as a dissident abroad.

Because armed conflict had broken out between members of the former SFRY, HSP soon began to build its own paramilitary units, known as *Hrvatske Obrambene Snage* (HOS), which took part in battles in Croatia and Bosnia and Herzegovina (BiH). Volunteer HOS units, which were strong in number, were a significant force and also received support from Far Right Croatian emigrants, making use of Ustaša symbolism. In spite of their good reputation as quality fighters, they presented a problem for the Tuđman regime from both an internal political and foreign-policy standpoint. HOS members often refused to obey the central authorities. They provided the Serbians with an easy propaganda target with which to paint the Croatian state as being Ustaša in character and contributed to a negative impression of the fight in Croatia abroad. In the case of BiH, the strategy of HOS further complicated the aims of the Tuđman administration, since local representatives had an entirely different picture of cooperation v. confrontation with the Bosnian Muslims. The Croatian Secret Service probably eliminated two HOS leaders, Paradžik in Croatia and Kraljević in BiH, albeit under the pretence of their having been caught in friendly fire.[1] HOS units were subsequently integrated into the Croatian army (HV) or, in BiH, into HVO, during the course of 1992. HSP thereby lost the significance and influence it had held in Croatia and Herzegovina.

The Serbian Far Right

The Serbian Far Right, represented by the Serbian Radical Party (*Srpska Radikalna Stranka*, SRS), has its political antecedents like the Croatian Right wing in the second half of the nineteenth century and the first decade of the twentieth century. Just in its name alone, the SRS harkens back to the National Radical Party (NRP), founded in 1881, and one of the chief political organizations in Serbia at the turn of the twentieth century. The NRP started out as a populist party more than a Right-wing party. It portrayed itself as parliamentarian but was also strongly nationalistic and, in its very first platform, declared one of its chief goals to be the unification of all Serbs in a single state. In spite of this Greater Serbia element of its platform, it was not the most radical nationalist entity in the Serbian environment and might even be called a fairly pragmatic party as regards participation in state governance. Its greatest influence derived from the personality of Nikola Pašić, one of its founders and the party's leader for several decades. The NRP became active again after the liberalization which took place in SFRY in 1990. But in its new incarnation, it did not enjoy the success of other parties and movements harkening back to their predecessors. Soon after coming into being, internal disputes led to its fragmentation and the chief faction, led by Tomislav Nikolić, joined the SRS of Vojislav Šešelj, which also took the NRP as its basis.

After 1908, the flag of Serbian ultranationalism was taken up by the National Defence (*Narodna Obrana*, NO), which set as its goals the elimination of party divisions within the nation and the all out struggle for Serbian unification. Among other things, the movement prepared volunteers for a future war with Austro-Hungry as it was convinced the war was inevitable and which motivated the creation of paramilitary groups. In 1911, the more radical representatives of NO founded the Unity or Death Society (*Ujedinjenje Ili Smrt*), which had a number of sympathizers in the armed forces. Its goal was to replace democratic parliamentarianism by an authoritarian regime with nationalist ideals more suited to realizing the dream of a Greater Serbia.

It is not until we come to the Yugoslavian National Movement ZBOR (*Jugoslovenski Narodni Pokret 'Zbor'*) associated with D. Ljotić that we have what we can term an authentic Far Right movement in the Serbian environment. The United Martial Labour Organization (*Združena Borbena Organizacija Rada*, ZBOR) arose from the impetus given by several Right-wing Yugoslav organizations during the Depression, which were striving for a prewar Yugoslavia. The movement was not purely Serbian. It also contained Slovenian elements and embodied the notion of Yugoslavia in its name. Its platform was close to that of Italian Fascism and corporatism, with ideological roots in the French *Action Française*, an antiparliamentary monarchist movement. However, it rejected both Fascism and national socialism. Despite its pan-Yugoslavian proclamations, it was based upon militant Serbian orthodoxy and Serbian peasant paternalism, and ZBOR advocated religiously (not racially) motivated adamant anti-Semitism. ZBOR's platform and activities centred around an authoritarian state, anticommunism, the Yugoslavia ideal, patriarchal and religious traditions of the Yugoslavian nation's and battling the Jewish conspiracy.

In spite of its opposition to parliamentary government, the movement took part in elections in 1935 and 1938. But it did not achieve any great success and was not represented in parliament, remaining in the opposition until April of 1941. It sharply attacked the regime in power and was persecuted by the ruling class of the day as a non-cooperative competitor in the Right of the political spectrum (Cohen and Riesman 1999:17).

After the defeat of Yugoslavia and the occupation of Serbia, ZBOR adapted its programme to the new conditions and became part of the collaborationist government, with the German occupiers deeming ZBOR to be the Serbian movement which was closest to the programme of National Socialism. With German support, ZBOR organized its own paramilitary organization, the Serbian Volunteer Corps (*Srpski dobrovoljački korpus*), which took part in operations against Communist partisans. But the defeat of the occupying powers also meant the collapse of ZBOR, which continued its ideological and physical existence only among a few activists living in exile. After the renewal of a pluralistic regime, there was no direct successor to the movement as in the case of the Ustaša in Croatia, since Ljotić's activity as a collaborationist had discredited him among Serbian nationalists, and there were other, better models available to follow. In terms of its ideology, ZBOR is currently close to the Obraz movement in the Serbian Right, a relatively marginal youth organization which, however, just like ZBOR, is based upon Serbian orthodoxy and nationalism, as well as resistance to parliamentary democracy. Between 1992 and 1995, the Serbian National Renewal movement created a paramilitary unit called White Eagles (*Beli Orlovi*), possibly a reference to the unit of the same name in Ljotić's ZBOR, which took part in battles in Croatia.[2]

The Macedonian Far Right

In contrast to other Balkan States, it is difficult to locate the historical roots and ideological examples used by the Far Right in Macedonia. This fact is directly connected to the complicated development of the Macedonian national identity, with Macedonia as one of the youngest nations in the Balkan region, even though reference is also made in this case to remote historical events. The movement may, however, be factually dated to the 1880s and 1890s, with the appearance of Macedonian separatism as a reaction to three sources of foreign propaganda (from Bulgaria, Serbia and

Greece) demanding the territory of the Macedonian provinces which were then under the control of the Ottoman Empire.

Because of ethnic and linguistic relatedness, this issue took on importance particularly in the Bulgarian environment, and it is somewhat difficult in a number of cases to differentiate nationalist tendencies of a pro-Bulgarian and pro-Macedonian character. For Macedonian nationalists and the Far Right, however, it is likely that the only usable model is the VMRO, probably established in 1893. But this organization lacked both political and ideological unity from the very outset. It included nationalist, socialist and anarchist factions (Stojar 2006:227). The only goal on which the ideologically fractured activists were able to find agreement was overthrowing the Ottoman Empire. As to what should happen next, both individuals and factions differed greatly in their notions. Some wanted to see direct incorporation into Bulgaria, following the Eastern Rumelia model (1881); others wished for a Balkan-wide federation. Inside VMRO, formation began gradually of a tendency to demand that an independent Macedonia be created, since almost half of the inhabitants were members of a non-Slavic ethnicity and ethnic Macedonian Slavs themselves lacked the kind of clearly defined identity possessed by ethnic Bulgarians.

The division of Macedonia after the First World War brought fundamental changes to the further development of VMRO. The disappearance of the Ottoman Empire meant the VMRO had lost its raison d'être, but the violent division of the historical territory, which ignored its natural geography and ethnic boundaries, supplied movement with another reason to fight, this time under Bulgarian tutelage, against Greek and Serbian administration in areas under their control. VMRO thus gradually turned into a pro-Bulgarian movement which actively took part in the fighting in the Second Balkan and First World Wars on the Bulgarian side, with some parts of VMRO fully integrated into the Bulgarian army and some leaders attaining leading positions in the Bulgarian officer corps.

After the defeat of the Central Powers, with which Bulgaria was allied, VMRO continued guerrilla actions against Serbian forces in so-called Vardar Macedonia, the land which today makes up the Republic of Macedonia, part of the Kingdom of SHS at that time. In spite of bloody factional fighting which claimed the majority of VMRO leaders, the organization carried out a number of successful attacks and, after beginning collaboration with the Ustaša in Croatia, took part in the Marseille assassination.

In the 1920s and 1930s, VMRO began to define itself ideologically and took on a semi-Fascist character, a by-product of its cooperation with the authoritarian regime of Bulgaria and its contacts with Italy and Germany. In the early 1920s, however, a Left-wing, socialist-oriented splinter group broke off and established its own VMRO, the so-called United. The result was a bloody factional war from 1924 to 1934, in which the nationalist VMRO refused to tolerate the use of its name by a competing group with diametrically opposed ideological principles. The total number of losses was never precisely determined. Various sources speak of hundreds to thousands of victims (Stojar 2006:238).

In the early 1920s, VMRO took an active part in developments in Bulgaria, where it had substantial support and a number of sympathizers inside the security forces. In 1923, it took active part in the coup d'état that brought down the Left-wing-oriented government of Prime Minister Stamboliyski and his Bulgarian Agrarian People's Union (BZNS). VMRO divisions fought the BZNS paramilitary formations and physically liquidated their leadership, including the prime minister. They took an active part in suppressing an uprising by BZLS remnants and Communists against the new regime that same year. Thanks to these actions, VMRO solidified its position to the extent that it obtained a safe base in the so-called Pirin area of Macedonia which went to Bulgaria after the Balkan Wars and which was not under the control of the Bulgarian authorities. This Pirin parastate was to become the Macedonian Piedmont. The region became practically independent of Bulgarian governmental control, and VMRO built up its own military and security structures, collecting taxes and administrative fees. The extent of the region's independence gradually exceeded what was bearable even in sympathetic Bulgarian governmental circles, especially when signs of Macedonian ethnic separatism began to become apparent (Tulejkov 2001).

After the 1934 coup, the new Bulgarian government dissolved all political parties and movements, including VMRO, which, however, viewed this as a purely formal move. But this was followed by a successful armed intervention on the part of Bulgaria, part of whose success was due to the fact that one of the pro-Bulgarian factions inside VMRO voluntarily put down its arms and ceased its activities because one of its leaders had been murdered by a competing group in the organization's leadership shortly before. A number of VMRO members were arrested and interned but their leader, Ivan Michajlov, was able to escape to Turkey with the help of sympathetic Bulgarian officers. Thanks to his pre-war contacts in the Ustaša, from 1941, he found himself in the NDH and, at the end of the war, briefly became an object of German policy interest in the Balkans.

Before withdrawing its troops from the Balkans in September of 1944, Germany declared Macedonia to be independent, with Michajlov formally in charge. Upon arriving in the country, however, Michajlov saw that the plans were impossible to carry out and distanced himself from them. In contrast to his predecessors in the VMRO leadership, he lived to grand old age, dying in 1990, the year before the Yugoslav federation fell apart and the Republic of Macedonia came into being.

VMRO, because of its revolutionary activities in its early years, became an ideological resource for the new Macedonian statehood, as it indeed had already been during the existence of the Communist regime in SFRY. The semi-Fascist, pro-Bulgarian VMRO of the 1920s and 1930s was ignored or condemned, being rehabilitated to a certain extent only after 2000 when the governing Internal Macedonian Revolutionary Organization–Democratic Party for Macedonian National Unity (*Vnatrešna Makedonska Revolucionerna Organizacija–Demokratska Partija za Makedonsko Nacionalno Edinstvoe*, VMRO–DPMNE) spoke in approving terms of its legacy and organized a commemorative ceremony at the memorial to the assassin of Marseille, among other things, or unveiled a memorial plaque dedicated to a suicide terrorist in the 1930s in Skopje.

Ideological and ethnic ambiguity, however, present certain complications for Macedonian nationalists and the Far Right wing in the case of VMRO. The lack of other models, however, makes ties to this tradition necessary. But tradition is also used by the Bulgarian Far Right, which rejects Macedonian identity, both national and state, and thus continues the tradition of diverse, hard-to-define directions under the VMRO standard.

The Albanian Far Right

Because of its archaic social structure and geographical isolation during the twentieth century vis-à-vis the rest of the European continent, Albania has taken a fairly specific developmental route, something which is reflected in the formation of its political outlook. As in other cases, here, too, tight ties between the extreme Right and extreme nationalist currents may be sought, arising in the Albanian environment during the first decades of the twentieth century as a reaction to regional development.

One organization which may be counted here is Homeland (*Atdheu*), a radical national association founded in 1922 by Avni Rustemi, a young nationalist with pro-Serbian sympathies who assassinated the influential Albanian politician and tribal leader Essad at a peace conference in France in 1920. He was set free, however, by the French courts, which accepted his defence that he acted under emotional duress. *Atdheu* and later Unity (*Bashkimi*) took as their goal the unification of all ethnic Albanians in a single state, as did, for example, the Serbian *Ujedinjenje Ili Smrt* in the case of Serbs. Contacts were initiated with Italian Fascists, and the organization later functioned as a strong competitor to the conservative government of Ahmed Zog. A member of *Bashkimi* attempted to assassinate Zog in February of 1924, leading to the reciprocal assassination of Rustemi, whose death became the impetus for the revolt which brought down Zog's government and forced his temporary exile. The new government consisted of an agglomeration of radical national and extreme Left-wing groups but was only a passing episode: with the support of the Yugoslavian government, Zog and his supporters returned to power the same year, and the opposition forces were put down.

In spring of 1925, those who had become political refugees the year before founded the National Revolutionary Committee (*Komiti Nacional Revolucionar*, KONARE), which sought the overthrow of the autocratic Zog republic in favour of a liberal democratic regime and an Albania with ethnic borders. Internal fault lines soon appeared within the organization, however, with the group's core oriented to the Left- and a Right-wing faction gradually separating from it. As early as autumn of 1925, the organization *Bashkimi Kombetar* (National Association) came into being, sympathizing with Fascism and opposing itself to Bolshevism and other ideologies which might threaten the base of traditional Albanian society, in addition to its opposition to the Zog regime. This group, too, however, saw the separation of members holding pro-Italian and chauvinist views, the so-called Zadar Group led by Mustafa Merlika-Kruja, a pro-Italian Fascist politician and admirer of Mussolini.

These groups survived in emigration until the occupation of Albania by Fascist Italy in April 1939, when some activists began to work with the Italian administration. Kruja became the head of the Albanian puppet government, and in June of 1939, the Albanian Fascist Party was organized (*Partia Fashiste Shqiptare*), seeing itself as an offshoot of the Italian Fascist Party. After the defeat of Yugoslavia by the Axis powers in April 1941, Albania's territory was expanded to include Kosovo and Western Macedonia, where Fascist volunteer youth corps sprang into being, systematically expelling the local Slavic population.

In November of 1942, a grouping of Republican and liberally oriented illegal opposition forces was founded under the name National Front (*Balli Kombëtar*, BK), led by former opponents of the regime of King Zog. This organization was very diverse both politically and socially. Its programme, however, was radical, calling for the creation of a modern Albanian state within ethnic borders. This was responsible for its later tilt to Germany, since the Allies still rejected Greater Albania and insisted on restoring the pre-war borders. BK vehemently rejected the Italian occupation and became one of the main sources of domestic resistance, establishing its own armed formations and achieving a relatively strong position in southern Albania in 1942–1943. The group also made contact with the British intelligence services, which explored the potential for cooperation with Albanian Communist and non-Communist resistance forces. The Italian occupation attempted to handle growing resistance both by using force and by revising its existing policy. The new party entitled the Greater Albanian Guard came into existence to replace the existing compromised Albanian Fascist party, and Mustafa Merlika-Kruja was replaced by a less prominent politician.

The break came with the capitulation of Italy and subsequent German military operations, with German soldiers occupying Balkan areas which had been under Italian influence up to that point. Full Albanian independence was renewed formally and the Germans declared their support for the Greater Albania project in return for political loyalty and cooperation with the Reich. BK's leadership also made contact with the Germans because of fear about the growing influence of the Communists. The original anti-Fascist guerrilla movement became a collaborationist organization, its units taking part in anti-partisan operations and anti-Serbian ethnic purges in Kosovo. After the withdrawal of German troops in 1944, BK, like other Albanian collaborationist organizations, was slowly liquidated by Communist forces, but some armed groups in northern Albania and Kosovo maintained resistance until 1946. BK was the only Albanian organization to be renewed after the fall of the regime. In its current incarnation, BK builds upon the ideas of the Ballists – on the thinking of Abdyl Frashëri, Isa Boletini and Avni Rustemi, used by BK in the period between the two world wars.

The Bulgarian Far Right

The Bulgarian Far Right has been significantly connected to military and paramilitary organizations in the past, during certain periods significantly influencing the internal political situation. During the interwar period, the fact that Bulgaria was among the vanquished in the First World War contributed to this development. It became necessary to give up an extensive land area which had been considered to belong within the borders of an authentic national Bulgarian state.

Because of demilitarization, room appeared for secret military structures and semi-legal or secret officers' associations to arise which, similar to those in Germany and Hungary, had a pronounced Right-wing character. In 1933, the Union of Bulgarian National Legions (*Sjuz na Bulgarskite Nacionalni Legioni*), a Fascist organization also known as the Legionnaires' Association, was found. At its head was Hristo Lukov, a Bulgarian general. At the outset, it was an anti-Communist monarchist movement which rejected the parliamentary system. Later, it began to draw inspiration from German National Socialism and had a strong pro-German orientation, becoming a tool of coercive diplomacy for the Germans in Bulgaria during the Second World War (Payne 2001:429). In practical terms, its activities came to an end with the assassination of Hristo in 1943 by the Bulgarian Communist resistance.

Some activists fled the country after the war, establishing the Anti-Communist Bulgarian National Front, active until the 1990s. After 1990, they continued to be active in Bulgaria but less radical in character. At the midpoint of the 1990s, however, one activist, Nikola Altunkov, established a Far Right party of the same name. In 1996, the party leadership made use of the VMRO label, founding the VMRO–*Bulgarsko Nacionalno Dvizenje* (*VMRO*–BNP) political party, which seeks to annex the Republic of Macedonia and rejects the existence of a Macedonian ethnicity separate from the Bulgarian nation. The party has little political support, gaining only a negligible vote share in the 2001 election (Mudde 2005:9). BNP is closely tied to a contemporary political party (with marginal parliamentary representation from time to time) whose political goal is the incorporation of Macedonia into Bulgaria – the VMRO.

There was also an attempt in Bulgaria during the interwar period to directly copy the German National Socialism model. In 1932, a political party called the National Social Movement (NSM) was founded under the leadership of Aleksandar Tsankov. Tsankov was originally a member of the governing Popular Block but was inspired by Nazism to establish his own party. This group espoused its own conception of 'social nationalism' which, to Tsankov, meant including support for the national workers' syndicate against class struggle. Although NSM was not able to obtain significant support with the public, it contributed to the rapid collapse of the coalition government. The subsequent government led by Pencho Zlatev opposed the Far Right and helped suppress NSM.

The Romanian Far Right

The historical roots of the Romanian Far Right go back to the end of the First World War. Although Romania was in the victors' camp under the Treaty and attained national goals that would have been beyond reach before the war, the country met with novel circumstances which contributed to increased influence for the Far Right movement. Worries about neighbouring Bolshevik Soviet Russia, which was unwilling to accept the loss of Bessarabia (now the Republic of Moldavia), formed the impulse behind the country's strong anti-Communist stance. The fact that the Romanian Communist Party was led by members of national minorities stirred up a powerful xenophobic reaction from the Far Right. Generational conflict also contributed to its radicalism, with young Right-wing adherents clashing with the already-established older generation they accused of corruption and betraying traditional values.

A number of Right-wing student organizations came into being at the start of the 1920s, becoming part of the National Christian Renewal League led by the adamant anti-Semite A.C. Cuza in 1923. In 1927, the Legion of the Archangel Michael was established (*Legiunea Arhanghelului Mihail*) under the leadership of the charismatic Corneliu Zelea Codreanu, with a number of former League members joining. The Legion began by organizing a propaganda campaign which brought a great response in poor and backward areas of Romania.

In 1930, the Iron Guard was officially established (*Garda de Fier*), intended to protect Legion members from repression by state bodies, but later transformed into a political party and terrorist organization. The key elements of the Legion's propaganda consisted of anticommunism, anti-Semitism and support for traditional Orthodox values.[3] The Garda also accepted a quirky philosophical direction which created a unique ideology within a European Fascist framework, based upon religious mysticism. The fight against the corrupt regime led the government to dissolve the Garda in 1931 and once again in 1932. But the movement obtained the sympathies of King Carol II, who thought the Garda might fit into his own plans. The Garda was also supported in influential financial circles, the royalist camarilla and the Ministry of the Interior. In the second half of the 1930s, the movement began to support Nazi Germany as part of its own diplomatic offensive in Southeastern Europe. Before the 1933 elections, however, the government declared the organization illegal and took repressive measures against it, leading to the Garda's first major conflict with state power. Some members of the Garda were killed, their leaders were arrested, and the Legion was forbidden to print its materials. In retaliation, a successful assassination attempt was carried out on Prime Minister Duca. As in other organizations of this type, internal dissension broke out shortly after its founding resulting in the creation of factions and the exit of other entities.

At the midpoint of the 1930s, the movement became less destructive and attempted to follow the Nazi example by promoting its goals using constitutional options, thereby allowing its activities to once again become legal. In the second half of the 1930s, volunteer camps popped up all over Romania, whose participants worked on projects for the public good at the same time they were exposed to Legion indoctrination. This approach was very successful. The movement began to receive mass support and became a symbol for curing societal ills, receiving the sympathy of a number of important intellectuals along the way. Silencing its violent side, however, did not mean the group's opinion had changed; it continued to be anti-Semitic and continued to have the character of an extremist organization. But it gradually lost the sympathy of the royal court and, with the coup of January 1938, moved underground.

Carol II, who was inspired by Fascist regimes, decided to do away with the system of government based upon political parties he could not manipulate to his liking. In the constitution of February 1938, he legalized royal dictatorship as the only legally permissible political structure. His relationship to the legionnaire movement, however, changed dramatically. Up until 1938, he had served as something of a protector. After the coup, he decided to join in its repression. In April of 1938, leaders were arrested and 2,000 legionnaires were interned. Codreanu was then sentenced to 10 years in prison in a manipulated trial. In November of that year, he and thirteen other Legion leaders were killed trying to escape. The legionnaires reacted with an assassination attempt on the life of the prime minister, which only lead to another wave of repression resulting in the internment of 252 legionnaires.

Germany's military successes and the weakness of the Western democracies led Carol II to re-evaluate his approach and by special decree in spring of 1940 to declare amnesty for all legionnaires and accept their new leader, Horia Sima, into the government. Thanks to its cooperation with the Nazis, the legionnaire movement became a significant element in Romanian internal politics thanks to the direct patronage of Heinrich Himmler and the SS. The 1940s saw the end of Greater Romania, as well, since the Romanian state had to give up an extensive amount of territory: Transylvania went to Hungary and Northern Bukovina and Bessarabia to the Soviet Union. Together they represented one-third of the country, with six million inhabitants. This development caused the breakout of an internal political crisis which ended in September of 1940 with the abdication of the King and the establishment of a national legionnaire state. The government may have been headed by an army general, General Antonescu, but the Legion and Garda controlled the Ministry of the Interior and the police and used them as tools to revenge the executed legionnaires. The Garda's leadership also attempted to build a cult around Codreanu. They considered canonizing him, renaming the unit of currency from the lei to the codreni, etc. The Garda's demands for cleansing society and state institutions, however, led to a confrontation with Antonescu and the army, ending in January of 1941 with a Garda rebellion which was put down by state forces, with 9,000 guardsmen arrested, one-third of whom were brought before a military court. But a number of leaders of the Legion and Garda found themselves under the protection of the German authorities, who saw them as a convenient tool for promoting German interests in Romania.

When Romania passed over to the Allies in 1944, Germany reacted by creating a Romanian National Socialist government in exile in Vienna, led by Horia Sima, and by forming Romanian SS units. This relatively complicated historical development contributed to the fact that current-day Romania's Far Right harkens to two mutually antagonistic directions: the Fascist legionnaire and Garda movement and the national authoritarian regime of General Antonescu, fighting on the side of the Axis against Bolshevism.

As we have seen, most current Far Right parties on the Balkan peninsula claim as their heritage nineteenth-century and twentieth-century formations – groups which dreamt about the 'unification of Croatian, Serbian, Albanian, Macedonia, Bulgarian or Romanian soil'. Some contemporary political parties draw on ideologies, some on Fascism and others on communism with nationalist overtones, as is the case with Romania. However, it is necessary to keep the historical context in mind, as these ideologies are not the main motivator; this is rather the existence of independent and 'Greater' states.

Notes

1 www.icty.org/x/cases/blaskic/tjug/bcs/000303.pdf.
2 More than ties to ZBOR, however, it was the use of the national heraldic symbol, the White Eagle. The name *Beli Orlovi* is not unique. The Serbian football team had also carried the name, for example.
3 The programme is summarized in Codreanu's manual entitled *For My Legionaries* and in *The Nest Leader's Manual*, which is relatively popular with current members of the Far Right, as well, and accessible in various versions on the Internet in several languages.

4

An overview of Far Right political parties in the Balkan region and political party selection

The aim of this chapter is to describe the overall Far Right scene in the region and indicate cases for further analysis. In order to be preselected for further investigation, the party must have been depicted by researchers as a Far Right party and must have gained at least one seat during parliamentary elections in the 2000–2010 period.

The Far Right in Croatia

In 1999, Ivan Grdešić noted that the presence of the Croatian Far Right was manifested in one of three dominant ways: as a faction of the Croatian Democratic Union (*Hrvatska Demokratska Zajednica*, HDZ), in the form of the Croatian Party of the Right (*Hrvatska Stranka Prava*, HSP) and, least significantly, in the form of a few organizations and political parties representing post-Second World War emigration, most of whose members were prominent during the Independent State of Croatia (*Nezavisna Država Hrvatska*, NDH) period.[1] This latter group was forced to emigrate and returned after Croatia declared independence (Grdešić in Ramet 1999:176–179). As many scholars point out, the leading post-war party, HDZ,[2] has transformed itself and shifted towards the centre of the Right–Left axis. It seems to be in the process of becoming a conservative party (see, e.g., Buljan and Duka 2003:15–22).[3] In looking at the two other streams envisaged by Grdešić, the fragmentation becomes clear at first glance. The most visible actors on the Far Right in Croatia are the HSP and the Croatian Bloc (*Hrvatski blok*, HB)[4]; other Far Right parties remain without political representation in parliament: the Croatian Pure Party of the Right (*Hrvatska Čista Stranka Prava*, HČSP),[5] Croatian Right–Croatian Right-Wing Movement (*Hrvatski Pravaši–Hrvatski Pravaški Pokret*, HP–HPP),[6] Croatian Party of the Right 1861 (*Hrvatska Stranka Prava-1861*),[7] Croatian True Revival (*Hrvatski Istinski Preporod*, HIP),[8] Croatian Right-Wing Brotherhood (*Hrvatsko Pravaško Bratstvo*, HPB),[9] Party of Croatian Right (*Stranka Hrvatskog Prava*)[10] and Croatian Party of the Right dr. Ante Starčević (*Hrvatska Stranka Prava dr. Ante Starčević*).[11]

In conclusion, there are essentially three parties described by researchers as Far Right parties which have been represented in the Croatian Assembly: the HSP, the HB and the HDZ (Grdešić in Ramet 1999:179, Šedo in Stojarová and Emerson 2010:79). The former depository of nationalism and xenophobia in Croatia, HDZ, has not been depicted as being on the Far Right since 2000 but has moved to the Right centre. The only party which has been elected to parliament since 2000 is the HSP – the maximum number of MPs elected from the party's list was eight deputies in 2003. In 2007 elections, the party won a single seat in the Croatian Parliament.[12]

The Far Right in Serbia

Many scholars have pointed out that most parties in Serbia at the beginning of the 1990s promoted an emotional species of nationalism: 'generally speaking, regarding the ethnicity-integrity dimension, the Serbian Radical Party (*Srpska Radikalna Stranka*, SRS) has taken an extremely nationalistic position, whereas the Socialist Party of Serbia (*Socialistička partija Srbije*, SPS), Serbian Renewal Movement (*Srpski pokret obnove*, SPO),[13] Democratic Party (*Demokratska Stranka*, DS)[14] and Democratic Party of Serbia (*Demokratska Stranka Srbije*, DSS)[15] assumed a moderate nationalist position' (Goati 2001:73). In addition to SRS, Pribičević includes the Party of Serbian Unity (*Stranka Srpskog Jedinstva*, SSJ) in the Far Right group[16] (Pribičević in Ramet 1999:202), while Stojiljković talks about the national-oriented politics of SPS (Stojiljković 2006:193). The party's policies during the 1990s were clearly nationalist, as Serbian politics, or more precisely those of Federal Republic of Yugoslavia (FRY), reveals, as does its conduct during the wars in Croatia, Bosnia and Herzegovina (BiH) and Kosovo. Nevertheless, no researcher has depicted the SPS as a Far Right party since 2000.

The relevant Far Right in Serbia is currently embodied only in the SRS, which has continued to be elected to parliament since the October revolution. During the regime of Milošević, the SRS was partially in the opposition and partially backed the regime as part of formal coalitions with SPS. Since 2000, the party has been very successful at attracting voters and has gained more than 27% of votes in all subsequent elections (2003, 2007, 2008). The then acting party leader, Tomislav Nikolić, was very close to the post of President of the Republic in the February 2008 presidential elections. In 2008, the party split due to the internal disagreements concerning Serbian accession to the EU, and the acting party leader formed a new party with other MPs – the Serbian Progressive Party (*Srpska Napredna Stranka*, SNS). Although the party never ran an election campaign, it is represented in parliament; the SNS focuses on social populism and is currently one of the most popular political parties in Serbia.

The Far Right in Montenegro

Since Montenegro ceded from the Federation of Serbia and Montenegro only in 2006, it is quite difficult to determine which of its political parties would qualify as Far Right. Both a state-building and nation-building process are going on – Montenegro was only recognized as a nation after the Second World War, while the Montenegrin language appears to have begun its existence in 2007, when the new Constitution of the Republic of Montenegro was passed. In 2003, 43% of people claimed Montenegrin identity, while 32% of inhabitants identified themselves as Serbian (*Popis stanovništva, domaćinstava i stanova u* 2003, 2004). These figures remain fluid as the nation- and state-building processes have not yet consolidated. Because of this, if we had looked at Montenegro politics prior to 2006, we would have had to take into account the fact that half the political scene had irredentist tendencies and was characterized by nationalism, xenophobia and welfare chauvinism, requiring most political entities to be entered into the analysis.

As Bieber points out, there are currently no extreme Right-wing parties defining themselves as ethnic Montenegrin – Montenegrin identity has so far been too inclusive to allow for such a political agenda (Bieber in Stojarová and Emerson 2010:122). When independence was declared, the only Far Right entities were subregional in nature (Albanian formations claiming Greater Albania) or sister parties of Serbian radical entities seeking the creation of Greater Serbia.

The SRS entered parliament in 1992 and then again, with one seat, in 2006. As it is the sister party of the SRS, its chief goal and strategies remain the same – the creation of a Greater Serbia. This applies to the SRS branch in Republika Srpska in BiH as well as to the Macedonian branch of the party. The SRS is the only party to have secured parliamentary representation since 2000 and to have been depicted in the academic literature as belonging to the Far Right family (Bieber in Stojarová and Emerson 2010:127). Since 1995, the party has carried the name Serbian Radical Party of Dr. Vojislav Šešelj (SRS CG).[17] Montenegro's proclamation of independence could lead to the assumption that SRS CG should be classified as an ethno-regional party, since it shows patterns similar to this party family; the conceptualization of Mudde excludes this, since the party does not call for autonomy within the larger state structure but instead strives for a suprastate within ethnic borders. We therefore speak about ethnic nationalism, which is one of the main preconditions for including the party in the Far Right party family.

The Far Right in Macedonia

Jovevska and Damjanovska include the Internal Macedonian Revolutionary Organization–Democratic Party for Macedonian National Unity (*Vnatrešna*

Makedonska Revolucionerna Organizacija–Demokratska Partija za Makedonsko Nacionalno Edinstvoe, VMRO–DPMNE),[18] Movement for All Macedonian Action (MAAK)[19] and the People's Party in the national and nationalist party category. Only VMRO–DPMNE has remained relevant; the other two formations still have no political representation. With the finalization of independence and the setting up of an independent Macedonian state, VMRO–DPMNE moved more to the centre of the political spectrum and gave birth to the marginal faction VMRO–People's Party (*Vnatrešna Makedonska Revolucionerna Organizacija–Narodna Partija*, VMRO–NP), sometimes referred to as a nationalist or radical Right party (Šedo in Stojarová and Emerson 2010:176). The party attained six seats in the 2006 elections; in subsequent elections in 2008 and 2011, it failed to gain a single seat. The party was founded by the former founder of VMRO and former Prime Minister, Ljubčo Georgievski, due to personal and ideological differences with the new VMRO leader, Nikola Gruevski. The party may be seen more as consisting of followers of the former prime minister, rather than having an ideology substantially distinctive from VMRO.

To conclude, VMRO–NP is the only party depicted by researchers as belonging to the Far Right ever to secure representation in parliament by democratic election after 2000.

The Far Right in Albania

There are a few political parties in the spectrum researchers consider to be nationalist parties or parties of the Far Right – the National Front (*Balli Kombëtar*, BK), Legality Movement Party (*Partia Lëvizja e Legalitetit*, PLL)[20] and the Albanian National Unity Party (*Partia Bashkesia Kombetare Shqiptare*, PBKSh)[21] (Biberaj 1998:66). BK is the only party with parliamentary representation. It won two seats in 1996 and three seats in 1997 and, in the 2001 elections, was part of the greater coalition of the Union for Victory (Democratic Party of Albania—*Partia Demokratike e Shqipërisë*, PDSh; Albanian Republican Party—*Partia Republikane Shqiptarë*, PRSh, and others), which won forty-six seats, while BK managed to win three. The BK did not win any seats in the 2005 elections, because the Central Electoral Commission denied BK's request to join the Alliance for Freedom, Justice and Well-Being, since it had missed the application deadline. It also failed to gain any seats in 2009. To sum up, the only party which has ever surpassed the threshold for entering the Albanian Assembly labelled Far Right by academics is the BK.

The Far Right in Bulgaria

Bulgarian Far Right politics was fragmented during the 1990s, only achieving low vote percentages in the elections and minor representation in legislative bodies. There are a few Far Right political parties which make openly xenophobic, racist, nationalist statements, mainly encouraging hate speech against the Turkish minority, local Romas and Jews, as well as against the USA. The Bulgarian National Radical Party (*Bulgarska National Radikalna Partija*, BNRP[22]), Bulgarian Christian Democratic Party (*Bulgarska Khristian Demokraticheska Partija*, BKDP),[23] Bulgarian Democratic Forum (*Bulgarski Demokraticheski Forum*, BDF[24]) and Bulgarian National Front (*Bulgarski Natsionalen Front*, BNF) are examples of political parties with strong xenophobic and nationalist appeal, though without political representation, leaving them on the fringes of the political spectrum (Ivanov-Ilieva in Mudde 2005:4–9).

The only group with relevance before 2005 seems to have been the VMRO – a nationalist political party whose political goal is the total and final resolution of the Macedonian question, since '*the Macedonian question forms an integral part of the Bulgarian national issue*' (Programa VMRO undated). The party has often been depicted as a strongly nationalist–populist Right-wing party (Karasimeonov in Karasimeonov 2004:55, Ivanov-Ilieva in Mudde 2005:4–9). VMRO won two seats in the 1997 elections as a part of the United Democratic Forces coalition and in 2005 gained five seats out of the thirteen won by the coalition Bulgarian National Union.[25] The party is quite successful at the local level (Ivanov-Ilieva in Mudde 2005:5). In the 2009 elections, the party failed to win a single seat.

A new nationalist force entered Bulgarian political space in 2005. The National Union Attack (*Natsionalen Sayuz Ataka*, Ataka)[26] was formed shortly before the 2005 elections by the National Movement for the Salvation of the Fatherland (*Natsionalno Dvizhenie za Spasenie na Otechestvoto*, NDSO), the Bulgarian National Patriotic Party (*Bǎlgarska Natsionalna-Patriotichna Partiya*, BNPP) and the Union of Patriotic Forces and Militaries of the Reserve-Defence (*Sǎyuz na Patriotichnite Sili i Voinite ot Zapassa-Zashtita*). In the 2005 elections, the party gained 8.1% (21 out of 240 mandates) and in 2009, it gained 9.4% (21 out of 240 seats). The party has often been described as a radical Right-wing party because of its xenophobic and nationalist statements (Stefanova 2007, Smrčková 2009).

In the 2009 elections, the winner was the new political party Citizens for the European Development of Bulgaria (*Grazhdani za Evropeysko Razvitie na Balgariya*, GERB), established in 2006. The party or, more precisely, its leader, the current (2009) Prime Minister of Bulgaria, is often depicted as a populist who employs nationalist hate speech in referring to Turks, Roma and pensioners in Bulgaria as '*bad human material*' and making discriminatory statements and threats against homosexual people. The party has, however, joined the European People's Party (EPP) in the European Parliament. The vice-president of the Socialist group in the EP, Jan Marinus Wiersma, maintains that Boyko Borisov 'has already crossed the invisible line between right wing populism and extremism'.[27] However, researchers prefer to call the party populist (anti-establishment) rather than classifying the party Far Right. In its preelection campaign, the party focused primarily on the issue of corruption, promising to 'bring the guilty to justice' and pledging to control the state bureaucracy and red tape and to streamline public administration. Because of its aspirations to join the European People's Party–European Democrats (EPP–ED) political grouping, GERB reshaped its programme from centrist–populist to centrist–Right (Stefanova 2008:570).

The Far Right political spectrum in Bulgaria is, then, embodied in two political parties depicted as parties of the Far Right by researchers which have found parliamentary representation, VMRO and Ataka.

The Far Right in Romania

One of the first nationalist formations to be so described by scholars was the Party of Romanian National Unity (*Partidul Unității Naționale a Românilor*, PUNR) registered in 1990 (Andreescu in Mudde 2005:186). During the 1990s, the party was represented in both chambers of the parliament and became an ally of the Democratic National Salvation Front. Nevertheless, a change in party leadership led to failure in further elections. PUNR has failed to gain a single seat since 2000 and has become a marginal political party. In 2006, the party merged with the Conservative Party (*Partidul Conservator*, PR).

The Greater Romania Party (*Partidul România Mare*, PRM), set up at the beginning of the 1990s by Corneliu Vadim Tudor, became the most successful party on the Far Right. The PRM is the only party on the Far Right described in the literature as being represented in the lower chamber of parliament since 2000 (Andrescu in Mudde 2005:188–189).[28] It is rather a one-man party in which Tudor plays first violin; his speeches contain anti-Semitic remarks and hate speech against Romas and Hungarians. He is also known for his wish to unite Romania and Moldova and is in contact with pro-unionist forces in Moldova like the Christian Democrat Popular Front (*Frontul Popular Creștin și Democrat*, FPCD).

In 2000, a new party called New Generation Party–Christian Democratic (*Partidul Noua Generație–Creștin Democrat*, PNG–CD; formerly *Partidul Noua Generație*, PNG) emerged on the Romanian scene around the former mayor of Bucharest, Viorel Lis, led by George (commonly known as Gigi) Becali since 2004 (Shafir 2008:154). The party has nevertheless never managed to surpass the electoral threshold. The party has alleged ties to the Noua Dreaptă.[29] Even though the party has never entered the Romanian Parliament, its leader, Becali, ran on the PRM ticket and won a seat in the European Parliament in 2009 which helped increase the party's popularity.

'Successes' and 'failures' of the Balkan Far Right parties

For the purpose of the analysis, the following parties were selected fulfilling the above-mentioned criteria: HSP, SRS, SRS CG, VMRO–NP, BK, VMRO, Ataka and PRM. Figure 4.1 shows that the representation of the parties in parliament differs markedly. The most successful in terms of percentage vote share has been the SRS, though it has never been part of the government after 2000 due to its nationalism and its alliances during the 1990s with the Milošević SPS.[30] Nevertheless, the party maintains its strong blackmail potential. The second-most successful party has been the Bulgarian Ataka, which from the time of its founding, has managed to secure twenty-one seats (out of 240) twice in the Bulgarian Parliament. The PRM reached its heyday in the 2000 elections, when it won eighty-four (out of 345) seats in parliament; its voting share decreased in the subsequent 2004 election, and the party won only forty-eight (out of 338) seats, while in 2008, the PRM failed to gain a single seat. Quite small are HSP and the Montenegrin SRS CG, each of which secured a single seat in the last parliamentary elections (Croatia 2007, Montenegro 2006); the Albanian BK has not been represented in parliament at all since 2005; the Macedonian VMRO–NP and Bulgaria's VMRO both failed to secure a single seat in the most recent elections. The only parties which have consistently won parliamentary seats since 1992 are HSP, SRS and PRM.

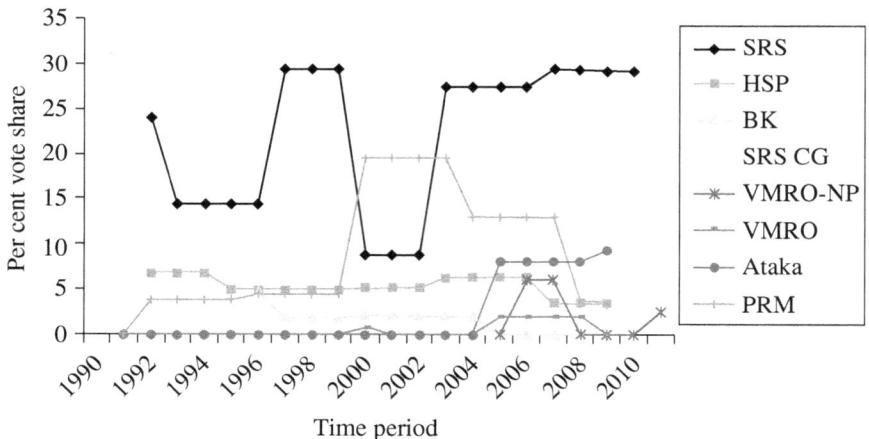

Figure 4.1 Percentage vote share of Far Right parliamentary political parties in the Balkans since 2000. (Data retrieved from the Adam Carr Archive and Šedo 2007 and rounded upwards. Data for 1992 Croatia related to the proportion of votes won, while data for the 1997 Albanian elections relates to the total per cent (both the proportional and majority components) of seats for the party)

As we have seen, none of the parties have been able to secure government representation since 2000. However, this was not the case during the 1990s. SRS, PRM and the PUNR are[31] the only parties with government representation. The SRS was in an informal coalition with SPS for a brief period in 1992, becoming part of the formal opposition in 1993. In 1998, the party created a coalition government with SPS which it left one year later, in 1999. The PRM appeared in the coalition government for a brief three months in 1995 as part of the so-called Red Quadrilateral coalition, while the PUNR secured two ministerial portfolios and several other important positions in the period 1992–1996. HSP has not been acceptable as a partner for any government though it indirectly supported the HDZ-led government between 2003 and 2007 (Antić and Gruičić 2007:754–755). In addition to this, the HDZ played the role of nationalist party during the 1990s.

Because two of the countries have gained entry to the EU, one must not forget elections to the European Parliament. PRM won five of thirty-five observers before the elections took place and then received no seats in the 2007 elections. Two years later, it increased its presence to three seats (out of thirty-three at that time) which put it in fourth place, together with the Democratic Union of Hungarians in Romania. Ataka received three out of seventeen seats in the European Parliament elections in 2007 and then, in 2009, two out of seventeen elected MEPs.

None of the leaders of the parties analysed have become president of the republic, though some came quite close. Volen Siderov won 21.5% of votes during the 2006 presidential elections, placing him second, and took part in the second-round runoff, where he won 24%. The winner, Georgi Parvanov, won 76% of the votes.[32] The Serbian presidential elections in 2008 were also very close for the candidate of SRS, Tomislav Nikolić, who won 40% of votes in the first round, as opposed to 35% for Boris Tadić, who came in second. Nevertheless, Nikolić was beaten in the second round, winning 48.8% to Tadić's win of 51.2%. The leaders of the SRS have had steady support, and there has not been a significant fluctuation in voters, with the results of previous elections being very similar.[33] The fate of coming in second in the presidential elections also befell the PRM leader, Vadim Tudor, who received 33.2% in the second round of the 2002 elections, with the winner, Ion Ilescu, gaining 66.8% of the vote.[34]

Minkenberg notes that Far Right parties in consolidated Eastern European countries (Baltic States, Poland, Hungary, Czech Republic) are weaker in terms of votes and organization than their counterparts in Western Europe (WE), especially Austria, Belgium and France (Minkenberg in Minkenberg *et al.* 2006:29). In comparison to the Balkans, Far Right parties in WE with a presence in parliament get more votes in national elections. But no Western European Far Right party has achieved the 29% share that SRS did in the 2008 and 2009 elections. One of the best results was obtained by Freedom Party of

Austria (*Freiheitliche Partei Österreichs*, FPÖ), which obtained almost 27% of the vote in 1999; another example of a successful party is the Swiss People's Party (*Schweizerische Volkspartei*, SVP), which won 26.6% of the vote in the 2003 Swiss elections and 28.9% four years later. In Central and Eastern Europe (CEE), Jobbik gained more than 12% of parliamentary seats in the 2010 elections in Hungary.

The chief goal of this introductory section has been to describe the political parties which will feature in further analysis based upon two criteria: being represented in the lower chamber of parliament (when applicable) after 2000 and being described as parties of the Far Right by researchers. At least one such party has been identified in every country upon which we have focused. In Croatia, the only party so identified is HSP, in Serbia SRS, in Montenegro SRS CG, in Macedonia VMRO–NP, in Albania BK, in Bulgaria VMRO and the Ataka and in Romania the PRM. Since the Montenegro SRS CG overlaps in terms of ideology, organization and affiliation to international organizations, strategy and tactics with its mother party in Serbia and claims to be only the local branch of SRS, the next section will focus on the SRS in Serbia while accentuating local differences whenever applicable.

Notes

1 NDH was established in 1941 and was governed by the Ustaša movement and its leader, Ante Pavelić, who adopted German policies and adapted them to Croatian circumstances – Serbs, Jews and Romas were the groups most frequently subject to persecution.
2 The HDZ was set up in 1989 in Zagreb and became the majority party in Croatia during the 1990s. It ruled from 1990 till 2000 and has been in power again since 2003. In the 1990s, the party, or more precisely governmental policy, was heavily influenced by the war in Croatia and in BiH. Heightened nationalism therefore became the dominant philosophy.
3 HDZ strives to take on the appearance of a pro-European, pro-democratic party but retains some characteristics of its nationalist past. For example, the party's current view on the nation focuses on protecting the Croatian minority in BiH and promoting its right to become a third entity; the party promotes the right for active as well as passive voting for Croats living abroad (HDZ 2002).
4 The HB was founded in 2002 and was thought to be more of a movement than a party. Since the party evolved as an HDZ faction, it was present in the parliament from 2002 until the elections of 2003, even though it has never gained a single seat in an election. In two subsequent elections, the party failed to enter the Croatian Parliament. (For more see HB and HIP 2003, HB 2006.)
5 The party was re-established in 1992 due to personal rivalries which had arisen in the original HSP. It struggles for 'the liberation of the entire Croatian ethnic space,

for a completely independent and free Croatia over the entire territory' (HČSP 2007b, par. 8, 2007a).

6 HP–HPP was founded in 2003 and 'refuses to renounce historically Croatian lands where genocide took place against Croatian citizens: BiH, the Gulf of Croatian Saints (Zaljev Hrvatskih Svetaca q. e. Boka Kotorska), Srijem and Bačka' (*Temeljna načela* HP-HPP). The party clearly signals its nationalism and xenophobia, directed in its writings mainly against the Serbs.

7 The party was founded in 1995. It pushes for the creation of a (con)federation with BiH in order to tighten relations with the Croatian minority there (HSP 1861, par. 6).

8 HIP was founded in 2001 and the son of the former president – Miroslav Tuđman – was its first leader. The party is against any detuđmanization, for preserving the dignity accorded to the Patriotic War, and against the Hague prosecution, for the protection of Croatian generals, and promotes special relations with BiH and the protection of the Croatian nation there (HIP 2001a, 2001b).

9 The party was set up in 2004 and promotes the dignity and values of Patriotic War; the merits of the first modern president, Franjo Tuđman; and the heroism of Croatian soldiers and HOS volunteers in the war (HPB 2004).

10 The party was formed in 2004 from ex-members of HSP who did not agree with the current HSP politics. The programme recalls Ante Starčević and does not really differ from the original HSP (http://shp.bizhat.com/onama.html).

11 The party was founded in 2009 as a splinter party of the HSP; the programme recalls Ante Starčević, and the party stresses cooperation with neighbouring countries and with the Croatian diaspora while adhering to international law (www. hsp-ante-starcevic.hr/index.php?option=com_content&view=article&id=2792&I temid=544).

12 For election results, see www.fpzg.hr/hip/. For election analysis, see Antić and Gruičić (2007:752–755).

13 At the beginning of the 1990s, the party sought for a Greater Serbia; since the fall of the Milošević regime and with the party's participation in the government, nationalist and xenophobic features have disappeared. The party is chameleonic in nature. One of the chief aims of the party at present is to restore the monarchy. The number of voters attracted by the party fell when some former members created their own party, New Serbia (*Nova Srbija*, NS), and some voters abandoned the party in favour of the more nationalistic DSS. The party is still controlled by its first leader and founder, Vuk Drašković.

14 The party openly announced the unification of Serbian territories in the early 1990s. It has been led since 1992 by its founder, Vojislav Koštunica, who became Yugoslavian president after the 2000 defeat of Milošević and, since 2003, has held the office of Prime Minister of Serbia. He appeared to be the main obstacle to the resolution of the problematic relationship with the EU because of his strong nationalist appeal and unwillingness to discuss the status of Kosovo. Koštunica's authoritarian manner and reluctance to compromise were partially responsible for the DS's choice of a partner which would have been unthinkable up to that time – the SSP.

15 The party also promoted nationalism at the start of the 1990s. However, it transformed itself into a modern pro-European political party.

16 Until his assassination, SSJ was led by Željko Ražnatović (commonly known as Arkan) and later by Borislav Pelević; its aim was the unity of the Serbian nation (Komšić 2006:172–174). The SSJ merged into the SRS in late 2007 (for more, see Komšić 2006: 171–175).

17 *Istorijat Srpske Radikalne Stranke*. Available online at www.srs.org.yu/onama/istorija.php. The acronym SRS CG will be used henceforth in the text to differentiate the mother party in Serbia.

18 VMRO–DPMNE recalled an old nationalist revolutionary organization operating in the late nineteenth and beginning of the twentieth century, which eventually transformed itself into a terrorist organization with elements of Fascist ideology (Stojar 2006:225). In the beginning of the 1990s, the party made historic claims to territory in Bulgaria and Greece, including Thessaloniki (Phillips 2004:80). VMRO–DPMNE was the leading party in the coalition in 1998–2002 and once again after 2006. Surprisingly, the two ethnic parties with the strongest nationalist tendencies were able to form a government in 1998. The party is currently led by Nikola Gruevski, Prime Minister of Macedonia.

19 MAAK – a nationalist radical party which demands the rapid withdrawal of Yugoslav troops and has proclaimed 12 August 1913 as a Day of National Catastrophe (the Treaty of Bucharest, which placed territories inhabited by the Macedonians under Serbian and Greek governance). However, the party was not successful in entering the political party system (www.b-info.com/places/Macedonia/republic/partiesMAAK.shtml)

20 The party supports restoration of the monarchy and the return to power of the House of Zogu. Crown Prince Leka returned to Albania in 1997 before the planned referendum on the restoration of the monarchy (the result of the referendum was that most voters favoured a parliamentary republic). Leka has been living in Albania since 2002 and has been trying to move opinion polls in favour of the monarchy. Even though he had been indicted for illegal weapons smuggling, after a long debate, he obtained a diplomatic passport as an expression of Albania's effort to reintegrate the royal family into post-communist society. The party advocates awarding the royal family special status and returning their property. It has very little support in society and should be classified as a monarchist party.

21 This party emerged from a 1997 split in BK which was chiefly motivated by internal disagreements of a personal nature between Hysen Selfo and Abaz Ermenji, with the former deciding to set up the new Democratic National Front. There have been repeated proposals to merge the two parties, but they remain unimplemented.

22 The BNRP was established on a clandestine basis in 1995 and officially registered in 1990. It defines itself as radically nationalist and maintains close ties to skinheads (Ivanov and Ilieva in Mudde 2005:6).

23 The BKDP seems to be a one-man party led by the former Orthodox priest Guelemenov, who was expelled from the Church before 1989.

24 The BDF was formed by the former *legionnaires* (the Union of Bulgarian National Legions, also known as the Legionnaires' Association, was a Fascist organization which was formed in 1933 in Bulgaria) and their progeny, claiming to be anti-Communist but with pro-monarchist tendencies. Their major action was probably

the joint petition with VMRO against ratification of the Framework Convention for the Protection of National Minorities and against United Macedonian Organization Ilinden–Pirin, a party of Bulgarian Macedonians (Ivanov-Ilieva in Mudde 2005:8).

25 http://vmrovr.dir.bg/_wm/pbasic/?df=186&GDirId=16f2f080e097b21bc1083453 a3cc1bff.

26 Referred to hereinafter as Ataka.

27 www.socialistgroup.eu/gpes/public/detail.htm?id=116844&section=NER&categ ory=NEWS.

28 See Strmiska Calls the PRM a Party of Radical Populist Continuity (Strmiska 2001b).

29 A neo-Fascist organization, see the chapter Far Right (paramilitary) organizations or the party's web page www.png.ro/.

30 In addition to SRS, the Arkan Citizens' initiative and later the SSJ won five seats in the 1992 elections and in 2000, together with other three parties, 14 seats in the 250-seated Serbian parliament.

31 The PUNR won thirty seats in the 1992 parliamentary elections (7.9% of the vote) in the lower chamber and fourteen seats (8.1%) in the upper chamber, enabling the party to take part in the governmental coalition. The 1996 elections were the most recent in which the party was able to secure any seats – eighteen seats in the Chamber of Deputies (4.4%) and seven seats (4.2%) in Senate.

32 www.izbori2006.org/results_2/.

33 30.1% for Nikolić and 27.3% for Tadić in the first round, as compared to 45% for Nikolić v. 53.7% for Tadić in the second round. In 2003, Nikolić obtained 47.9%, but the elections were declared invalid as voter turnout did not surpass 50% (this requirement was removed only before the 2004 elections). The 2002 elections were also declared invalid (for the second time in a row that year). Vojislav Koštunica won with 57.7% over Vojislav Šešelj who received 36.1% of the votes. In the 1997 presidential elections, Šešelj also came in second.

34 In 2004, Tudor came in third with 12.6%.

5

International supply side: brief presentation of political parties in terms of ideology

In Western Europe (WE), some Far Right parties favour the abolition of affirmative action, see plebiscites and referenda as an important corrective to representative democracy, would like to lower taxes and favour abolition of subsidies for industry and agriculture, and cuts in areas of public sector spending. The point of all these demands is to radically reduce the scope of the state and thus to deprive established political parties and the political class of power resources (Betz and Immerfall 1998:5). Minkenberg points out that the ideology of the Far Right in Eastern Europe is more historically oriented than its counterpart in WE. In most countries where democracy is not yet the only game in town, the Far Right enjoys openings not available to similarly positioned parties in WE (Minkenberg in Minkenberg *et al.* 2006:29).

The ideological core depicted by the researchers for both Western and Central and Eastern Europe (CEE) has already been discussed in foregoing chapters. But what about the Far Right in the Balkans – can we identify a single common ideological core for Far Right parties and, if so, is it identical with that in WE? Does the ideology of the Far Right party family in the Balkans contain any specific features? The primary aim of this chapter is to analyse those parties which are supposedly on the Far Right of the political spectrum and explore their ideological core, focusing on nationalism, xenophobia, law and order and welfare chauvinism. Due to the peculiarities of the Balkan region, additional specifics and regional idiosyncrasies will also be explored: the position of the party towards communism, anti-Semitism and revisionism, populism, the stance on the church and religion, the party's foreign affairs orientation and its stance on the North Atlantic Treaty Organization (NATO), the EU and International Criminal Tribunal for the former Yugoslavia (ICTY), and the party's economic policy.

Croatia: Croatian Party of the Right (Hrvatska Stranka Prava, HSP)

The HSP (founded in 1990 as the descendant of a party set p in the nineteenth century) was on the extreme Far Right end of the spectrum in the early 1990s. HSP organized the Croatian Defence Forces (*Hrvatske Obrambene Snage*,

HOS), one of the first *defence forces* organized by Croats at the onset of the Croatian war, later absorbed into the Croatian army (HV). Party members wore black shirts, with the open display of Ustasha symbols and calling to mind the leader of the Independent State of Croatia (*Nezavisna Država Hrvatska*, NDH), Ante Pavelić. The core of the HSP ideology during the war was the *nationalist* conception of Ante Starčević[1] which focused on the creation of a Great Croatia incorporating the whole of Bosnia and Herzegovina (BiH). Bosniaks were perceived as Croats with Islamic beliefs. After the war, the rhetoric became less radical and the party's leaders started to talk about the right of a decentralized BiH to form its own state created from three nations. Nevertheless, even fourteen years after the war, the leader of the party likes to emphasize Starčević's ideals and still includes *xenophobic* anti-Serbian rhetoric in his speeches, presenting the Serbs as the chief enemies of Croats. Great Serbian ideals and expansionism are always mentioned by the party's leaders.[2] To expand the party's coalition potential, its leadership began to distance itself from the NDH and the Ustasha regime somewhere around 2000 and placed more emphasis on the Patriotic War and Starčević's ideals (Buljan and Duka 2003:52). The party has nevertheless never denounced the Fascist Second World War regime and its policies as such.

In terms of the party programme, HSP presents itself as a party promoting ethnic nationalism (early party policies could be labelled externally exclusive – seeking the inclusion of all members of the Croatian ethnic community within a single Croatian state). Even though some party representatives have presented themselves as pro-European, the party programme contains anti-EU components, advocates referenda as a precondition for joining any other (supra-)state structures and paraphrases the *Father of the Homeland*, Ante Starčević: *Not Hague, not Brussels, not Dayton, but a free, independent Croatia!*[3] During the 2007 party congress, the leader of the party declared that 'Croatia must accept the Europe of Christian values, but if Europe does not have those values, if the EU means losing Croatian identity and losing traditional values, economic perspectives, having to accept an inferior role and having to accept the criminal character of the Patriotic War and repudiate our heroes, then we do not need the European Union because it does not bring us anything good' (*Govor predsjednika Hrvatske stranke prava na konvenciji* 16.IX.2007). HSP promotes greater centralization of the country and a stronger position for the government and is currently the only relevant party promoting a presidential model of democracy (Buljan and Duka 2003:52–55). *Law and order* is one of the core demands – a strong state is presented as necessary for fighting organized crime, corruption and the mafia.

After approximately 2000, the party started to reform and presented itself as a modern (sometimes even pro-European) conservative Right-wing party similar to the Christian Social Union (*Christlich-Soziale Union,* CSU) in Germany. In place of controversial issues like the ICTY and the Patriotic

War, the party began to deal with legal issues of state, protection of the environment, pollution of the Adriatic and the use of genetically modified food (Pleše 2003). Ecological topics were the domain of party vice-chairman Tonči Tadić, a nuclear physicist who had studied in Japan and was considered to be the chief specialist in these areas. However, Tonči Tadić left the party, and with the election of a new chairman in 2009, the party reverted back a focus on issues to do with nationalism – one example would be the Vukovar Declaration or the Open Letter to the Prime Minister, the first focusing on the role of Serbs in Croatia and the latter on the role of Serbia in the international community.[4]

The party has abandoned revisionism and tries to avoid Ustasha issues. Its leaders very often employ antiparty sentiment directed mainly against the two leading parties – Croatian Democratic Union (*Hrvatska demokratska zajednica*, HDZ) and Social Democratic Party (*Socijaldemokratska Partija Hrvatske*, SDP). There has been an attempt to move towards the centre of the Right–Left axis, thereby abandoning some features which had previously been key – the creation of Greater Croatia, xenophobia and conspiracy theories – while still trying to attract Right-wing voters by focusing on welfare chauvinism and populist antiparty sentiment. However, with the new leadership, the party returned to its previous political profile and style.

As for economic issues and party's stance towards *welfare chauvinism*, the programme is a mixture of Leftist and Rightist concepts. Small private firms are seen as the basis of economic development, but, by contrast, the party is against privatization and against selling property to foreigners and has even proposed a law on ethical privatization designed to ensure the return of companies sold unlawfully to the Croatian fund for privatization.[5] Croatian national interests are heavily accented in the economic programme, and the HSP uses the term *Croatian national wealth.*[6]

Serbia: Serbian Radical Party (Srpska Radikalna Stranka, SRS)

The ideology of the branch parties in Croatia, BiH and Montenegro does not differ from the ideological core of the mother party in Serbia. We will therefore focus only on the official SRS programmes. The initial SRS programme was based on the heritage of the Chetniks',[7] *xenophobia* (aimed mainly against Kosovo Albanians,[8] Croats and Muslims) and the promotion of patriotism, anticommunism, church conservatism and *nationalism* – it seeks the unification of all Serbian territories and the protection of all Serbs; this entails unifying Serbia, Republika Srpska, Republika Srpska Krajina, Montenegro (the SRS does not mention the Montenegrin nation), of course Kosovo and potentially Macedonia as well.[9] One book put out by the SRS is called 'Roman-Catholic Serbs, So-Called Croats' (*Srbi rimokatolici takozvani Hrvati*), in which the existence of a Croatian nation is denied; some of the most radical members promote the annexation of the entirety of Croatia.[10] Some radicals go even further, claiming that since Serbs once lived in Romania, Greater Serbia should encompass Romania as well.[11] A very good example (one of thousands) may be found in Šešejl's book Hunting the Heretic (*Hajka na Jeretika*), in which Šešelj states that Slovenians have no right to secede, since there is no precedent of a sovereign, independent Slovenian state in history. He blames them for making war with the Serbs and concludes by saying: 'Well, let the Slovenes go – it will be better for them, better for us. And for us Serbs, it means a million and a half fewer outraged enemies within state borders' (Šešelj 2002:917, cf. Šešelj 2000, 2007).

The programme of the SRS (SRS undated) is negative from the outset, stating that the Serbian nation has been divided into three states because of Serbia's traditional enemies – the Croats[12] and Muslims; it demands the return of refugees and unification of Serbian territories (SRS Program, Article 7). The SRS is very active in publishing journals and books in which the party attacks *the Albanians who are committing genocide on the Serbian nation, the international community which is helping them and which wants to destroy the Serbian nation, the current government – quislings cooperating with the international community, etc.* The main idea of the SRS's ongoing campaign is that those who are not with us are against us or, better put, those who are not Serb are against us. The party promotes traditional values and is strongly against abortions, gay marriage and supports the model of the traditional family and the Serbian Orthodox Church.[13]

The SRS programme from the Milošević era does not directly address the economy, but only mentions several features related to *law and order* – fight against corruption and organized crime. It further claims that the current (socialist) system has only produced instability, uncertainty and wage differences to the liability to the regime (*Program SRS u* 100 *tačaka* undated). The economic policy in the newer programme is then enlarged but reveals socialist as well as liberal components. On the one hand, the SRS states that state economic policy should be protectionist, aimed at economic colonialism, with the key industrial and natural resources controlled by the state and the state having a great role in redistribution, including higher pensions and free education at all levels. The SRS then offers 'the best social programme, one which will secure work for the poor' (SRS Programme, undated). On the other hand, the party supports small business and privatization. The party strongly rejects the integration of Serbia into the EU and NATO and strongly opposes the ICTY. The only organization the party does not see negatively is the UN but accepts it only with reservations. Regarding the party's position towards *welfare chauvinism*, the party does not trust foreign investment and is against globalization.

The deputy party president, Tomislav Nikolić, tried to position the SRS more towards the centre, emphasizing social and economic issues, campaigning for the losers in the economic transition and fighting organized crime and corruption, and trying to break from the past and the SRS leader, Šešelj. The break of Nikolić with the party also means confirmation of the previous nationalist orientation with its claims to create a Greater Serbia including territory currently in the possession of Croatia, BiH, Montenegro and Kosovo.

Macedonia: Internal Macedonian Revolutionary Organization–People's Party (Vnatrešna Makedonska Revolucionerna Organizacija–Narodna Partija, VMRO–NP)

The party defines itself as a Right-wing conservative and patriotic party, with a Christian democratic orientation. The programme is mainly populist, in opposition to the main parties in Macedonia. *Nationalism* may be identified; however, the party does not propose an ethnically clean Macedonia or even Greater (i.e. United) Macedonia. VMRO–NP supports the Euro-Atlantic integration, which is seen as a natural process for Macedonia. The leader, Ljubčo Georgievski, proposed ethnic division of the country and territorial exchange to settle ethnic tensions between the Macedonians and Albanians. Under this plan, the Albanians would move from Skopje, Kumanovo, Kičevo and Struga by exchanging money and real estate since 'the Albanians have always been a source of problems for Macedonians, and have taken more from the state than they gave'.[14] The VMRO–NP also demands in its public speeches a strong state which would be able to fight against organized crime and secure *law and order* for the Macedonian citizens.

The party claims that 'the capabilities and initiatives of individuals are the highest value for the party and one's position in society is determined only by the achievements of each person and their contribution to the community or society'. Because the party is very small and seems not to be particularly active, it is very difficult to obtain more information about its policies. The party's interviews and writings include *xenophobic* statements directed mainly against the Albanian minority (VMRO-NP 2006). The party would partially fulfil the Mudde criteria for being positioned somewhere between the Far Right and conservative parties. The party could likely be depicted as a kind of soft Far Right party or, in Mudde's terminology, as approaching the populist radical Right. VMRO–NP nevertheless by no means reaches the extremes of its counterparts in regions striving for monoethnic states, whose nationalism is clearly evident in their fight for external exclusivity. VMRO–NP does not seem to be overly concerned with the property of nonethnic Macedonians or selling property to foreigners and does not actively promote *welfare chauvinism*.

Albania: National Front (Balli Kombëtar, BK)

BK follows on its historical predecessor from the Second World War of the same name, which opposed the return of King Zogu, uniting various political elements which were mildly liberal and republican – supporting the programme of agrarian reform – and strongly nationalist, united by anticommunism (Karagiannopoulou 2004:170). The programme recalls the Abdyl Frashëri and Dekalogue written in 1942.[15] The main slogan of the new 2002 programme is *Albania for Albanians* (BK undated). The party states that Albanians are not chauvinist nationalists, and BK is oriented towards a Western political vision, supporting American politics in the Balkans.

Regarding *nationalism*, the party's programme is Janus-faced and ambiguous: according to the programme, BK does not wish to fight for the creation of a Greater Albania; on the other hand, it asks for compliance with international charters and respect for the right of the Albanian nation to place its frontiers where its natural borders lie (i.e. creation of Greater Albania). The programme calls 'for an Albania where no one lives at the expense of someone else and where farmers have adequate land for themselves and the economic system serves the needs of the Albanian people'. The articles available on the BK website are full of *xenophobic* statements directed at Slavs and mainly focus on the Serbian, Montenegrin and Macedonian occupation of Albanian lands. Sometimes they are directed against Turks who, it is claimed, 'reduce Albanian space in Macedonia'. The party seeks integration into Europe.

The party rails against traitors, those who are not patriots, spies and invaders and those who hinder the development and progress of Albania (BK 2006). According to a party statute, the BK brings together Albanian citizens residing within and outside the state borders of the Republic of Albania. Communist, Fascist, antinationalist and former communist security agents are not allowed to become party members, and the party has a strong anti-Communist stance (BK 1998).

As regards the economy, the party promotes a market economy and restitution of property and strongly supports the interests of farmers. *Welfare chauvinism* is partially present in the party's claims that foreigners should not be allowed to buy land, which should instead be designated for Albanian farmers. The party dedicated one entire section of its programme to farmers and agrarian issues and sees agriculture as the basis of the future Albanian economy and the country's future well-being. On the other hand, the party supports foreign investment in tourism, but only if tourist spots are not sold to foreigners but rather leased to them for a definite period of time. As regards *law and order*, the party is against bureaucracy and corruption and would like to provide security for all citizens and public order while fighting the mafia and crime (BK undated).

Bulgaria: the Internal Macedonian Revolutionary Organization (Vutreshno-Makedonska Revolusionna Organizatsija (VMRO)–Bulgarsko Nacionalno Dvizenje)

The party claims it would like to accommodate all ethnic Bulgarians in a single state by peaceful means, since the Treaty of Berlin in 1878 left millions of compatriots outside Bulgaria. Its basic document is clearly *nationalist and xenophobic* – the programme promotes unification of Macedonia and Bulgaria via European integration – the future phase of this process would be the establishment of a federation between Macedonia and Bulgaria based upon the German model. Its programme states that the biggest problem the 'country is facing' is posed by 'Bulgarian Muslims and Gypsies'. Currently, VMRO's chief foreign policy priorities are support of Bulgarians abroad, countering Islamic fundamentalism and developing contacts with the Bulgarian diaspora (VMRO undated).

VMRO has always supported the integration of Bulgaria into NATO as well as the EU and also supports reducing the state bureaucratic apparatus to a minimum. The party wishes to introduce referendums to resolve issues important to the country and increase the efficiency of state bodies. It supports decentralization and greater autonomy for institutions on lower levels. In regard to *law and order*, the programme talks about 'the urgent problems of the present: demographic collapse, organized crime, low income, corruption, the country's reduced capacity, the integration of minorities'. VMRO thinks a special law must be adopted to combat organized crime. The party also proposes the creation of a special unit to combat crime under the direct authority of the president.

The VMRO promotes the introduction of a flat tax, thinks the redistribution of GDP should be reduced from 40% to 30%, wishes to establish scholarships for all students with a progressive funding scale dependent upon on their success, reduces the degree of state intervention in social relations and would like to create a more mobile, accountable, cheaper state. VMRO thinks the state should protect Bulgarian culture, tradition and the Bulgarian heritage. In terms of energy, the party wants to make Bulgaria a significant regional logistic and energy hub and establish a 10% tax rate on profits for companies producing software and hardware as well as companies whose capital is in Bulgaria and whose profit is reinvested in the national economy. The party would like to support the birth of ethnic Bulgarian children, since 'the birth rate of Gypsies is more than five times that of ethnic Bulgarians'. It supports introducing religion in Bulgarian schools and claims to be one of the first parties to propose a law declaring Orthodox Christianity to be the official state religion (Programa VMRO undated).

In terms of *welfare chauvinism*, the party is not that explicit. It makes only vague intimations about promoting the protection of Bulgarian firms challenged by European and world markets. The party also wishes to regulate demography – to promote marriage and increase birth rates for ethnic Bulgarians, to settle

---

people of Bulgarian origin from abroad and to increase contraception among non-socialized segments of the population – and wishes to suspend allowances to the families of non-socialized children.[16]

Bulgaria: National Union Attack (Natsionalen Sayuz Ataka, Ataka)

The twenty principles of Ataka are *nationalist* at their very outset, claiming that the use of languages other than Bulgarian is unacceptable in national media supported by the state budget and that ethnic parties and separatist organizations should be prohibited. Emphasis is laid on national values, tradition, culture and education. The principles contain antiparty sentiments and call for a reduction in state administration in favour of the people. Ataka demands the withdrawal of Bulgarian troops from Iraq while promoting total neutrality and an exit from NATO. The party wishes to revise the unfavourable conditions Bulgaria agreed in EU negotiations, explicitly mentioning the contract for closing Kozloduy Nuclear Power Plant.

In regard to *welfare chauvinism*, the programme stipulates that Bulgarian farmland should not be sold to foreigners and that Bulgarian investors should have priority over foreigners until the Bulgarian living standard reaches the average level of the EU: 'Bulgarian production, commerce and the banking system should be in Bulgarian hands'. The principles also include some articles partially related to *law and order* demanding 'a clean hands campaign' to investigate criminal activity and shady transactions involving politicians. The programme ends with the proclamation 'Let's bring Bulgaria back to Bulgarians!' (20 Principles of the ATAKA Political Party).

After the 2009 elections in Bulgaria, when the populist party Citizens for the European Development of Bulgaria (*Grazhdani za Evropeysko Razvitie na Balgariya*, GERB) experienced a landslide victory, the leader of Ataka, Volen Siderov, declared that nationalism was no longer a taboo in Bulgaria and that the topic was becoming increasingly important. He demanded that GERB fight Islamization, the robbing of the country and corruption: 'We want to see GERB investigate the entire criminal clique of the DPS, which is connected to Turkey's secret services, the Turkish mafia, and to stop the advancing islamisation'.[17] Ataka promotes an official religion and the involvement of the Bulgarian Orthodox Church in the legislation process. The *xenophobic* anti-Turkish appeal seems to be powerful, since it is included in most Ataka statements and its leaders quite often refer to the suffering of the Bulgarian nation under the Ottoman yoke. The campaign for the 2005 elections contained slogans such as 'Turks and Romas out!', 'Bulgaria back to the Bulgarians', 'Stop the Gypsy Terror' and 'Labour Camps for Sentenced Gypsies'. Immediately before the elections, the party published a list on its web page featuring Bulgarian Jews, with the title 'The Jews Are Contaminated with the Plague and Should Be Uprooted from Birth' (Maegerle 2009).

Romania: Greater Romania Party (Partidul România Mare, PRM)

The PRM does not claim the Iron Guard, the Fascist movement in the 1930s in Romania, as part of its heritage, but rather takes its inspiration from the communist regime, that is, the regime of Nicolae Ceauşescu. PRM's core ideology, according to its program, lies in the preservation of national values, traditions, the defence of the national interest, culture and religion.[18] The main aim of the party is to protect people of Romanian nationality. Regarding *nationalism*, the party spoke quite openly about the incorporation of Moldova[19] and part of Ukraine into Romania at the beginning of the 1990s. But because the party feared these demands might justify counterdemands by the Romanian Hungarians in Transylvania, it has become less outspoken on the topic (Hollis 1999:283, cited from Smrčková 2009). As for Euro-Atlantic integration, the party is not openly against Romania's EU membership, but stresses state and national interests. Membership in NATO is seen as an instrument for protecting Romanian strategic interests (PRM 2008).

From the beginning, the party has adopted anti-Semitic and *xenophobic* postures, targeting Jews, Hungarians and Romas, and sees Nicolae Ceauşescu as a national hero who fought for the country's independence and sought to deliver it from the clutches of Jewish, Hungarian and other international conspirators (Shafir in Ramet 1999:234). In one interview, Vadim Tudor openly denies the Holocaust (though claiming he does not hate Jews: 'God has prevented me from hating Jews'...'I believe that all those who hate the people of Israel have been punished by God') and then describes his opinion about Jews in an interview: 'Jews are like warts on a man's body. Ideally, a man should learn to live with them. But when the warts grow so big that they darken the man's eyesight, or prevent him from speaking or using his hands and legs and the man decides to have the warts removed, it's too late because these cancer cells have by that time spread throughout his body, and in a short time the man will die. This is what has happened to all those who confront Jews or do not comply when they demand this or that. With few exceptions, these brave men have lost everything, even their lives.' The Jews are then lumped together with the Hungarians and Gypsies as 'they got all the power after the dramatic change in the National Destiny in 1945' (Humoreanu undated). But Vadim Tudor began changing his anti-Semitic image before the presidential elections in 2004. He paid a visit to Auschwitz with another one hundred PRM members, where he openly declared that it is important to preserve the memory of the Holocaust and said the most terrible tragedies of the twentieth century occurred in Europe, as the two world wars started. In the same year, he also commissioned, paid for and unveiled a statue of former Israeli Prime Minister Yitzhak Rabin in the Romanian town of Braşov.[20] These two moves fit in perfectly with Taggart's definition of populism as a political tactic and strategy, including the chameleonic nature of the parties.

The PRM programme supports the features of *law and order* – a fight against corruption, nepotism, discrimination and economic crime – and promotes a strong state which provides security to all its citizens. In this sense, it would like to punish all who are guilty of economic and moral crimes in *post-December Romania* (i.e. after the fall of the Ceauşescu regime). The party also supports compulsory military training, so the entire nation would be available for defence against the threat of international terrorism (PRM 2008). As regards economic policy and the party's stance towards *welfare chauvinism*, PRM supports the full nationalization of industry, stresses a fear of the open market and criticizes the impact of globalization. It promotes income parity between social classes and keeping Romanian property in Romanian hands.

Interim conclusion: Far Right parties in the Balkans, core ideologies and specific features

Significant nationalism may be observed, accompanied by xenophobia, a desire for law and order and populism in the ideology of all the parties under study. Table 5.1 shows that welfare chauvinism is present in full in four cases, partially in two cases and not at all in one case. The only parties not demonstrating one key feature of the Far Right described under all definitions – nationalism in the form of external exclusivity – are the VMRO–NP and Ataka. The nationalism of the Macedonian VMRO–NP is restricted to hate speeches against the Albanian minority and does not seek the creation of a United Macedonia, while Ataka does not wish to create Greater Bulgaria. VMRO–NP is populist in terms of ideology as well as strategy and tactics and is the closest to the political centre of the cases under analysis. The *softer* radical Right group encompasses VMRO–NP and Ataka (and possibly the new Slovak National Party (*Slovenská národná strana*, SNS) in Serbia) – the only parties to display nationalism purely in terms of internal homogenization, as opposed to external exclusivity. The *harder* extreme Right includes the SRS, HSP, Serbian Radical Party of Dr. Vojislav Šešelj (SRS CG), BK, VMRO, PRM and New Generation Party–Christian Democratic (*Partidul Noua Generaţie–Creştin Democrat*, PNG–CD) – all parties exhibiting nationalism both in terms of external exclusivity and internal homogenization, thus taking an anti-system position. However, the position of the parties may change over time – some parties may be labelled extremist, but over time, their ideology softens permitting their placement in the radical Right group.

Since the parties of the Far Right have a nationalist core, their substance is country specific; only some have had experience with the Italian or German puppet states of the Second World War, and each country has specific national minorities and specific issues the radical Right is focusing on. The position of the parties towards the West differs – if the West sided with the nation in the

Table 5.1 Ideological core and specific features of Far Right parties in the Balkans

	HSP	SRS	VMRO–NP	BK	VMRO	Ataka	PRM
Nationalism – external exclusivity	X	X	–	X	X	–	X
Nationalism – internal homogenization	X	X	X	X	X	X	X
Xenophobia	X	X	X	X	X	X	X
Law and order	X	X	X	X	X	X	X
Welfare chauvinism	X	X	NN	Partially	Partially	X	X
Populism	X	X	X	X	X	X	X
Anti-Semitism	X	X	–	–	–	X	X
Anticommunism	–	X	–	X	X	–	–
Glorification of communism	–	–	–	–	–	–	X
Affiliated to church/religion	X	X	–	–	X	X	X
Negative towards EU, NATO, USA	X	X	–	–	–	X	X
Negative towards ICTY	X	X	–	–	–	–	–
Second World War revisionism	X	–	–	–	–	–	–
Supports integration into EU	–	–	X	X	X	–	X
Supports integration into NATO	–	–	X	X	X	–	X
Islamic fundamentalism as enemy	–	X	–	–	X	X	–
Economic neoliberalism	NN	NN	Not fully elaborated	–	Partially	–	–
Socialist values (equal wages, nationalization, etc.)	NN	NN	–	–	–	X	X
Against FDI	NN	NN	–	Partially	–	X	X

X Applicable.

– Not applicable.

NN Not known or not an issue for the party.

Balkan Wars, then the nationalist formations support integration into Euro-Atlantic structures, whereas if the West stood against the nation (country), the formations are against the EU, NATO, ICTY, globalization, etc. Another feature mentioned by some authors – revisionism – is an issue only in countries where the Nazi regime was present; this should be valid for Croatia but need not be so, for example, in Serbia. In addition, the Romanian PRM does not tie its existence to Second World War Romania but rather to the Ceauşescu regime,[21] while it is Gigi Becali and his PNG–CD who glorify Antonescu Romania. Similarly, Ataka shares little in common in terms of Fascist ideology (see, e.g., Frusetta and Glont 2009).

Just as in WE, key representatives of the party family do not hold neoliberal views on the economy, and their economic programme is a secondary feature of their ideologies (cf. Mudde 2007:119). The political parties differ in their views on the economy. Some prefer neoliberal values and others equal wages and property nationalization at the same time they claim post-1990 governments have reduced the population to poverty. A typical example of Leftist ideology in terms of the economy is PRM, which coexisted with the Socialist Labour Party in government during the 1992–1995 period and later maintained a voting affinity with the Social Democrats. As for the chauvinist welfare state, most parties are against having property in the hands of nonnationals; only BK and VMRO see foreign ownership as a challenge to the development of the internal economy.

Each case observed includes core features of nationalism, xenophobia and law and order in its ideology, with welfare chauvinism present in some cases, sometimes attaining boundary values. If we take populism to be a core ideological feature, it is apparent that all parties feature populist ideologies, making the second revised conception of Cas Mudde, which includes nativism (in the form of nationalism and xenophobia), authoritarianism (in terms of law and order) and populism, better suited for defining minimalist criteria for the Far Right. But since populism seems to be present in the ideologies of other party families, it is probably wiser to view it as a complementary feature. The issue deserves further research – at present, it may only be concluded that parties on the Far Right share similar ideological patterns with their counterparts in WE.

Notes

1 A Croatian politician who lived in the nineteenth century and was one of those who helped to gain recognition for the Croatian language and nation and laid the foundations for the Croatian state. Being a Croatian nationalist, Starčević also became known for his nationalism, racism, anti-Semitism and rejection of the Serbian language and the Serbian nation (Miščević 2006).

2 For example, the party's position on voting for national minorities: 'Croatians are second-rate citizens. In parliamentary elections, a few hundred voters elect

representatives of the national minority. But the HSP representative needs to obtain 93,000 votes to be elected. In other words, a few hundred members of a national minority are worth as much as 100 thousands Croats! ... But in Croatia nobody should have greater rights than ethnic Croats!' Govor predsjednika HSP na konvenciiji 2009. http://hsp.hr/content/view/23/40/.

3   www.hsp.hr/content/view/6/6/lang,hr/.

4   HSP. *Vukovarska Deklaracija*. 18. rujna 2010. http://hsp.hr/content/view/997/138/. HSP. *Otvoreno pismo*. 2.9. 2010. http://hsp.hr/images/stories/otvorenopismo.pdf.

5   *HSP predlaže zakon o 'etičkoj privatizaciji'*, www.totalportal.hr/article. php?article_id=83925&action=rate&type=article&thumb=down.

6   Govor predsjednika HSP na konvenciiji 2009. http://hsp.hr/content/view/23/40/.

7   The Chetniks were Serbian nationalist and royalist guerrilla fighters mainly known for operating during the Second World War. Also the Serbian Renewal Movement (*Srpski pokret obnove*, SPO) claims heritage of the Chetniks, and the SRS has placed less emphasis on rehabilitating the Second World War Chetniks.

8   'Albanians always fought against the Serbs on the side of the Turks, Mussolini and Hitler and now want to create a Greater Albanian narco-mafia state and expel the Serbs from Kosovo'.

9   The Macedonian nation was recognized by the Serbians only after the Second World War. Prior to this, Macedonians were perceived to be Serbs and Macedonia was seen as Southern Serbia.

10   The blame is usually laid on the Roman Catholic Church, as is evident from the title of another book by Vojislav Šešejl: Roman Catholic Criminal Project of the Artificial Croatian nation (*Rimokatolički zločinački projekat veštačke hrvatske nacije*).

11   Conversation with the representative of government of Republika Srpska Krajina Slobodan Jarčević. Belgrade 3.5.2007. One of the most recent books of Mr. Jarčević, *Ex-Serbs. Roman-Catholics, Muslims, Romanians, Montenegrins (Bivši Srbi. Rimokatolici, Muslimani, Rumuni, Crnogorci)*, lays out the historical reasons for Greater Serbia and maintains that Croats, Bosniaks, Romanians and Montenegrins used to be Serbs, ruling over ancient Illyria.

12   The Croats are seen as stealing the language and the land of the Serbs and being responsible for all wars and conflicts in which Serbs have suffered since the seventeenth century (Šešelj 2002). In Šešelj's own words: 'We're not fascists. We're just chauvinists who hate Croats' (October 1997). *Vojislav Seselj in his own words*. BBC News Europe 7/77/2007. http://news.bbc.co.uk/2/hi/europe/2793899.stm.

13   Ties between SRS and the Serbian Orthodox Church were not always close, and the party is not necessarily as much emphasizing its proximity to the church than other parties (DSS) or groups (*Dveri*).

14   www.accessmylibrary.com/article-1G1–100447387/macedonian-party-leader-georgievski.html.

15   *BK fights for the red and black flag, for the rights of the Albanian nation; BK fights for a free Albania, ethnic and democratic on the basis of a modern state, etc. (Dekalogu. Programi i Ballit Kombëtar 2006, cf. BKK 2001).*

16 *Bulgarija 2050 – projekt za demografska programa.* VMRO 2010. Available online at www.vmro.org/index.php?option=com_content&view=article&id=321 &Itemid=49.

17 *Ataka Leader Siderov: Nationalism Not Taboo in Bulgaria After Elections.* Available online at www.ataka.bg/en/.

18 Even though Vadim Tudor claims adherence to the Romanian Orthodox Church, he is allegedly sectarian (Informal conversation with Romanian political scientist Andreea Maierean in Wien 2009).

19 The demands to create Greater Romania were present in Moldova as well, so annexation would probably not be the most suitable term.

20 Transitions Online: *Romanian Leopard Changing Spots.* The Centre for South-East European Studies. 19.1.2004. Available online at www.csees.net/?page=country_analyses&country_id=6&ca_id=988.

21 Antonescu is seen by PRM as a national hero, but the party does not tie its existence to this fascist heritage. PRM has also proposed naming military academies after Antonescu and suggested he be declared a saint.

6

External supply side: the roots of success and political opportunity structures in successful cases

This chapter is devoted to variables which might potentially influence the success of Far Right political parties. After reviewing scholarship focused on the roots of success and political opportunity structures, we will closely explore the Serbian, Bulgarian and Romanian milieu and try to apply potential variables for these cases.

Some scholars suspect the good fortune enjoyed by the parties has mostly resulted from a profound, and largely psychological, crisis of the 'popular classes' whose hard work and determination form the backbone of the post-war recovery, of mass affluence and of the social welfare state. Seen from this perspective, xenophobia is a response to perceived competition from labour immigrants. Betz and Immerfall say blue-collar workers defect from Left-wing parties when party organizations modernize (creating a transformation from essentially religious-, class- and regionally based 'mass parties' to programmatically open, moderate and electorally expansive 'catch-all' parties or 'Volksparteien') and due to changes in the fabric of society (social alienation, isolation and deprivation). Newly emerging parties find it easier to establish themselves due to changes in technology and the availability of new resources which make it difficult for the established parties to pre-empt opportunities for the emergence of new competitors (Betz and Immerfall 1998:251–253).

As for explanatory models, Minkenberg notes the cultural context for mobilization of the radical Right, including demographic, immigration-related and religious characteristics as well as political culture. Political opportunity structures then include the effects of election laws on new parties, major cleavages, the behaviour of elites, the structure of party competition, major convergence and trends towards polarization and the degree to which parties are either open or closed to accepting demands from outside the system (Minkenberg 2008:20–28).

Herbert Kitschelt argues that an advanced capitalist democracy is a necessary precondition for a strong radical Right. The second condition relates to the behaviour of the major parties on both the Right and Left of the political continuum. When the two chief Left and Right parties converge, it creates a space on the edge of the Right–Left continuum, allowing the Far Right party to be successful, as voters look for an alternative and see no clear difference between the two main players. Last but not least, 'the extreme Right can do well in this configuration provided it finds the winning formula to attract right-authoritarian support, namely a resolutely market-liberal stance on economic issues and an authoritarian and particularistic stance on political questions of participatory democracy, of individual autonomy of lifestyles and cultural expressions, and of citizenship status' (Kitschelt 1995:25, 275).

Some authors (e.g. Carter 2005, van der Brug and Fennema 2007) focus on the political continuum while emphasizing the position of the chief Right-wing party, accompanied by the convergence of both Left and Right as envis-aged by Kitschelt – 'the ideological proximity of the parties of the mainstream right (the extreme right parties' nearest competitors) determines how much political space is available to the parties of the extreme right, and this space may well be related to how successful the extreme right parties are at the polls. In other words, the degree of ideological convergence between the mainstream right and the mainstream left may well affect the right-wing extremist party vote' (Carter 2005:7). Similarly, Bonnie Meguid claims that the strategies of the electorally and governmentally dominant parties shape the electoral fortunes of the *niche* parties.[1] Moreover, when the actions of the mainstream parties on the niche party's new issue dimension are taken into account, the standard institutional and sociological factors fail to exhibit a consistently signi-ficant effect on Green and radical Right party vote levels (Meguid 2005:357). Meguid claims that mainstream parties are able to shape the electoral fortunes of their niche party opponents and uses the case of the USA to show that 'niche party fortune depends on the behaviour of mainstream and – contra standard spatial models – especially nonproximal mainstream parties' (Meg-uid 2010:272).

Many research articles point to the fact that Fascism as well as Nazism came to power as their leaders took advantage of structural flaws in a parlia-mentary system where the traditional Right parties were too weak to provide an effective alternative (see, e.g., Griffin 2000:9). Other explanatory theories include radicalization of the political space which regards radical Right voting as a product of political opportunities conducive to the politicization of new cleavages (Koopmanset *et al.* 2005 cited from Stefanova 2007:5) or a single-issue thesis which sees the Far Right as a response to salient issues in society, such as unemployment or immigration.

Terri Givens claims that the electoral system, coalition structures, factional-ism and the varying electoral rules and coalition structures provide differing incentives for voters to vote strategically and for parties to coordinate on coa-lition strategy. Her central argument is that the Far Right has more problems attracting voters and winning seats in countries whose political systems encourage voters to vote strategically. For example, the two-stage election system in France makes it hard for a Far Right party to win any seats in the second round. These parties may win votes in the first round as voters protest incumbents, but the voters will abandon them in the decisive second round. In Germany, Far Right parties might pick up some seats in the party-preference vote, but they cannot win any seats in the constituency votes. In contrast, the grand coalition between the two biggest parties encouraged Austrians to cast protest votes for the Far Right, and this eventually propelled the Freedom Party into government (Givens 2005:4).

Some researchers believe proportional representation helps Far Right parties obtain popular support (this claim is based on Duverger's Law, which stipulates that single-member majoritarian districts tend to foster a two-party system, while proportional representation fosters multipartism (Duverger 1972)). Others deny this (Jesuit and Mahler 2004:26, van der Brug et al. 2005:568); some conclude that electoral systems matter in specific ways. Jackman and Volpert claim that a lower effective electoral threshold is associated with increased support for Far Right parties (Jackman and Volpert 1996:516) or find, as did Golder, that populist parties do better in countries where district size is larger and more seats are allocated in upper tiers. They also believe permissiveness in the electoral system mediates the effect of immigration on populist parties (Golder 2003:461).[2] Arzheimer and Carter report their findings that Far Right voters are not responding to the psychological effects of electoral systems in the way we might expect. In addition, the effect of unemployment is negative, perhaps because voters turn (back) to the more experienced mainstream parties in times of high unemployment (Arzheimer and Carter 2006:439).

A link has often been noted between religion and the Far Right. There is a common belief that Catholics are more prone to radical/extreme Right politics and Protestants are immune to voting for Far Right parties, though, as Jean-Yves Camus remarks, the situation is actually more complex; the New Right is also on the rise in countries such as Denmark and Norway which are predominantly Protestant, though without a single example of a Protestant extreme Right political party having risen anywhere in Europe. Protestant voters do not have confessional parties and consequently split their vote between various competing parties. Camus further remarks that Pagan movements are oriented towards the Far Right, while relations with Islam have become a point of conflict within the extreme Right: one stream considers Islam to be an ally in the fight against the West, another stream is strongly Islamophobic, and a third group opposes both Islam and Israel/Judaism, calling both alien to European culture. As for Judaism and anti-Semitism, there are few extreme Right parties which may be said to be genuinely free of anti-Semitism. Some other religious or ethnic minorities seem to tend towards the Far Right, as well,

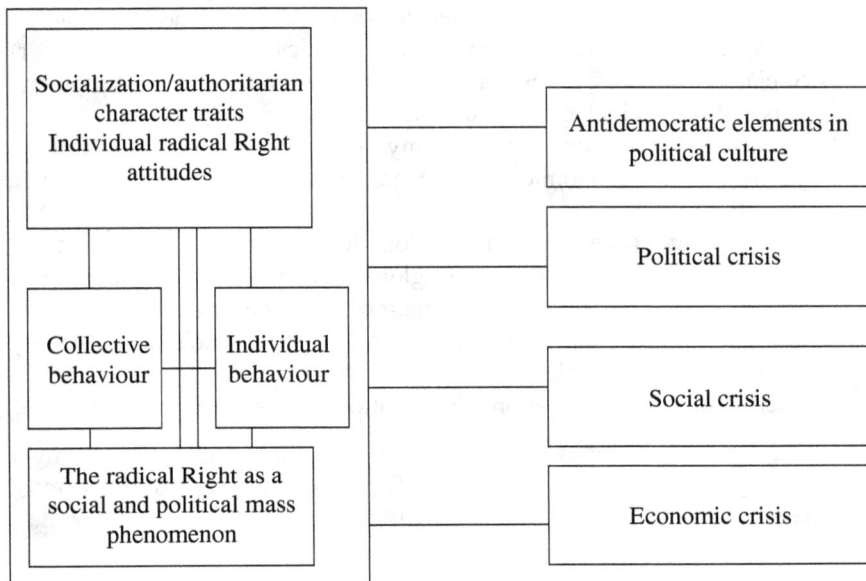

Figure 6.1 Causes of radical Right behaviour (Stöss, R. (1991). *Politics Against Democracy: Right-Wing Extremism in West Germany.* Oxford: Berg, cited from Williams in Ramet 1999:31)

something true of the Hindutva movement or the Jewish extreme Right. Camus concludes that extreme Right family in general is today a largely secular movement, though it retains an interest in religion because it sees religion as one component of national identity; he then identifies three streams in the extreme Right family in terms of religion: (1) a group which defends free-thinking and libertarian values, (2) a group which promotes European civilization against the threat of Islamization and sees Christianity as a cultural cornerstone of European civilization and (3) a group which sets religion aside and promotes a European identity based upon ethnicity and 'racial awareness' (Camus 2007).

Richard Stöss claims that radical Right behaviour has societal and individual causes, while the success of the radical Right relies upon the relations between these two. Periods of political, social and economic crisis, then, form a breeding ground for the emergence of anti-democratic elements (Figure 6.1).

From the above discussion, one may divide the variables into five categories (Betz and Immerfall 1998, Williams in Ramet 1999:37, Minkenberg 2008):

1. Political (political discontent, convergence/polarization/fragmentation of the party system, electoral system, emergence of Green parties and New Left movements, referenda that cut across the old party cleavages,

creation of a new state, perceived internal/external threats, the political expression of nationalism, regime change, political culture, elite behaviour)
2. Social (dissolution of established identities, middle-class discontent, existence of social tension or conflict)
3. Economic (post-industrial economy, rising unemployment, welfare payment cuts, economic crisis, war, foreign domination, economic transition)
4. Ethno-cultural (cultural fragmentation, demographic fragmentation and multiculturalization, the impact of globalization, reaction to the influx of racially and culturally differing members of the population, popular xenophobia and racism, religion v. secularization, one's own ethnicity living outside the borders of a mother state)
5. International context (national humiliation, desire for higher status)

The next section will focus on the above-mentioned variables which might potentially influence the success of Far Right political parties in the most successful cases – Serbia, Romania and Bulgaria.

The context of the most successful Far Right parties: Serbia, Romania and Bulgaria

Political, social and economic variables

Political variables in Serbia

The Romanian, Bulgarian and Serbian transitions are usually depicted as being complex and arriving late. Nationalist parties had a fair amount of popularity in Serbia at the beginning of the 1990s. The nationalist card was played by the Socialist Party of Serbia (*Socialistička Partija Srbije*, SPS) during the wars in Croatia and Bosnia and Herzegovina (BiH), and Milošević found favour with many voters. The Serbian Radical Party (*Srpska Radikalna Stranka*, SRS) rose to power in the 1997 elections. The party's success is usually credited to a deteriorating economic and social system and disaffected voters unhappy with the defence of national interests at the end of the war in Croatia and BiH, particularly the Dayton Peace Accord. Serbia's GNP at the close of 1997 was barely half that of 1989. Average real wages paid to employees were approximately 40% of those paid in 1989. At the end of 1997, there were 2,328,000 workers in the Federal Republic of Yugoslavia (FRY) with about 700,000 laid off as part of 'mandatory furloughs'. Employment agencies had 800,000 persons registered (mostly under the age of 30), and the number of pensioners was 1,477,663. The revival of nationalism in Serbia is usually presented as a result of systematic propaganda, an exceptionally severe economic social situation and dramatic worsening of the political circumstances in Kosovo. As Goati remarks, the SRS addressed the same target groups as did the SPS, in an attempt to attract *wandering voters* (Goati 2001:128–129). The unemployment rate in Serbia was not excessive despite unfavourable conditions on the labour market, remaining fairly stable between 1995 (12.9%) and 2003 (14.6%), with a slight increase towards the end of that period (for all unemployment rates see International Labour Organization statistics at http://www.ilo.org/global/statistics-and-databases/lang--en/index.htm).[3]

The overwhelming victory of democratic parties in 2000 meant total loss for the SRS. The fragmented coalition responded by making controversial moves (e.g. sending Milošević to the Hague, which sparked controversy in both society and the *polity*, the issue of Šešelj and the International Criminal Tribunal for the former Yugoslavia (ICTY), the unresolved situation in Montenegro and relation towards Republika Srpska). Events after the assassination of prime minister Zoran Djindjić[4] helped the SRS to consolidate and become the de facto victor (on the level of political parties, not coalitions) in every election (2003, 2007, 2008), although remaining isolated in opposition. Prtina remarks that the success of the SRS is doubly motivated. On one hand, there is a populist–nationalist programme with easy, attractive solutions aimed at voters who lost jobs during privatization, the middle class which happened to be economically on the edge of society and refugees from BiH, Croatia and Kosovo. The second reason lies in protest votes. Voters showed their disagreement with government policies which focused on disputes within the governing coalition rather than on the problems of everyday Serbs (Prtina 2004:11–12).

The Serbian party system has been quite stable – four areas of conflict have evolved around the main poles. As noted above, it is not really possible to distinguish Left from Right in the Serbian political environment. At one directional extreme, we have an authoritarian nationalist pole represented by the SRS and at another, a party with a communist past – the nationalist SPS. The nationalist Democratic Party of Serbia (*Demokratska Stranka Srbije*, DSS) might have played a certain role for the voters of the SRS; the fourth pole is then occupied by the Democratic Party (*Demokratska Stranka*, DS) and the G17 Plus, these being pro-European, modern, democratic players. The SRS seems to have replaced the SPS in the key position after 2000, since the SPS has not been achieving high numbers. Of note, though, is the fact that SPS was accepted into the coalition government after the 2008 elections,[5] while the SRS remains excluded from coalition talks as an infeasible partner. It seems that the SRS does not profit from DSS voters – DSS has been in continuous decline since 2007, while the SRS has steady support, with stable election results since 2003, when both parties made their best showing in the electoral race. Kitschelt's rule cannot be applied in the case of Serbia, since the most proximate party, DSS, does not seem to create space for SRS voters. Polarization of the system could play a part in the success of the Serbian Radicals – the main extreme poles are occupied by SRS and SPS and then by DSS and DS and G17

Plus. Voter opinions regarding all four of these points of the political compass are quite stable, with little fluctuation between them, except for SRS and SPS voters, who do not much differ in ideology. The SRS replaced the SPS in dominant position with a charismatic leader and a focus on the same themes, those of nationalism, nationalization of the economy, and law and order.

In 2008, a new player made its presence felt in Serbian politics, the Serbian Progressive Party (*Srpska Napredna Stranka*, SNS), created by former SRS Deputy President Tomislav Nikolić and his supporters, because of internal disagreements over party direction with the party's leader, Vojislav Šešelj. Probably the chief difference is that the party promotes the accession of Serbia to the European Union (EU) and its nationalism has been softened. The party says it does not wish to create a Greater Serbia nor does it wish for any region to be annexed. Its only claim is to Kosovo, which it sees as an integral part of the Republic of Serbia. The relations with the Serbs in Croatia and BiH are to be defined by economic unity with Serbia. The party's programme also calls for ethnic and religious tolerance, military neutrality on the part of Serbia and a fight against crime and corruption. Its economic policy leans left on issues to do with social justice and the welfare state.

The SNS is becoming very popular with the Serbian public, and it has begun to call for early elections. February 2011 opinion polls showed that 34.4% of voters would vote for SNS and its allies,[6] 29.1% would vote for DS, 7.1% for the SPS, 6.1% for the Liberal Democratic Party (*Liberalno demokratska partija*, LDP) and 5.7% for DSS, and SRS would struggle to get past the 5% threshold.[7] If voters vote in the upcoming elections as the opinion polls show they will, there would be a complete shakeup of the currently stable political party system, and new configurations would emerge. SNS is also very unpredictable as a new political player, something which might lead to lack of commonality with the EU during the accession process.

Political variables in Romania
The Romanian transition was a bit delayed as well.[8] Until 1996, post-communist parties[9] dominated – the National Salvation Front (*Frontul Salvării Naţionale*, FSN) proposed a very cautious approach to economic reforms, accompanied by an expensive social system. Necessary structural reforms were therefore bypassed in the name of social cohesion. The 1996 elections were then run by parties situated on the Right end of the political continuum. These began economic reforms (liberalization, privatization, restructuring and an end to business subsidies). The centre-Right ruling coalitions managed to hold on to power despite a lack of cohesion, the internal frictions, decisional paralysis and leadership change (Romania had three prime ministers in the space of four years).

The 2000 elections brought the Left back to power (Social Democratic Party) and Iliescu as President of Romania. From 2004 until 2008, Rightist parties came back to power in the governing Justice and Truth coalition, which had a parliamentary majority composed of the National Liberal Party (*Partidul Naţional Liberal,* PNL), Democratic Party (*Partidul Democrat,* PD) and the Democratic Union of Hungarians in Romania (*Uniunea Democrată Maghiară din România,* UDMR). In 2008, the government was formed by the Social Democrats and the Democratic Liberal Party (*Partidul Democrat-Liberal,* PD-L),[10] while the coalition ally of the latter, PNL, entered the opposition. The Romanian party system consisted of two main poles and two to three complementary ones in the 1990s. After the upheaval, the chief pole was occupied by the successor to FSN – Democratic National Salvation Front (*Frontul Democrat al Salvării Nationale,* FDSN), the party which would occupy the second main pole, the Christian-Democratic National Peasants' Party (*Partidul Naţional Ţărănesc Creştin Democrat,* PNŢCD), was confirmed by the elections in 1996. Supplementary poles were occupied by PD, the nationalist Greater Romania Party (*Partidul România Mare,* PRM), the Party of Romanian National Unity (*Partidul Unităţii Naţionale a Românilor,* PUNR) and the UDMR, as the party representing the Hungarian ethnic minority (Strmiska 2000).

PRM voters came partially from supporters of the PUNR, which was part of the National Celebration Front. But it was only with the collapse of the fledgling Romanian centre-Right at the end of the 1990s that the PRM got its chance to seek power. The PRM was not at that time addressing the issues which Carter says should be addressed by Right-wing parties; instead its rise took place because parties of the Right had become discredited in the eyes of their voters. Voters saw no difference between the clientelist Right and Left; PRM was to become the alternative for voters on the Right end of the continuum and voters whose standard of living had fallen after 1990, that is, the *losers* in the economic and political transformation.

Opinion polls in 2000 showed great voter dissatisfaction with politics, accompanied by authoritarian sentiments: only 34% of the respondents had faith in political parties, 50% preferred equality to liberty and 57% believed that people behaved as they should if governed by an iron hand (Mungiu-Pipidi-Althabe 2002 cited from Gallagher 2003:32). The Romanian case shows certain similarities with the Serbian case in the cooperation of the political parties operating at the end of the political continuum – a government composed of former communists was supported after the 1992 elections by the PRM and PUNR – the xenophobic discourse and rigidly centralized unitarian concept of the state hindered the emergence of democratic pluralism and of a Western Europe-oriented foreign policy (IDEA 1997).

Data released by the World Bank in 2000 showed that in 1999, 41.2% of Romanians lived at or below the poverty line, compared with 25.3% in 1995. Meanwhile, Romanians living in extreme poverty comprised 16.6% of the population in 1999 compared with less than half that (8%) in 1995. Overall poverty, then, contrasted with the fact that the parliament approved salary increases for Members of the Parliament (MPs) of 16% (Gallagher 2003:14, 22), leading to a further lack of public confidence in political institutions and a deepening of the gap between politicians and their voters.[11] The missing political culture and the swapping of ideology for personal ambition and public benefit for private benefit contributed to the overall dissatisfaction of the populace with politics. Statistics show that the number of people claiming their standard of living compared to that of 1989 was much worse rose sharply from 20% in 1997 to 35% in 1999 and the number of respondents who assessed the post-communist change as definitely negative rose from 7% in 1997 to 17% in 1999 (Marginean 2004:195–196).

The PRM was also able to draw votes from that portion of the population which was better off during the regime of Nicolae Ceauşescu, who was glorified by the party. One in thirty members of the population was an informer to the state secret police, Securitate (Deletant 2000, cited from Gallagher 2003:20), so the party was able to draw upon a large number of people who were not satisfied with the new situation after 1989. The public was quite aware of the fact that former Securitate collaborators operated within PRM.[12] The party refused to hand over the candidate list for verification by the National Commission for the Securitate Archives (CNSAS), whose task was to uncover collaborators with the former regime before they were allowed to run for office. However, there were no consequences. The commission published an incomplete list of candidates with compromising links to the former regime, and PRM candidates went on to run in the elections (RFE, cited from Gallagher 2003:29).

The process of Romanian accession to the EU had a great impact on the strategy and tactics of PRM. The continued popularity of the EU with the public forced PRM to recognize that there was no alternative to EU accession and the party moved to a more positive line on European integration. But even this pro-integration move did not add votes. PRM never repeated its success in the 2000 elections, when it had won 84/345 seats – 19.5% of the vote. Instead, the party experienced a steady decline, winning forty-eight seats (13% of the vote) in 2004 and failed to gain a single seat in the 2008 national elections.

One additional phenomenon must be mentioned in relation to PRM as well – the existence of the other Far Right party within the system, the New Generation Party–Christian Democratic (*Partidul Noua Generaţie–Creştin Democrat*, PNG–CD; formerly *Partidul Noua Generaţie*, PNG) or, more precisely, its leader, Gigi Becali, who is very popular (*inter alia* Becali placed 13th in the 2006 TV show 100 Greatest Romanians).[13] Becali recently joined the PRM and was elected an MP to the European Parliament as an independent on the PRM list. This has been seen by many as the reason the PRM has gained popularity recently and is viewed as very significant within the political context.[14] The chief difference between the two parties is that the PRM retains its leftist orientation as regards the state's role in the economy. PNG–CD, by contrast, accords the major role to the market. The PRM also leans more to the Social Democrats, while PNG–CD leans in the direction of the Liberal Democrats (Sum 2008:4) and employs more nationalist, racist and xenophobic rhetoric. The existence of the second party on the Far Right must not be overlooked when speaking of elections. In the 2007 elections to the European Parliament, the PRM received 4.2% of the vote, while PNG–CD received 4.8%, with neither surpassing the electoral threshold. PNG–CD might also be seen as a potential new rival to the PRM which is taking its voters away and contributing to the party's decline. This may prove true even bearing in mind that each party has a radically different perspective on the economy since, as Mudde has noted, the economy is not a particularly salient issue for Far Right parties.

Political variables in Bulgaria
Bulgarian voters, like their Romanian counterparts, had become alienated from political parties due to corruption scandals, and the government was unpopular because it had implemented stringent economic and social reforms. In the European elections of 2007, with the success of the National Union Attack (*Natsionalen Sayuz Ataka*, Ataka) and the PRM, public opinion polls showed around 75% of Romanians were dissatisfied with their government's anticorruption programme. The same proportion of Bulgarians reported dissatisfaction with their government's policies as well (Stefanova 2008:567). Scepticism and distrust in Bulgaria was quite visible in the confidence rating in Gallup polls from before and after the elections (June–July 2005). While parliament received only 14–15% confidence and the cabinet 19–23% confidence, the president received 70–71% and the army 55–56%.[15]

Bulgaria used to have a highly stable multipolar system which was mostly classified as a limited multipartism or as a 'two-and-a-half' party system at the start of the transition (cf. Strmiska 2001a). Two main political players emerged over time – the Union of Democratic Forces (*Sayuz na Demokratichnite Sili*, SDS) on one side and the Bulgarian Socialist Party on the other. The 2001 elections brought a new player to the scene – the National Movement of Simeon II (*Nacionalno Dviženie Simeon II*, NDSV)[16] which noticeably upset the existing electoral competition and destabilized the party system. The permeable nature of the electoral system and voters' lack of patience with the governments in power allowed the system to be disrupted based upon a division between the *post-communist Left* and the *anti-communist Right*. However, the success of NDSV was only temporary and was not repeated, in spite of the party's being accepted into the coalition government with the Socialists and the Movement for Rights and Freedoms (*Dvizhenie za Prava i Svobodi/Hak ve Özgürlükler*

Hareketi, DPS) in 2005. The new government led by Simeon Saxe-Coburg-Gotha was instead composed of technocrats without any political experience, sometimes described as a government of lawyers and yuppies.[17]

Bulgarian politics is extraordinary in that no government was able to achieve re-election until 2005. In addition, despite a large Turkish minority and high transformation costs, the nationalist parties remained at the edge of the political spectrum until 2005, when Ataka won twenty-one seats out of 240. The fragmentation and fluidity of the party system led to an increased number of parties represented in the parliament and party switching: 'For instance, the 40th National Assembly began its term in 2005 with seven parliamentary groups but by the end of the mandate in 2009 it had ten parliamentary groups plus independents' (National Assembly of Republic of Bulgaria 2005, 2009 cited from Barzachka 2009). The 2005 election made polarization among voters clear. Public opinion was divided between an expectation for radical change in government policy and preservation of the overall policy framework with certain amendments made. Supporters of these two positions added up to approximately 42–43% of poll respondents, while 12–13% of voters believed no change at all should be made to the way the country was governed (mainly DPS and NDSV voters) (Karasimeonov 2005:22).

The 2007 European elections in Bulgaria showed how tired Right-wing voters had become. There was a lack of credible candidates on the Right side of the spectrum and an inability on the part of Right-wing parties to get along. These were the chief reasons cited for the emergence of the new political formation Citizens for the European Development of Bulgaria (*Grazhdani za Evropeysko Razvitie na Balgariya*, GERB) (Yordanova cited from Maškarinec 2008:125). The socialist camp then lost support as the result of a corruption scandal which broke out during the month of elections, disputes within the coalition government and the prioritization of EU requirements for accession in 2007 over domestic issues such as the social security system and healthcare (Savkova 2007:2). The elections to the European Parliament in 2007 also meant success for Ataka – the party received 14.2% of the votes (three seats). The mobilization of anti-European and anti-Turkish voters, along with the low turnout in the European elections, was behind the gain of Ataka as the party de facto placed fourth in the race. Dissatisfaction among voters on both sides of the political spectrum led to the fact that the elections of 2009 were won by the populist formation GERB, while Ataka confirmed its position by gaining the same number of mandates as in previous elections. The main competitor to Ataka since 2007 seems to have been GERB due to the similarities in their campaigns and the same target group of voters. Both parties use anti-Turkish and Eurosceptic sentiments in their campaign and aim at voters dissatisfied with the current state of politics in Bulgaria on both sides of the political spectrum.

Other common variables: unemployment, electoral systems,
the post-material dimension and anarchism
The level of unemployment does not correlate with the gains of the Far Right
parties in any of the cases. In Romania, PRM's biggest success came only
when the unemployment rate began to drop.[18] At first glance, the level of unemployment does not seem to matter in Serbia – SRS seems to have a stable voter
basis, and the numbers do not differ much with the decreasing unemployment
rate, though they might have affected voter behaviour in the 2003 elections
where the unemployment rate slightly rose. The year 2009 shows a slight
increase in unemployment in Bulgaria and a slight increase in the support for
Ataka, though in the previous elections, this relationship was not visible.
Unemployment expectations in Bulgaria prior to the 2005 elections were also
optimistic – the number of people who thought unemployment would rise fell
(from 29% in January 2009 to 15% in June 2005), while the number of people
thinking unemployment would drop increased (from 15% in January 2005 to
20% in June 2005).[19] The same optimism was visible in a poll by the same
agency regarding living conditions for families – an increase from 9% to 11%
from January 2005 to June 2005 of those who claimed the economic conditions of their family had gotten better, with a slight decrease in those who
claimed economic conditions had worsened compared to prior year (from 36%
to 35% over the same time period).[20] The numbers given for unemployment
rates are nevertheless inaccurate because of the existence of the grey economy.
The unemployment rate does not seem to be the main factor in explaining the
increase of support for Far Right parties, though in some cases, it might play a
certain role. This would be especially true for Serbia, where the economic situation had been bad for an extremely long period of time (Figures 6.2 to 6.4).

The Serbian *electoral system* for parliamentary elections has remained
essentially the same since 2000, with the exception of rules on ethnic minority
representation. The parliament is comprised of 250 seats, and its members are
elected for a four-year term by closed-list proportional representation with the
D'Hondt formula in a single national district, with a 5% threshold (Jovanović
2005). The Serbian case shows a trend towards worsening conditions for
smaller parties (since 2000, Serbia has had only one electoral district on the
state level; earlier it had 9 in the 1992 elections and 29 in the 1997 elections)
and, since 2007, improving conditions for parties of national minorities by
abolition of the threshold for these parties. The Bulgarian electoral system
resembles the Serbian system. Bulgaria adopted a proportional system in 1991
for 240 seats, with members elected to a four-year term with a 4% threshold
using the D'Hondt formula on the national level (then apportioning mandates
into thirty-one districts). The Romanian electoral system has changed with almost
every election. Until 2008, there was a palpable trend towards continuously
increasing barriers for smaller political entities and a steady positive approach

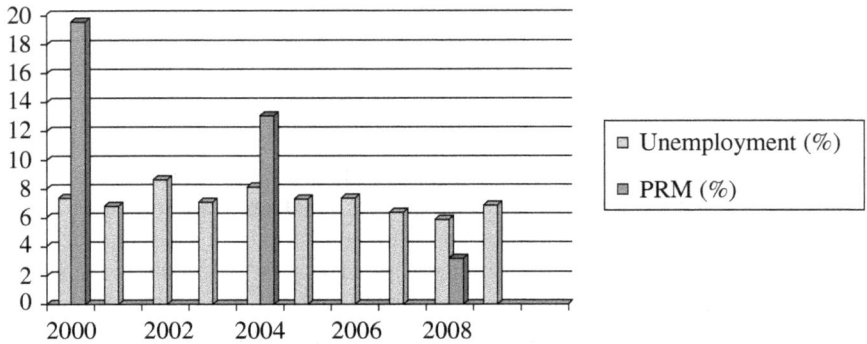

Figure 6.2 The Romanian unemployment rate and gains by Far Right parties after 2000
(Source: Eurostat, http://epp.eurostat.ec.europa.eu/statistics_explained/index.
php?title=File:Table_unemployment_rates.PNG&filetimestamp=20100602100039)

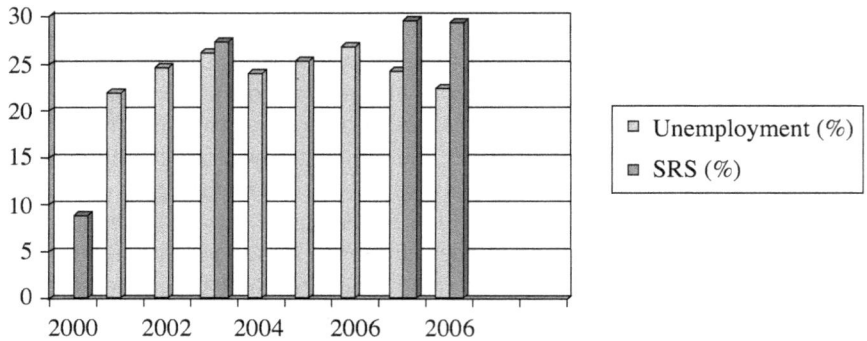

Figure 6.3 Serbian unemployment and the gains of SRS (Source: Statistical Office of
the Republic of Serbia, http://webrzs.stat.gov.rs/axd/en/god.htm)

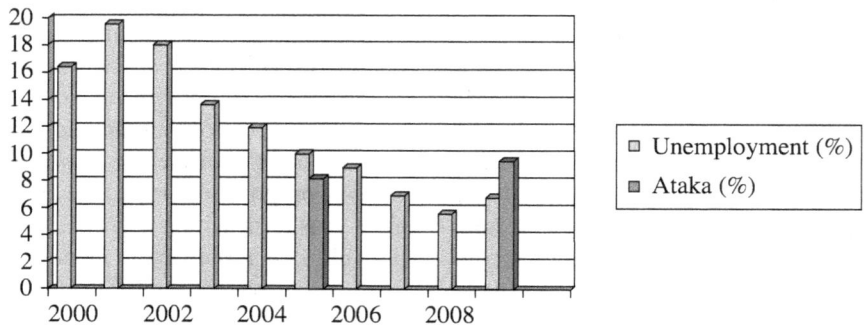

Figure 6.4 Bulgaria and the Far Right and the unemployment rate (Source: Statistical
Office of Bulgaria, www.nsi.bg/ORPDOCS/Labour_3.2.3_EN.xls)

towards national minorities which would not otherwise have a chance at gaining a seat (proportional representation, in 2004 the number of MPs dropped to 332 from 345 in 2000, while the seats reserved for national minorities were kept at 18; the single party threshold was set at 5% and the two-party coalition threshold at 8%. Multiparty coalitions had to pass a 10% threshold. The D'Hondt formula was used in forty-two electoral districts) (Šedo 2007:80–83).

In 2008, Romania introduced a new electoral system which replaced party-list proportional representation and introduced single-member constituencies in which candidates need an absolute majority of the votes in order to win a seat. The overall distribution of seats in each chamber is then carried out by proportional representation among parties surpassing a 5% nationwide threshold or winning a minimum number of seats (3 in the Senate, 6 in the Chamber of Deputies). National minorities have guaranteed seats if they fail to obtain a constituency.[21] Bulgaria is the second country which reverted back, adopting a mixed electoral system for the 2009 elections which introduced thirty-one single-member districts (SMDs), overlapping and identical in size to the existing thirty-one multimember districts (MMDs). Two hundred and nine out of 240 parliamentary seats are distributed according to the proportional system and thirty-one according to a first-past-the-post system. Voters cast two ballots – one for the party list and another for the SMD candidates, with candidates able to run in both districts. The method used to calculate results in the MMDs was changed from D'Hondt to Hare–Niemeyer (Stenographic Diaries 2009, cited from Barzachka 2009:4).

The regional trend towards transition from a mixed electoral system to a proportional system was maintained until 2008, when Romania and, in 2009, Bulgaria decided to revert back to include a majoritarian component in their electoral systems. In all cases, there are barriers in the form of an electoral threshold for smaller parties to enter parliament, though these are not extraordinarily high; the Bulgarian case is most open towards new smaller political entities. The distribution of mandates on the national level, accompanied by the D'Hondt formula in the Serbian (and Bulgarian case until 2009), then favours bigger parties, while Romania and Serbia (since 2007) have promoted better conditions for the parties of national minorities (reserved seats for national minorities in the Romanian case and the abolition of the threshold for these parties in the Serbian case). Despite the fact that Bulgaria has been most receptive towards new political parties, the only gain of mandates before 2000 was that of VMRO in 1997 (2 mandates as part of the coalition United Democratic Forces), whereas in the more restrictive rule environment in Serbia and Romania, Far Right parties scored much better and SRS and PRM and the PUNR were parties with government representation.

The 2008 elections in Romania under new predominantly majoritarian rules (not strictly first-past-the-post) were the first elections in which the PRM failed to gain seats to either the Senate or the Chamber of Deputies. Some political scientists assign the new electoral system a large role in hindering the PRM's access to parliamentary representation, since only one year later, in the 2009 European Parliament (EP) elections, during which the proportional system was used, the PRM did quite well, coming in fourth with three seats (out of thirty-three Member of the European Parliament (MEP) seats).[22] The 2009 parliamentary elections in Bulgaria also resulted in no mandates in SMDs for Ataka (9.36% of the votes in the proportional section of the system), whereas under the fully proportional system, 12% of votes were cast in the EP elections for the party (i.e. two mandates). The electoral system made a difference in both cases – the majoritarian component was a hindrance to Far Right parties in these two countries, and the electoral rules in the two countries played a certain role in creating the party systems.

The post-material dimension, which is usually mentioned in regard to Far Right parties in Western Europe, does not seem to play a role in these three countries either. In Bulgaria, the Green Party had already emerged in 1989 but only participated in local elections until 2005, when it was part of the Leftist Coalition for Bulgaria. In spite of the coalition's gains, none of the seats were allocated to it. The same outcome was repeated in the 2009 elections. The Romanian Green Party was only established in 2009. Before that, the Ecological Movement of Romania (*Miscarea Ecologista din Romania*, MER) won twelve seats in the 1990 elections, when the euphoric boom and the electoral system allowed the party to enter parliament. Since that time, no other Green Party has won a seat. The Green Party of Serbia was registered as a political party only in 2010.[23]

Anarchists in Serbia show some activity[24] but do not seem to have any influence yet on the voters of the extreme Right. Bulgarian anarchists try to follow in the famous Bulgaro-Macedonian anarchist tradition and seem to be the most active anarchists in the three countries; the Anarchist Federation of Bulgaria is a member of the International Anarchist Federations,[25] and anarchist protests are usually met with resistance from the Bulgarian extreme Right.[26] At present, however, the Left-wing movements lack the potential to significantly influence voters' decisions.

Ethno-cultural variables

Ethno-cultural variables in Serbia
There is a very *extensive Serbian diaspora* living outside of central *Serbia*; the last pre-war Yugoslavian census counted 581,663 (12.2%) Serbs in Croatia, 1,365,093 Serbs (31.2%) in BiH, 57,453 Serbs (9.34%) in Montenegro[27] and 209,498 (13.2%) Serbs in Kosovo.[28] There is also a tiny group of Serbs living in Albania and Macedonia – the 2002 census registered 35,939 (1.7%) Serbs.[29]

The censuses which took place after the war show quite different numbers – a significant drop in the ethnic Serbian population in Croatia and a slight increase in Serbs in BiH – 201,631 (4.54%) Serbs in Croatia, according to the 2001 census, while the 1996 United Nations High Commissioner for Refugees (UNHCR) population census registered 1,484,530 Serbs (37.9%) in BiH.[30] In 2004, 198,414 (32%) declared Serbian ethnic affiliation in Montenegro[31] – the enormous increase in number of Serbs in Montenegro may be explained by the fluid notion of the national concept and the processes of nation and state building which culminated during the declaration of independent Montenegro in 2006.

The extensive Serbian diaspora was also part of the reason behind the wars in the 1990s. Ethnic Serbs in Croatia and BiH (or their political representations) did not sympathize with the motion for an independent Croatia and BiH and felt part of Yugoslavia. The Serbian autonomous region (SAO) Krajina had already been declared in December 1990, and its representatives announced their will to stay in Socialist Federal Republic of Yugoslavia (SFRY) or with Serbia. Croatian forces were gradually winning the territory inhabited by Serbs; the territory around Knin was reintegrated into Croatia only after Operations Storm and Flash, and the final part of the region was integrated in January 1998.

Serbs in BiH declared their republic to be affiliated to Serbia in January 1992 – three months before the European Communities acknowledged the independence of BiH and at a time when the country was already flooded by refugees from Croatia and Yugoslavian National Army was withdrawing. The leadership of Serbs both in BiH and in Serbia declared their will to fight for the unification of Serbian lands so that all Serbs could live in a single state. The war only ended after the engagement of the USA and North Atlantic Treaty Organization (NATO) and the enormous Croatian offensive, all aimed against the position of Bosnian Serbs. The Dayton Peace Accord was signed after complicated negotiations in November 1995.

Kosovo had already been a problematic region during the Kingdom of Serbs, Croats and Slovenes, the Yugoslavian Kingdom, the Italian occupation during the Second World War and in Tito's post-war Yugoslavia. The poorest province needed a huge influx of funds, and the lowest standard of living in Yugoslavia resulted in periodic nationalist conflicts which were regularly suppressed by state forces. The conflict came to a head in 1999 after the conference in Rambouillet in which Milošević refused to accept the presence of foreign military forces in Kosovo. Kosovo was provisionally put under an international protectorate until the issue was solved after seventy-seven days of an *air campaign* at the conclusion of which a Military–Technical Agreement was signed in Kumanovo in Macedonia. Kosovo then declared unilateral independence in February 2008.

Ethno-cultural variables in Romania

Romania is a special case in which the public acquires dual identities based on pro-Europeanism and nationalism[32]: 'today, unsure of how to communicate effectively with the social groups that make up their electoral base, unsuccessful reformist parties are tempted to use nationalism to preserve minimal respect in the eyes of electorate disillusioned by the mediocrity and corruption of Romanian politics' (Gallagher in Light and Phinnemore 2001:114). Despite being described as a party of the Far Right, the PRM glorifies the previous communist regime. This is made possible by the fact that the Ceauşescu regime in Romania was special in promoting nationalism rather than internationalism, unlike in other communist countries in Central and Eastern Europe, which were complete vassals to the Moscow leadership. Ceauşescu was (next to Enver Hoxha) the only leader in the Warsaw Pact able to stand against the USSR – in particular, during the Prague Spring. Romania also was the only country in the Soviet Bloc which did not boycott the 1984 Olympic Games in Los Angeles and so became beloved by the West.

The communist regime was the regime which began to Romanianize the *Hungarian minority in Romania* (Hungarians make up 6.6% of the total population according to the 2002 census; in Transylvania, Hungarians make up almost 20% of the population).[33] Many Hungarian schools merged with Romanian schools and the teachers were Romanianized.[34] Shortly after the change of regimes, interethnic clashes between the Romanians and Hungarians broke out in the town of Târgu Mureş. The violent clashes broke out in March 1990 and left five people dead and hundreds injured. Regarding the scale and format, there have been no other interethnic disputes similar to this one since that time. Nevertheless, the relationships between ethnic Hungarians and ethnic Romanians remain problematic and are full of stereotypes and prejudices on both sides. Relations between the Hungarian minority and state authorities are characterized by mutual distrust.

However, it is not only the Hungarian minority; in Romania, a *Roma minority* may be recognized as well and smaller groups of other national minorities ranging from several thousand to 100,000 members. According to an Ethnocultural Diversity Resource Center (EDRC) poll, most Romanians believed minorities had sufficient rights in 1995 and 2002, in contrast to Hungarians, who saw them as insufficient; heated public disputes centred on both the issue of bilingualism and minority language use in public administration – 37.5% of respondents from the Romanian community disagree with any form of university study in the Hungarian language funded by the Romanian state (Bâdescu *et al.* 2005:19–27). Hungarians in Romania are represented in politics by the UDMR, which plays an important role on the Romanian political scene, being a member of almost every governmental coalition after 1996. The radicalization of some members led to the creation of a moderate wing, represented by Béla Markó and the radicals led by Tökés.[35] As some authors note, the Romanian media are very often against the Hungarian minority and present the demands of ethnic Hungarians as *insolent* and government attempts to meet them as *unacceptable concessions* (Light and Phinnemore 2001:100).

The *Moldovan card* might have played quite an important role in the case of the PRM. Moldova joined Romania in 1918, only to be occupied in 1940 by the Soviet Union on the basis of the Molotov–Ribbentrop Pact and was split between the Ukrainian SSR and the Moldavian SSR, remaining in the USSR until independence came in August 1991. The nationalist regime of Ceauşescu had already condemned the Molotov–Ribbentrop Pact in November 1989 at the XIVth Congress of the Communist Party of Romania, which basically constituted a claim to territory under the jurisdiction of the USSR. From time to time, there are voices in Moldova calling for unification with Romania[36]; the newly emerging Moldovan identity was only evolving in the 1990s, which was evident in the issue of language.[37] Even though PRM's founding statute speaks of the 'realisation of Greater Romania in its historical boundaries' (*Statutul partidului România Mare*, Article 3), the party only actively promoted the issue during the first half of the 1990s; since that time, it has not emphasized the issue but focuses instead on socioeconomic tasks and the Hungarian question. The PRM did not even take advantage of the opportunity to demonize the bilateral treaty with Russia in July 2002, which draws a veil over the Molotov–Ribbentrop Pact of 1939 which prompted the loss of the province of Bessarabia to the Soviets (Gallagher 2003:3).

Ethno-cultural variables in Bulgaria

The *Bulgarian ethno-cultural context* resembles that in Romania. The biggest national minority consists of *Turks*, who constitute 9.4% of the total population, followed by the 4.7% who are *Roma inhabitants*.[38] Turks have always been seen as former occupiers and Turko-Bulgarian relations have been rather hostile. The Todor Zhivkov regime pressured for Bulgarization of Turks, forced many to accept the Slavic ending (-ov, -ova, -ev, -eva), closed Turkish schools or merged them with Bulgarian schools, banned use of the Turkish language both in public and at home and renounced Turkish customs. It is estimated that around 310,000 Turks left the country in 1989[39] and 500–1,500 people were killed when they resisted assimilation measures; others were forcibly resettled.

After the fall of Zhivkov regime, the parliament restored the cultural rights of the Turks – they were able to begin using their original names once again and speak their mother tongue and some Turkish-speaking schools were reopened. The new regime also restored property rights and citizenship rights. The latter brought about heated discussions as some Turks had already acquired Turkish citizenship and settled down in Turkey. The new provisions led to many Turks living permanently in Turkey resolving to ask for Bulgarian citizenship. Turkish migrants with dual Bulgarian and Turkish citizenship form a community of around 380,000 people. Under the 1998 citizenship law, these migrants have the Right to retain their Bulgarian citizenship while keeping their Turkish citizenship. As dual citizens, they develop and share dual loyalty, rights and obligations. The main disputes centred around a law which enables Turks to vote in elections in Bulgaria at all levels – local, parliamentary and presidential, as well as for the European Parliament. Opponents of these extensive rights were successful in the 2007 election, after a new law had been introduced requiring residency be indicated on ID cards. But the Turkish minority living abroad possessed ID cards and the electoral tourism this allowed continued (Smilov and Jileva undated:228–229), although according to some sources, 85,000 ethnic Turks were denied the right to vote (Savkova 2007:4). Despite the fact that Bulgarian law does not recognize reserved seats for national minorities, the DPS scores well in every election and so took part in governance led by NDSV in 2001 and Socialists in 2005.[40]

The second issue is similar to the Romanian case as well. The *geographical region of Macedonia* was divided after the fall of the Ottoman Empire between Bulgaria, Yugoslavia, Greece and Albania. Bulgaria claimed some of the territory during the First World War. Its claim was based on the commonality of the Bulgarian and Macedonian languages and identities. The Macedonian language and nation are products of the twentieth century, and many perceive the Macedonian language to be a dialect of Bulgarian. In 1961, Bulgaria recognized that a new Macedonian nation had emerged after the Second World War, while in 1971, relations improved to the point that Bulgaria even agreed to sign bilateral documents in both the Bulgarian and Macedonian languages. After Macedonia's declaration of independence, Bulgaria was one of the first countries to recognize the new country. Bulgaria nevertheless refused to recognize the Macedonian nation or Macedonian language, and some began to speculate that Bulgaria viewed annexation as the easier alternative. The Bulgarian policy regarding the acquisition of Bulgarian passports based on the concept of *Bulgarian by origin* is perceived negatively by the official Macedonian representation though welcomed by the inhabitants of Macedonia for its advantages in travelling freely throughout the EU without visa requirements.[41] The Bulgarian law could be also interpreted to mean that Macedonian inhabitants are de facto ethnic Bulgarians, which in a way threatens the sovereignty of Macedonia. Nevertheless, Macedonia does not penalize its citizens for holding dual citizenship.

The nonrecognition of the Macedonian language may serve as a pretext for retaliation by the Macedonians or as a source of discontent with Bulgarian politics and poor bilateral relations. These are then reflected in Macedonian claims that Bulgaria is violating the rights of Macedonians in Bulgaria,

in particular the Right to association and assembly, since the Bulgarian Constitutional Court banned the nationalist Macedonian party OMO – Ilinden in
2000 as a threat to the integrity of the state. This reasoning was judged to be
in violation of the European Convention on Human Rights by the European
Court of Human Rights in 2006. Since then, Bulgarian authorities have been
denying registration to the party on various grounds. Mobilization against the
ethnic Macedonians was then used in Bulgaria chiefly by the populist VMRO
and only rarely by Ataka (Smilov and Jileva undated: 231–232).

Ataka does not play the Macedonian card much but chooses to pick on the
Turkish minority instead. The Turks and Romas are accused of being responsible for the poor economic situation of the Bulgarian inhabitants. The party
advocates the expulsion of Turks or at least their Bulgarization as already
carried out under the Zhivkov regime. Similarly as with the PRM, many Ataka
deputies are former members of the security forces and win votes from former
members of the security apparatus during the communist regime.

Other common variables: Roma population, identities and immigration
Besides the largest national minorities, there is a *large Roma population in
the region*. In Bulgaria, the official numbers state that 4.7% of the population
are Roma inhabitants[42] and in Romania, they make up 2.5% of the total
population.[43] The 2002 census in Serbia revealed that 1.44% of the total population (central Serbia and Vojvodina) is of Roma origin.[44] However, all these
data are open to dispute and researchers believe the number of Romas to be far
higher than the official data shows. Roma faces discrimination on the labour
market – the unemployment rate among the Roma population is somewhere
between 60% and 90%, their housing and living conditions are far below average
and discrimination in education is widespread.

The PRM and Ataka use the anti-Roma issue in their campaign, while the
SRS does not focus on the issue. One of the reasons may be that, in Serbia, the
perception of Romas is a bit different. Romas are second-class citizens as
elsewhere in the region, but they are not seen as a threat in terms of criminality
or as parasites of a welfare state. The other reason is that the SRS has always
focused more on the *enemies* of the Serbian nation and those *who are Serbs
but do not know it*. In this regard, the SRS always sees Croats, Bosniaks and
Albanians as the biggest threat to Serbian identity or claims that Croats and
Bosniaks are Serbs of different beliefs. The party then claims the territory of
Croatia, BiH, Montenegro, Kosovo and sometimes even the state of Macedonia.
This argument is aided by *affinity between the nations and languages*.

Pre-Second World War Yugoslavia recognized Slovenes, Croats, Serbs and
Albanians, while the Macedonian and Muslim (Bosniak) nation was a product
of the Tito regime. The Montenegrin nation also experienced a revival, and
after the declaration of independence, more people started to identify

themselves as having Montenegrin nationality. Nationality is narrowly tied to religion, and the proximity of religion and nation is extremely visible in the case of the Orthodox Churches, where the Church equals the nation. The Serbian Orthodox Church granted autonomy to the Macedonian Orthodox Church in 1959 but insisted on canonical unity with the Serbian Church in recognizing the Serbian Patriarch. Autocephality of the Macedonian Church was then declared in 1967 but condemned by the Serbian clergy as schismatic and never recognized. The same took place with regard to the Montenegrin Orthodox Church, which declared autocephality in 1990 and was never recognized by any of the Orthodox Churches.[45]

Under the Tito regime, a common Serbo-Croatian language was introduced, and a national renaissance of the Croatian language started only in the 1970s, when a Croatian spelling and grammar textbook came out (*Hrvatski pravopis, Croatian Orthography*). The book was initially banned, but the fourth edition came into use as a definitional standard for the Croatian language. The Bosnian language emerged as a by-product of the war; the Montenegrin language then emerged as a political necessity for the new state.

The Croatian war for independence did not help but only stirred anti-Croatian feelings among Serbians and anti-Bosniak sentiments during the war in BiH. The revival of Croatian nationalism which praised the Ustasha regime and Operations Storm and Flash meant a drop in the Serbian population in Croatia from 12% to 5% of the total population and de facto created an ethnically homogenous country. The nationalism in Croatian and Serbian society was nourished by the official media, which did not provide objective information and helped the regimes of Milošević and Tuđman to sustain themselves. The war facilitated anti-Bosniak propaganda as well. Albanians were held responsible through the entirety of the 1990s for the economic downfall and lowered living standards of Serbian inhabitants. Kosovo was responsible for keeping Albanians in the sights of Serbian nationalist propaganda.

Immigration figures show quite clearly that the immigration rates do not matter in the case of Eastern European countries to the extent they do in Western Europe. In Romania, there were 1,685 refugees[46] in 2000, while in Bulgaria in 2005, when Ataka scored for the first time, there were 5,218 refugees and asylum seekers seeking shelter in Bulgaria. In 2003, there were 480,040 refugees and Internally Displaced People (IDP) in Serbia totalling 6.4% of the overall population (7.5 million inhabitants). That figure dropped from 542,510 in 2002 (data for 2001 is available only as a total including Kosovo and Montenegro).[47] These data nevertheless seem to be irrelevant, since most refugees are ethnic Serbs who fled Croatia, BiH or, more recently, Kosovo and are therefore not seen as an alien element by the local population. What is more, the cause is different – the ethnic Serbs who came to Serbia during or after the wars often have been core voters for the SRS (Milanović 2004).[48]

International variables of Serbia, Romania and Bulgaria:
state humiliation and the EU accession

The international context of the three cases differs markedly. In Serbia's case, the international context was rather favourable for the rise of an extremist party, something which was made use of in the 1990s by the SPS and, after 2000, by the SRS, which was the most successful party in the elections. Serbia played the role of the black sheep until the fall of Milošević and remained in disfavour with the international community until the end of his regime. The presence of the international community (i.e. the USA and EU) was used by the Far Right, which demonized it and presented its members as the *Serbia's greatest enemies*. In spite of this, support is quite high for integration of the country into the EU. A 2005 survey in Vojvodina showed 77.1% of voters in a potential referendum would vote for accession, with only 6.7% against and 16.2% saying they were not sure (Mihić 2005).[49]

Unlike Serbia, Romania and Bulgaria were candidate countries for the *EU membership* which they finally joined in 2007. In Bulgaria as well as Romania, public opinion on EU membership was very favourable, and the European card was not used by the Far Right parties until accession. The slow accession process and tough EU requirements had a bit of a negative impact on public opinion, and the 2007 EU elections saw the issue of the European Constitution in the pre-electoral campaign – the governing parties saw the European Constitution as a mechanism for strengthening the position of European institutions, which was beneficial to the country, while Ataka perceived the Constitution as a document that facilitated the transfer of power from the national to the supranational level and was in conflict with Bulgaria's national interests (Savkova 2007:4). The restrictions on the right of Bulgarian citizens to work freely in some EU states (e.g. UK, Ireland) and the right for EU citizens to buy land in Bulgaria and[50] the closure of two reactors in a nuclear power plant in Kozloduy were interpreted by many Bulgarians as losses for Bulgaria, and many felt themselves to be second-class citizens in the EU. The expected increase in standard of living did not materialize immediately after accession, and many Bulgarians felt betrayed. Ataka and GERB made use of Eurosceptic feelings and nourished them further in the pre-election campaign in 2009, by promoting the Bulgarian national interest, fear of losing national sovereignty and promoting *Bulgarianship* – similarly as the Hungarian Jobbik, which profited from Hungarian accession to the EU and the rise of Euroscepticism.

The Far Right in Bulgaria saw success only in the 2005 elections, while its Romanian counterpart, the PRM, won almost 20% in the 2000 elections and the party's steady decline was visible. Both countries joined NATO and Romania has aligned itself extensively with the USA in its war on terrorism. This was not the case for Serbia, which was de facto at war with NATO in

1999 and never really had any intent of joining the organization. The international context was not really used by the PRM. It employed neither Romania's engagement in the war on terror in the Middle East nor the inclusion of the Hungarian UDMR in governing arrangements as a precondition for application to the EU. The PRM considers NATO to be the only tool capable of protecting and safeguarding the country and its strategic interest, unlike Ataka, which calls for revision of the accession treaty, non-participation in military operations, neutrality and no military bases in Bulgaria.

Ataka uses the anti-Turkish card in its programme towards the EU, advocating standing in the way of *Turkey in its accession to the EU*. All the chief political parties in Bulgaria support the accession of Turkey into the EU (GERB, Bulgarian Socialist Party, NDSV, Union of SDS, DPS[51]), which enables Volen Siderov to make use of anti-Turkish sentiments: 'Turkey currently has a population of 70 million. The Muslim country will rule the EU; it will have the greatest number of Members of the European Parliament (MEPs), the most votes. It will tell everyone what to do and what not to do. I will tell you what they are going to do – they will build mosques all over, they will place a minaret on top of the Eiffel Tower. This is what Turkey will want in the EU. As far as Bulgaria is concerned, we are doomed to extinction. When Turkey joins the EU, the Turkish yoke, the one our national heroes fought against, will resume once again.'[52] In the electoral campaign before the elections to the European Parliament, the party stressed the threat from immigration and the tide of cheap labour from Turkey, unlike the governing parties, which saw Turkish membership in the EU as a chance to assert Bulgaria's regional role (Savkova 2007:4). A video clip then showed the European capitals and their symbols (Eiffel Tower, Big Ben, etc.) reverting to mosques. The anti-Turkish campaign was also present in the 2009 European elections, where Ataka's main slogan was 'No to Turkey in the EU'.[53]

Interim conclusion: the overall context of successful cases

What is it, then, that makes the Far Right successful in Serbia, Romania and Bulgaria? Our analysis has shown that one of the most important political variables is the position, tactics and strategy of mainstream parties – in Serbia's case, the SPS plays the dominant role in success of the SRS, since the parties do not differ in their ideology and, to a certain extent, share a voting base. In the case of Romania, it was the Right pole of the spectrum which lost credibility for the voters and created the space for a new Far Right formation, while, in Bulgaria, voters were also tempted to vote for a change from the established but discredited political parties. A proximate party may play a role only in certain cases – it does not play any role in the case of voters for DSS and SRS, while it plays a certain role in the case of PRM and voters for PUNR and PNG–CD. Another important political variable is electoral systems – as can be observed, the inclusion of majoritarian components in the Bulgarian and Romanian systems meant no gain for Far Right parties in SMDs. Significant voting for new politics might play a certain role in the case of Bulgaria, with the low level of political culture then being supportive in all three cases.

Ethno-cultural variables seem to be very important in the context of successful Far Right parties – in the case of Serbia and seen from the particular ethno-centred perspective of Romania and Bulgaria, ethnic borders are not aligned with national borders. In the Serbian context, the SRS plays the Greater Serbia card; the PRM (despite its name and the inclusion of Greater Romania in its party statute) and Ataka do not focus on issues to do with ethnic borders. The case of a strong ethnic Turkish minority in Bulgaria, the Albanian ethnicity in Kosovo and the Hungarian minority in Romania, with its capable and qualified political representation, seems to be of great importance to the success of the Far Right parties. The issue of the Roma population is used only by the PRM and Ataka but not by SRS. The international dimension played a great role in the success of the SRS and in the case of Ataka and the EU integration process but could reduce gains by the PRM in Euro-optimist Romania. The Bulgarian context is multidimensional, as the topic of Turkey's accession to the EU could also increase the electoral basis of Far Right formations. Unemployment and economic expectations might be also supportive, though they do not seem to be the main motives for the Far Right voters. As may be seen, the post-material dimension plays no role, as it is still non-existent.

Notes

1 Meguid defines as *niche parties* new parties which reject the traditional class-based orientation of politics. Instead of prioritizing economic demands, these parties politicize sets of issues which previously lay outside the scope of party competition (e.g. Far Right parties and green parties) (Meguid 2005:347).

2 Golder differentiates between populist parties and neo-Fascist parties, claiming that their fortunes depend on different factors (Golder 2003).

3 For unemployment rates since 2004, see www.mfin.gov.rs/UserFiles/File/tabele/maj/Tabela percent201percent20Osnovni percent20indikatori percent20makroe-konomskih percent20kretanja.pdf.

4 Zoran Djindjić was a founder and chief of the Democratic Party and became Prime Minister of Serbia in 2001. He was assassinated in 2003 by people related to the Serbian organized crime scene. The then-acting President of Serbia, Nataša Mičić, declared a state of emergency, and the new government led by Zoran Živković arrested hundreds of people by irregular means.

5 The SPS had already supported the first Koštunica minority government in 2004/2007.

6 The Strength of Serbia Movement (*Pokret Snaga Srbije* PSS), New Serbia (*Nova Srbija*, NS) and Socialist Movement (*Pokret Socijalista*, PS). The only parliamentary

party is the monarchist NS, while PS emerged only in 2008 and PSS a year later. A possible coalition partner in terms of ideology might be DSS (cf. Light and Phinnemore (2001).

7 *Trećina Gradjana za Prevremene Izbore.* In: Politika online, 28.2.2011. www. politika.rs/rubrike/Politika/Trecina-gradjana-za-prevremene-izbore.it.html.

8 A partial cause for this, it should be noted, is the legacy of the previous regime. There was widespread distrust of the political process by citizens, anxiety about taking the initiative on an individual level, an atomized society, distrust of any organized process and widespread nepotism and clientelism.

9 The label post-communist does not imply that National Salvation Front was a direct successor party but that the leaders of the party were mostly former communist officials.

10 PD-L was created by merging the Democratic Party and the LDP.

11 The lack of public confidence in the parties registered at 77% and 74% for the parliament in 1999 according to a poll carried out by the Metro Media Institute (Adevârul 28.11.1999, cited from Gallagher 2003:22).

12 For example, Eugen Barbu was a prominent novelist during the communist regime and the co-founder of PRM.

13 Note that an important party for PRM during the 1990s was PUNR. The rivalry between the two ceased when PUNR's leader, Gheorghe Funar, left for PRM and took radical supporters along with him. This move partially paid off in the 2000 elections.

14 Informal conversation with Romanian political scientist Andreea Maierean.

15 Gallup Institute 2005. *Confidence in Institutions in Bulgaria.* Available online at www.gallup-bbss.com/images/freeindex/free1.gif.

16 Known since 2007 as the National Movement for Stability and Progress.

17 *The Government of Lawyers and YUPPIES. Prime Minister Simeon Saxe-Coburg-Gotha Relying on the Youth.* 10 August 2001. Available online at www.aimpress. ch/dyn/trae/archive/data/200108/10810-004-trae-sof.htm.

18 The highest rates were in 1993–1994 and then again in 1998–1999. For the rate of unemployment in Romania in the 1990s, see Bâdulescu (undated).

19 Gallup Institute. *Unemployment Expectations.* www.gallup-bbss.com/images/freeindex/free4.gif.

20 Gallup Institute. *Family Economic Conditions.* www.gallup-bbss.com/images/freeindex/free3.gif.

21 Rivera, M.A. *Romania Votes Under a New Electoral System.* Available online at http://globaleconomydoesmatter.blogspot.com/2008/11/romania-votes-under-new-electoral.html.

22 Informal conversation with Romanian political scientist Andreea Maierean.

23 http://zelenisrbije.org/english/?lang=lat.

24 See, for example, Pokret za Slobodu. http://pokret.net/cms/.

25 For activities of Bulgarian anarchists, see, for example, http://anarchy.bg/istoria.html, http://flag.blackened.net/revolt/ws/bulgar48.html, http://sm.a-bg.net/.

26 See Anarchist Federation in Bulgaria. *Protests.* http://anarchy.bg/deynost/protest.html.

27 Statistical Agency BiH. Census 1991. www.bhas.ba/arhiva/census1991/Etnickapercent20obiljezjapercent20stanovnistvapercent20biltenpercent20233.pdf; Montenegrin Censuses from 1909–2003. www.njegos.org/census/index.htm.

28 Data from 1981. All data from this period remains questionable due to a boycott by ethnic Albanians (Petrovic and Blagojevic 1992).
29 According to 1989 census, there are 100 people of Serbo-Montenegrin identity, while the overall population is 3,182,417. OSCE 2004. www.osce.org/publications/ hcnm/2004/10/10605_14_en.pdf. Statistical Office of Macedonia www.stat.gov. mk/PXWeb2007bazi/Dialog/Saveshow.asp.
30 http://en.academic.ru/dic.nsf/enwiki/967300. A new census is expected in April 2013. The CIA World Factbook estimates 37.1% of Serbs live in BiH. CIA World Factbook. www.cia.gov/library/publications/the-world-factbook/geos/bk.html.
31 Croatian Statistical Agency. 2001 Census in Croatia. www.dzs.hr/Eng/censuses/ Census2001/Popis/E01_02_02/E01_02_02.html; Montenegrin Statistical Office www.monstat.org/EngPrva.htm.
32 There are some similarities with Croatia.
33 Census in Romania 2002. http://recensamant.referinte.transindex.ro/?pg=8. Romanian Statistical Office www.insse.ro/cms/files/RPL2002INS/vol5/tables/ t16.pdf. Hungarians in Romania were not alone. Mention must be made as well of the Transylvanian Germans (*Siebenbürger Sachsen*) who were repressed after the Second World War.
34 Hungary reacted by appealing to the Conference of Security and Cooperation in Europe (CSCE) which provoked anti-Hungarian feelings in Romania.
35 The split may be seen, for example, on the issue of university courses taught in the Hungarian language, where moderates would be happy with departments in the Hungarian language but radicals demand a university.
36 The question of unification with Romania was quite ardent in the first half of the 1990s, but the idea almost died with the adoption of a new constitution. Pro-Romanian voices have been heard most recently in the anti-communist demonstrations of April 2009. The entry of Romania to the EU gave many Moldovans a chance to seek a Romanian (EU) passport, though the process was speeded up after the unrest in spring 2009. Romanian law stipulates that anyone with a great-grandparent who was once a Romanian national may apply for Romanian citizenship and expect an answer within five months. *Alarm at EU Passports for Moldova.* 4.5.2009. http://news.bbc.co.uk/2/hi/8029849.stm.
37 The declaration of independence designated the official language to be Romanian, while the constitution of 1994 declares that the national language is Moldovan. Researchers agree that the Moldovan and Romanian languages are identical, though the will for creating a nation dictated a need for a language to be created to match. Nevertheless, Prime Minister Vlad Filat was the first to officially announce that his mother tongue was Romanian. *Moldovan Premier Wants Clear EU Perspective, Financial Aid.* 30 September 2009. www.rferl.org/ content/Moldovan_Premier_Wants_Clear_EU_Perspective_Financial_ Aid/1839909.html. *Declaratia de independenta a Republicii Moldova.* www. moldova-suverana.md/index.php?start_from=&ucat=7&subaction=showfull&i d=1156426235&archive=1156767681&; *Constitution of the Republic of Moldova,* adopted in July 1994, Article 13(1). http://confinder.richmond.edu/ admin/docs/moldova3.pdf.
38 Nacionalen Statisticeski Institute. *Census 2001.* www.nsi.bg/Census/Ethnos.htm.

39 http://countrystudies.us/bulgaria/25.htm.
40 In 2001, the party scored 7.4%, in 2005 14.07% and in 2009 14.45% and in the 2007 elections for the European Parliament 20.26% (data retrieved from Central Electoral Commission. www.cikbg.org/). The success of the party in the 2007 elections was brought about mainly by lower turnout (28.6%), and the absolute numbers were not that bad for DPS because of the discipline of its voters and the mobilization of DPS against attacks by GERB and Ataka before the elections. For the issue of the party's legality as regards its ethnic basis, see chapter 8.
41 The EU lifted visa requirements for citizens of Macedonia in December 2009.
42 Nacionalen Statisticeski Institute. Census 2001. www.nsi.bg/Census/Ethnos.htm.
43 2002 Census in Romania. www.recensamant.ro/pagini/tabele/t47.pdf.
44 Census 2002 in Serbia. http://webrzs.stat.gov.rs/axd//en/popis.htm.
45 The dispute continues between the Churches and is not reflected by the state institutions. The Montenegrin Ministry of Finance accepted the demands of the Serbian Orthodox Church for titular rights over churches and monasteries, despite the resistance of the Montenegrin Orthodox Church. Also the Serbian Supreme Court has annulled a ministry's refusal to list the Montenegrin Orthodox Church in the Register of Churches and Religious Communities. *Serbia Lifts Ban on Montenegrin Church*. 12 June 2008. www.balkaninsight.com/en/main/news/10958/.
46 UNHCR 2000. *Statistical Year Book*. www.unhcr.org/3d4e7bec5.html.
47 UNHCR 2003. *Statistical Year Book*. www.unhcr.org/cgi-bin/texis/vtx/page?docid=41d2c1a9c.
48 However, for example, Jelena Grujić claims that 'in communities with more incomers from BIH the domicile population tends to support the Radical political option, while in areas with more incomers from Croatia, the Radical votes come from the refugees themselves'. She bases her argument on the fact that BiH incomers are more educated, come from urban areas, share more of the *Yugoslav identity* and have integrated better than refugees from Croatia.
49 The same survey showed that 52% of SRS voters believe Serbian accession to the EU to be a bad thing, in contrast with 1.8% of DS voters.
50 UK firms are the chief investors in Bulgaria and pressure is therefore built to introduce countermeasures in retaliation for work restrictions in the UK, in the form of a ban on buying land by British nationals (Savkova 2007:3).
51 *Dvizhenie za Prava i Svobodi*; *Hak ve Özgürlükler Hareketi*. The party consists predominantly of ethnic Turks. Nevertheless, party bylaws stipulate that the party is open to all Bulgarians. Therefore, the Constitutional Court affirmed the constitutionality of the party in 1992.
52 *Nationalist Ataka Leader: Minaret Will Top Eiffel Tower After Turkey Joins EU*. www.novinite.com/view_news.php?id=101662.
53 *No to Turkey in the European Union*. 15 May 2009. www.ataka.bg/en/index.php?option=com_content&task=view&id=49&Itemid=1.

7

External supply side: the roots of success and political opportunity structures in the less successful cases

This chapter analyses the less successful cases. The first section focuses on countries where Far Right parties have steady but marginal representation in national parliaments – Croatia, Montenegro and Albania – with the second section devoted to Macedonia, where the Far Right is almost non-existent.

Countries where Far Right parties have steady but marginal representation in national parliaments: Croatia, Montenegro and Albania

Political, social and economic variables

Political variables in Croatia

The elections in 1990 in Croatia were the first pluralistic elections which confirmed the overall will for secession. The elections in 1992 took place in the midst of the despair over the war, and those of 1995 were held in an atmosphere of post-war euphoria (Šiber 2007:153, Barić 2005). The Croatian Democratic Union (*Hrvatska demokratska zajednica*, HDZ) triumphed over other political parties in all the elections of the 1990s and dominated the political scene. The cards were re-dealt in 2000, with the elections which launched a new phase in the Croatian democratic transition. The rejection of nondemocratic practices and strengthening of competitive elements in the *Croatian party system* was confirmed by the victory of the Social Democratic Party (*Socijaldemokratska partija Hrvatske*, SDP).

The elections in 2003 and 2007 then confirmed the bipolar tendency of the Croatian political party system. On the Right side of the spectrum, we find the HDZ, which was dominant during the 1990s and further to the Right than the Croatian Party of the Right (*Hrvatska Stranka Prava*, HSP).[1] The Left side of the political continuum is occupied by the SDP, and the centre is taken by several smaller political formations (the Croatian Social Liberal Party (*Hrvatska socijalno liberalna stranka*, HSLS), Croatian Peasant Party (*Hrvatska seljačka stranka*, HSS), Istrian Democratic Assembly (*Istarski demokratski sabor*, IDS), Liberal Party (*Liberalna stranka*, LS), Croatian People's Party (*Hrvatska Narodna Stranka*, HNS) and Croatian Party of Pensioners (*Hrvatska stranka umirovljenika*, HSU)). The main political players were quite distinctive until the new millennium – the cleavage was at first conformity with the old regime and the new independent Croatia, which then transformed into a cleavage between the Tuđman vs. anti-Tuđman regime. The change in HDZ leadership meant a slow movement by the formation towards the political centre; the final years of the first decade of the new millennium have shown that it is hard to distinguish between the programme and position of the main political players. Now it is clearly evident that none of the main political groupings in Croatia offer a clear, precise political solution for the chief issues facing Croatian contemporary society (Milardović *et al.* 2007:35).

HDZ is the main rival to the HSP in terms of voters, as both parties have been defined as national parties with Christian-Democratic values promoting protection of traditions and the identity of Croatian society and the nation. Ivan Šiber described Croatia as a national state in which the church has great influence, where conservatism prevails and community is important, unlike in European countries where civic, secular and liberal values prevail in society (Šiber 2007:180). The war for independence and traditional conservatism were then behind the fact that Croatian voters opted for parties with conservative, national and authoritarian tendencies. The change in HDZ after 2000 might have led to a small increase in the percentage of HSP voters in the 2003 elections. HSP voters show almost no volatility, and therefore the slight drop in voter preferences in 2007 may be explained by the basic accomplishment of nationalist formations – the creation of an ethnically homogenous country, movement of the party towards the political centre, ever-emerging new formations on the Croatian extreme Right and, importantly, the European Union (EU) agenda, as Croatian society was formerly very much in favour of the integration of the country to the EU.[2]

Political variables in Montenegro
Despite the fact that the *Montenegrin party system* has been quite stable, it was deformed, being overpowered by the ultra-dominant successor party Democratic Party of Socialist (*Demokratska Stranka Socijalista,* DPS), led by Milo Đukanović, which was able to retain power since its transformation from Communist League of Montenegro in 1991. The party experienced a schism in 1997. The wing led by Momir Bulatović founded the Socialist People's Party (*Socijalistička Narodna Partija,* SNP), and it seemed the Montenegrin party system was moving in the direction of a two-party system. However, the success was only temporary and was tied to the main Montenegrin cleavage till 2006 – either being pro-Serbian and voting SNP or being for independence and voting DPS. Since then, the dominant dividing line has been whether one is pro-Đukanović or against him. Đukanović hegemonizes Montenegrin

politics – he served three consecutive terms as Prime Minister from 1991 to 1998, then was elected President of Montenegro from 1998 to 2002 and then again became Prime Minister from 2003 to 2006 and from 2008 until his resignation in 2010.[3] The Đukanović family runs politics, controls entrance to the Montenegrin economy and is very often blamed for nepotism, widespread corruption and close links to organized crime. The hegemony of DPS is also possible due to the fragmentation of the opposition parties. If we place DPS on the Left side of the political continuum (the Montenegrin party system is not about ideology but rather about personalities or ethnicity), the Right side remains vacant – the only conservative parties are the ethnic Serbian parties. Consolidation of the political system is awaited with the loss of pro-/anti-Serbian cleavage and depersonalization of the Montenegrin politics.

Despite the deficiencies of Montenegrin democracy, the Montenegrins are among the most satisfied with their lives and material situation and are among the most optimistic about the future. This positive outlook stems mainly from the inflow of foreign capital into Montenegro and the economic boom in the country as it impacts upon the inhabitants' mood. People are satisfied with the performance of state institutions, and around 60% of respondents in the 2009 survey were convinced that their country is doing *well* or even *very well*. Across the region, this rate of satisfaction is only surpassed by Kosovo (Gallup Balkan Monitor 2009:8).

Political variables in Albania
The Albanian party system has been highly polarized, with two dominant political parties – the Socialist Party of Albania (*Partia Socialiste e Shqipërisë*, PSSh, in power 1997–2005) and the Democratic Party of Albania (*Partia Demokratike e Shqipërisë*, PDSh, in power 1992–1997 and since 2005, cf. Biberaj 1998; Schmidt-Neke 2001). These two parties make up a strong component of the party system, but the same cannot be said of their coalition partners. The main political party on the Right of the political continuum is the Republican Party, while the main partner on the Left until the 2009 elections was the SDP. Since 2004, there has also been the Socialist Movement for Integration (*Lëvizja Socialiste për Intigrim,* LSI), set up as a splinter party from PSSh and since 2009 in the coalition government with PDSh. The PDSh draws most of its support from northern Albania, while the PSSh is more successful in the south.[4] The Albanian party system is highly personality-driven – PDSh is the one-man party of former President (1992–1997) and current Prime Minister (since 2005, reassumed office in 2009) Sali Berisha. For a long period, PSSh was led by Fatos Nano, who was then replaced by the charismatic mayor of Tirana, Edi Rama. LSI is personified by long-time politician Ilir Meta.

Albanian politics is not only highly personalized, but there is great gap between the people and politicians, as the political debate grows away from the everyday concerns of the electorate and distrust by the electorate towards politicians grows. The parties in power have an absolute monopoly on power and have ostracized their political opponents from power for the time being. Albanian politics is usually described as being a partitocracy with a high level of corruption, inefficiency, abuse, authoritarian tendencies and a hybrid democracy with democratic institutions but autocratic political behaviour (cf. Biberaj 1998, Kajsiu in Karasimeonov 2004, Jano 2008). This lack of trust is then reflected in a drop in turnout for elections – from almost 99% in 1991 to 50.77% in 2009 – the lowest turnout was registered in the 2005 elections, where 48.8% of the electorate turned out to vote. The ideology and policies of the two main rival parties are rather blurred, and, as we have already noted, the politics is dominated by party leaders and disputes between them. Contemplating the convergence of Left and Right for the position of the dominant player on the Right would seem to be senseless in light of the partitocracy.

Other common variables: electoral systems, unemployment
and the post-material dimension
The Croatian *electoral law* reflects the regional trend in moving from a majority system towards a proportional one. The majority system is preferred by the strongest parliamentary party and has enabled the creation of a one-party government; systems before 2000 favoured the election victors, while that after 2000 favours strong entities. In spite of the electoral system, HSP has not managed to win representation commensurate with its share of the vote (Šedo 2007:222). HSP showed constant results until a slight drop in 2007. The electoral law has remained pretty much the same since 1999[5] and therefore had no impact on the performance of HSP in 2007. Albanian electoral law was unique in its regional context by virtue of having a mixed system with a prevalence of the majoritarian element. This was maintained until 2009, when a fully proportional system was introduced. Every election brought a new electoral system or made changes to the old one. The prevalence of a majoritarian component led to the establishment of a two-party system; changes after 1997 led to fragmentation of small parties in the parliament. Since 2001, Albania has had a personalized proportional system. Despite the fact that the proportional system was introduced in 2009, fragmentation decreased mainly due to the fact that the electoral districts were too small and, though the electoral threshold was set at 3% for parties and 5% for coalitions, in some districts, the real electoral threshold was far higher.[6] The new electoral law then caused large parties to win 35% more seats and to be overrepresented in the parliament (Kneblová 2009). Montenegro changed the rules with every election, but the changes did not affect the main formula (proportional representation), and changes made since 1998 might rather be described as cosmetic (Šedo 2007:71). Montenegro uses a system of proportional representation, having a single electoral unit for parliamentary elections. Only half of the

seats must be allocated according to the candidate lists; the remainder may be freely assigned by the parties which, together with the single electoral unit, favour a strong role for parties and their leadership (Bieber in Stojarová and Emerson 2010:120).

The *economic situation* in Croatia and Montenegro was impacted by the wars and the imposition of UN sanctions against the Federal Republic of Yugoslavia; the economic infrastructure in Croatia sustained massive damage – factories, power lines, bridges and buildings were destroyed, and 520,000 people in Croatia were displaced (IDMC 2008). The international sanctions not only affected the economy but also had an impact on the rise of organized crime and its links to state structures. The mishandled privatization, as in other countries, was not really beneficial to the overall state of the economies of the region. In all these countries, nepotism was very widespread, and many new businesses, with the backing of state authorities, acquired previously state-owned companies and firms at extremely low prices. These were then sold for much larger sums, and a new business elite closely tied to the new political nomenklatura emerged, while most of firms which have been sold went bankrupt. Nepotism was endemic in all post-communist countries, though in most Balkan countries, the situation was special as the transition was somehow embodied in a single man and his family, not really following the democratic pattern and establishing semi authoritarian rule – in Croatia, this was Franjo Tuđman,[7] in Albania Sali Berisha[8] and in Montenegro Milo Đukanović.[9] Despite high transformation costs, Croatians seem very optimistic – within the EU, higher optimism is found only in the Scandinavian countries (UNDP Hrvatska 2007:92).

Albania was the last country in the region to start political and economic reforms; its starting point was incomparable to those of the former Yugoslavian states. However, despite the existence of a great Albanian population in the region behind Albania's borders, the politicians in Tirana never really attempted to create Greater Albania and always tried to secure the state from war with its neighbour (cf. Hradečný and Hladký 2008:577). Still, the transition was very difficult, as the country had to wrest itself out of the late nineteenth century and join the late twentieth century to catch up with other states. Initially, Albania's results were encouraging and it seemed the country had set out on a good path. Nevertheless, the failure of the so-called pyramid schemes in 1997 and subsequent looting and anarchy showed that it was just an illusion; the balloon deflated just as it did in Bulgaria and other Eastern European countries or is doing at present in the USA. Albania has been struggling for a long time with the impact of the fall of Ponzi schemes and has been recovering only very slowly.

The unemployment rate in all three countries is among the lowest in the region: the official unemployment rate for Croatia in 2008 was 13.7%, Montenegro 14.7% and Albania 12.5% (CIA WorldBook).[10] Nevertheless, these data are misguided: the actual rate of unemployment differs from the official rate due to the existence of the grey economy. For example, in the agricultural and tourist sectors, there is a tendency for seasonal workers not to register as employed to avoid taxes and social contributions. The welfare network mechanism also contributes to official numbers, since some people may be employed in the grey economy but still register as unemployed. Thus, the data are far from being accurate and in some countries or regions may significantly differ – either higher or, in some cases, lower. For example, the official unemployment rate in Albania is only 12.5%, while estimates speak about 30%.

The *post-material dimension* has no impact in any of the three countries, since none of the Green parties, even where they do exist, have succeeded in entering the local parliaments.[11] The Left movements do have a certain potential in the three countries for the future but currently do not significantly influence voters' decisions.

Ethno-cultural variables

Ethno-cultural variables in Croatia
The fight for a *Croatian identity*, for the highest degree of differentiation from its surroundings of the Croatian language, culture and religion, culminated in 1990 and represented a security threat to the Serbian ethnic minority. The vicious circle of the Croatian national identity is tied to the identity of the state. In 1990, it was believed that the only modern example of Croatian statehood had been the Croatian Independent State of 1941–1945, tied to the personality of Ante Pavelić and the Ustasha regime. Many Croatians differentiated between a good side of the state (the fact that it was an independent Croatian state) and a bad side (the Ustasha regime). Some Far Right parties regarded the Pavelić regime as a point of national pride and a symbol of resistance.

The only significant *national minority* in Croatia is composed of Serbs. Changes in the Croatian constitution in 1990 repealing the status of the Serbian language as a state language forestalled further development. Nationalist feelings were ignited on both sides, and between 300,000 and 350,000 left their homes in Croatia during the 1991–1995 war (Human Rights Watch 2003). The Tuđman regime was not really receptive to the return of the Serbian minority, and many remained abroad, even after the end of the war. The 2000 political change also meant a change in the situation of ethnic Serbs. The number of seats reserved for ethnic Serbs in the national parliaments was raised to 3, while the rights of national minorities incorporated in the Constitution began to be regarded and implemented. In 2005, the government signed the Sarajevo Ministerial Declaration on regional refugee returns and agreed to develop national strategies to resolve outstanding refugee issues by the end of 2006. Human rights organizations, however, continue to point out that the sustainable return of displaced Serbs to Croatia remains difficult, something evidenced by the fecklessness of housing programmes and discrimination against Serbs on the job (Mikić 2006). This has also often been pointed to by the EU during the accession process, with EU representatives repeatedly stressing that Croatia must guarantee the rights of the Serbian minority in the country, in addition to cooperating with the International Criminal Tribunal for the former Yugoslavia (ICTY).

There is also a large diaspora immediately inside the Croatian borders – the CIA World Factbook estimates that 14.3% of total population in Bosnia and Herzegovina (BiH) are Croatians.[12] The Croatian war was seen by some as more than just a war for independence. They saw it as a war for the unification of the Croatian ethnicity. The Serbian and Croatian President had allegedly planned the division of BiH before the outbreak of war in Croatia. Secret negotiations in April in Croatia embraced the idea of parcelling off Bosnia, and the results of the meeting were compared to the *Cvetković–Maček* Agreement of 1939.[13] The end of the war brought the ethnic homogenization of Croatia and an end to plans for incorporating the idea of unifying the Croatian element in the region. Contemporary Croatian representation in BiH seeks only equal treatment or, more precisely, the creation of a third entity within BiH. However, the *Croatian diaspora* plays an important role during elections to the Croatian Parliament as Croatians living abroad are entitled to vote and, since 1995, have had a special electoral district. The party then in power, HDZ, was governed by its own interests as Croatians from BiH voted massively for HDZ.[14] And the second reason was to give the BiH Croats the impression that they were part of the total 'Croat national corpus' – or a potential Greater Croatia. This relic of representation without taxation was preserved and still impacts greatly on election results. In the 2005 presidential elections, diaspora votes forced a second round of elections and allowed the HDZ candidate, Jadranka Kosor, to be saved from humiliation in the first round.[15]

Ethno-cultural variables in Montenegro
The process of creating a *Montenegrin national identity* was in many ways delayed. In 1918, Montenegro was incorporated into the Kingdom of Serbs, Croats and Slovenes, and the formation of a national identity was delayed to certain extent.[16] The wave of nationalism which passed over Yugoslavia in the 1960s and 1970s was displayed in the form of Serbian nationalism (Bieber 2003:11). Many ethnologists class Montenegrins with the Serbs and stress that for centuries the region had been a sanctuary for refugees from the Ottoman Empire.[17] This statement is rationalized by the use of a common language and the possession of a common faith and traditional culture (Pavlović 2003:84).

The delay in the national identity formation process results from several factors. First of all, Montenegrin society identified with clans rather than with the political nation. Another reason lies behind the political representation of the first decade of the twentieth century. The National Party (*Klubaši*) supported unification of Montenegro with Serbia, and most perceived Montenegro to be part of Serbia and Montenegrins to be ethnic Serbs. The True National party (*Pravaši*) supported the idea of an independent Montenegro, but many of its party members thought of themselves as Serbs from Montenegro. Similarly, *Zelenaši* promoted unification with other south Slavic nations but with recognition of Montenegrin nationality. *Bjelaši* perceived the unification process of Southern Slavs as natural, and its members felt themselves to be Serbs.[18] Post-war Yugoslavia tried to create one Yugoslav nationality, and the proclamation of Montenegrin identity was perceived as a reactionary ideology. The discussions about Montenegrin sovereignty, independence and identity were rare up until the 1990s. Montenegro was usually taken to represent a nostalgic sentiment rather than a real state and the Montenegrins as the poorest Serbs. The problem lies with the concept of a Montenegrin identity and territorial identification with the national identity seen as Serbian. The question of identity contributed to the change of the ethnic structure of the inhabitants and the cleavage in society regarding the national identity and staying with Serbia or secession (Figures 7.1 and 7.2).

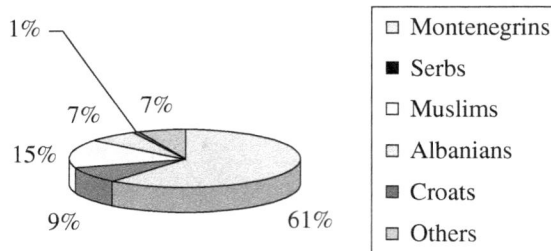

Figure 7.1 1991 Montenegro census

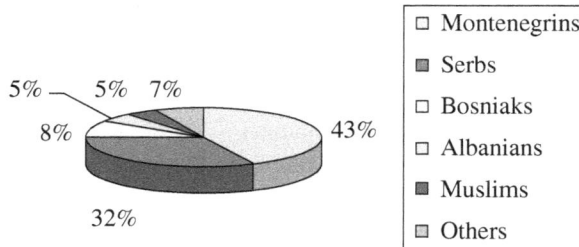

Figure 7.2 2003 Montenegro census

A significant change is the rise in people claiming to be Serbs and the drop in Bosniaks and Muslims, who total 3% less than had been true in 1991. The decrease was caused partly by emigration and partly by the move towards Montenegrin identification. The enormous increase in the number of Serbs is explained by the fact that the overall context of 1991 (a common agreement within Montenegro politics and society to remain in a single state with Serbia) created no pressure to consider strong differentiation and identification with either the Montenegrin or Serbian ethnicity.

Despite the decision of the Badinter Commission that Montenegro had the right to secede, the political representation decided to remain in a single state with Serbia[19] (Federal Republic of Yugoslavia) and was loyal until 1997, when the change in the leadership of the DPS took place and the pro-secessionist Milo Đukanović became President of the country. The German mark was introduced as the official currency next to the Yugoslav dinar, and the country started to open consulates in European states. A fundamental rupture was caused by the Kosovo conflict when Montenegro decided to stay neutral and was labelled traitorous by Beograd. Serbia's Prime Minister at the time, Vojislav Šešelj, claimed that Montenegro's declaration of independence would end in a bloody conflict. The EU then assisted during the negotiation process and another Balkan Solania was created – a new state, Serbia and Montenegro, emerged, while the name Yugoslavia vanished after eighty-four years of existence. Montenegro then declared independence in 2006 after a very tight referendum. The Montenegrin constitution approved in 2007 was controversial on issues tied to identity – official languages and state symbols.[20]

Ethno-cultural variables in Albania
There are approximately 6.5 million Albanians living in the Balkans and only around 3.6 million live in Albania. The *Albanian national question* has been pushed by Albanians since the League of Prizren in 1878 but decreased in importance after the creation of an independent Albania in 1912 and the incorporation of large regions inhabited by ethnic Albanians in the Kingdom of Serbs, Croats and Slovenes. Nevertheless, the question of the unification of territories inhabited by Albanians periodically rose to the surface. The sealed border between Tito's Yugoslavia and Hoxha's Albania caused the Kosovo Albanians to dream of a better life in Albania. The end of both regimes and opening of the borders meant facing the reality in Albania for the Kosovars and pushing for more rights within Yugoslavia initially by pacifist means. The emergence of the Kosovo Liberation Army then led to war by the Albanians with the Serbs and subsequently to the North Atlantic Treaty Organization (NATO) air campaign. Despite the fact that UN Resolution 1244 kept Kosovo under Serbian formal jurisdiction (and only temporarily be placed under international jurisdiction) pending a final settlement, subsequent steps by the

international community led to a unilateral declaration of independence by the Kosovo Parliament. The International Court of Justice (ICJ) then delivered an advisory opinion that 'the declaration of independence of the 17th of February 2008 did not violate general international law, Security Council Resolution 1244 (1999) or the Constitutional Framework. Consequently the adoption of that declaration did not violate any applicable rule of international law' (ICJ 2010). However, the ICJ decision is only advisory and plays no relevant role.

According to the 2002 census in Macedonia, there are 509,083 ethnic Albanians, accounting for 25% of the total population.[21] The Albanians initially demanded cultural, educational and administrative autonomy and, in 1992, proclaimed the Republic of Ilirida. The UN sent a small stabilization contingent, and Macedonia then remained an oasis of peace for a prolonged period and was held up as an example of viable multiculturalism in the Balkans. The situation escalated once again in 2001. Peace negotiations took place in Ohrid, where constitutional changes were negotiated and most Albanian demands were essentially met. In addition to Macedonia, there is also a significant diaspora in neighbouring south-eastern Serbia in the Preševo Valley, where the Ground Safety Zone was formed after the Kosovo conflict and the territory was given back to Serbia after the fall of Milošević regime. The Liberation Army of Preševo, Medveđa and Bujanovac was dissolved, and many of the fighters went back to Macedonia or Kosovo. The region is sometimes mentioned as one which might be swapped with Kosovo for the region in former Serbian autonomous province around Mitrovica.[22] There is also a significant Albanian diaspora in Montenegro and in Greece, where the phantom Liberation Army of Çameria (*Ushtria Çlirimtare e Çamërisë*, UÇÇ)[23] allegedly operates.[24]

The Albanians are divided into two subgroups: southerners (Tosks, Labs and Chams) and northerners (Gegs), with a border formed by the river Shkumbin. The Gegs live in the north of the country, in Kosovo, Montenegro and in Macedonia, while the Tosks, Chams and Labs live in southern Albania. Gegs are usually depicted as a traditional conservative people obeying traditional law and adhering to Islam, while the Tosks are cosmopolitan and modern professing Catholicism or the Albanian Orthodox religion. Enver Hoxha succeeded in creating an atheist state as the relation of Albanians towards any religion remains lukewarm and adherence to the church does not create cleavages in society. Since Socialist support was based in the south, the Tosk dialect became the basis for the codified Albanian language. Currently, there is a debate between Kosovar linguists as to whether or not to codify the Kosovo Albanian variant according to the Geg dialect. Dual Albanian identity is manifested in the fact that Kosovars use both flags – the newly created one always accompanied by the flag of the Republic of Albania, which is perceived to be the flag of all Albanians rather than the flag of a neighbouring state.

Having free movement of people, Albanians on both sides of the frontier do not strive to redraw the border.

Albania is an ethnically homogenous country[25]; the only larger national minority consists of the Greeks. The last census, in 1989, declared 3% of the population to be Greek. The Greeks themselves estimate the number to be much higher – some even put it at 12% (Barjarba 2004:233).[26] The next census is expected in Albania in 2012. During the rule of King Zogu, ethnic Greeks in Albania were repressed, Greek schools were closed and the monasteries of the Greek Orthodox Church were changed into mental institutions. After the end of the civil war in 1949, many Greeks settled down in Albania and many of them succeeded in political circles. After the declaration of first atheist state in the world, the Greek Orthodox Church became a target. Many churches and monasteries were destroyed and Greek religious books were banned. The liberalization of the region in 1989–1990 also brought an improvement in religious conditions. The Greek Orthodox Church was revived and took over confiscated property. Albanian law prohibits parties based on ethnicity and therefore the Greeks set up the Party for Unity and Human Rights (*Partia Bashkimi për të Drejtat e Njeriut*, PBDNJ, Κόμμα Ένωσης Ανθρωπίνων Δικαιωμάτων) which is pro forma open to all Albanians but primarily represents the interests of ethnic Greeks (Stojarová *et al.* 2007:25). The Greeks sought better conditions which sometimes spur tensions, and anti-Greek feelings are on the rise. A typical example would be the case of the ethnically Greek mayor, Vasil Bollano, of the town of Himara, who in 2007 ordered that road signs be removed because they were not bilingual and caused traffic chaos. Bollano was then indicted by the courts and sentenced to a six-month prison term and 500,000-Lek (€3,800) fine.[27]

Other common variables: Roma and immigration
Similar to its neighbours, Croatia has a significant *Roma minority*. The 2001 census put the Roma population at 9,463, but the real number is probably much higher, since they often do not declare their ethnicity for fear of discrimination. Unofficial estimates place the Roma population at 30,000–40,000, with some up to 60,000.[28] It is estimated that there are around 50,000 Romas in Albania not residing in one compact territory (the largest communities are concentrated in and around Tirana and the towns of Fier, Gjirokaster, Berat and Korçe) and dwell under poor living conditions. Similar as in Croatia, Roma are not recognized as a distinct minority – only ethnic communities with existing kin states were recognized, which is not the case for Roma (CEDIME-SE 2000), though it is without significant impact, unlike in Croatia, where Roma did not have reserved seats for the national parliament until 2003, unlike the other national minorities.[29] At the time of the 2003 census, 2,875 people declared their identity as Roma in Montenegro. Some experts estimate

the real number is around 20,000, which would make the Roma the fourth
largest national minority group in the country (after the Serbs, Bosniaks/Mus-
lims and Albanians). The standard of living and education achieved are far
below the Montenegrin average (UNDP undated document).

All three countries are countries of origin rather than countries of residence
as regards *migration*. The number of refugees and, even more, of Internally
Displaced People (IDP) was quite high during the 1990s in Croatia. But the
number is gradually decreasing, and in 2010, United Nations High
Commissioner for Refugees (UNHCR) registered only 1,238 refugees and
2,285 IDPs in Croatia. Albania has a very low number of people seeking
refugee status – in 2010, UNHCR registered only 20 applications for asylum.
The only difference is Montenegro, where the number of refugees makes up
more than 4% of the total population.[30] As is the case with Serbia, the cause
is once again different. It is the ethnic Serbs from Kosovo, Croatia and BiH
who are seeking shelter in Montenegro or Croatians living in BiH who have
the right to vote in Croatia, a potentially important factor in the success of
radical Right parties.

International variables: EU accession

The *foreign relations of Croatia* were not optimal during regime of Franjo
Tuđman; the country was not accepted into Euro-Atlantic structures and was
repeatedly criticized for non-compliance with human rights principles, poor
cooperation with the ICTY, non-standard relations with the Croatian entity in
BiH and putting obstructions in place for Serbian returnees. The death of the
Croatian President and the new government of Ivica Račan started a new
period in the Croatian transition and relations with the EU and NATO. Croatia
applied for EU membership in 2003 and was granted candidate status in 2004.
Continuous criticism from the EU led to the capture of General Ante Gotovina
indicted by the ICTY in Tenerife in 2005.

As regards accession to the EU and NATO, bilateral relations with Slovenia and Italy should be noted. Croatia has been in a long-term dispute with
Slovenia over the borders in the Bay of Piran, where Slovenia's main goal is
to reach international waters without having to leave Slovenian territory. The
Slovenian presidency in the EU in the first half of 2008 was not welcome in
Zagreb, since Croatia was instructed to abandon plans for a new fishery
protection zone in the Adriatic Sea and restructure or shut down Croatian
shipyards if the country wished to remain in negotiations with the EU. Poor
relations with her neighbour also led to the lowest support for EU accession
by Croatian inhabitants – only 33%.[31] Even though Croatia hoped to join the
EU in 2010, in spring of the same year, Slovenia was still blocking the opening of the *Foreign, Security and Defence Policy* chapter. Finally, a referendum was held in Slovenia which accepted the ruling of international

arbitrators on the dispute. The heated pre-referendum campaign was observed by many Croatians, and anti-Slovenian sentiments, accompanied by anti-EU sentiments, were growing.[32] The road to resolving the problematic relationship was opened when 51.54% voted for the international arbitration and 48.46% were against.[33] A similar scenario was awaited before Croatian accession to the NATO. Some politicians from the Slovenian Democratic Party announced that they would not vote for the accession of Croatia into NATO during a parliamentary session. However, a two-thirds majority was found and the law was passed. Croatia became a full NATO member in 2009.[34] Croatia also had strained bilateral relations with Italy regarding the purchasing rights of Italian citizens in Croatia. The issue was resolved in 2006, when both countries agreed that Croatians could buy land in Italy and vice versa. Croatians were also most critical of the EU at the end of the first decade of the twenty-first century. The Euro-optimist Croatia has evolved with the long accession process into a Eurosceptic party – it is the only country in the Western Balkans where a relative majority are not supportive of EU membership and where a majority does not consider the consequences of EU accession to be beneficial to the country (Gallup Balkan Monitor 2009:10).

Montenegro plays both sides of the game – on the one hand, it claims to rank integration into the EU and NATO as priorities. On the other, relations with Russia are very close and Montenegro's economy is secured more and more in Russian hands.[35] Support for the EU reflects the ethnic composition of the country: only 36% of Montenegrin Serbs consider the EU to be a *good thing*, while roughly six in ten respondents from other groups support EU accession (Gallup Balkan Monitor 2009:8). Relations with Serbia are based on the fact that Montenegro had already recognized the independence of Kosovo in October 2008 and on other multiple factors such as the status of Serbs or of the Serbian Orthodox Church in Montenegro.

Albanians have the highest expectations and support for integration into the EU and NATO of the Balkan countries – according to the 2003 survey, 98.31% of respondents were very supportive and said that they would vote for Albanian integration into the EU in a referendum on this issue, while another survey from 2007 showed that 89.4% of respondents support integration of the country into NATO (AIIS 2003, IDM 2007).[36] Albanians are also probably the most enthusiastic nation in Europe as regards the USA. The USA and its policy are highly admired; one boulevard in Prishtina bears the name of former President Bill Clinton and one street in the centre of Tirana the name of George Bush. Albania's relations with its neighbour Greece are not optimal and become very tense from time to time due to the living conditions of ethnic Greeks living in Albania and the large Albanian diaspora living in Greece.

Interim conclusion: overall context of the unsuccessful cases

Why is the Far Right so weak in Croatia, Montenegro and Albania? Some of the most important variables seem to be political–cultural ones – the national card in newly created states Montenegro and Croatia was played by the mainstream political party (in Montenegro's case, DPS; in Croatia, HDZ) which left no space for Far Right formations. The tactics and strategy of HDZ and DPS were important determinants in the failure of the Far Right parties in these countries. Both parties openly promoted independence. HDZ even secretly negotiated for the division of BiH and the creation of Greater Croatia. The chief political players promoted nationalism and left no space for Far Right political parties.

Albania, with a large Albanian population outside its borders could present a grand opportunity for the Far Right – if so, why is the Far Right so weak? The explanation lies in the international context. Albania was pressured to stay back from the national question in exchange for financial and political assistance from the USA. Politicians were aware of the state's weakness. It was not even able to retain control over its own territory, let alone fight a war against its stronger neighbour, so the issue of Greater Albania was never pushed. Politicians as well as citizens fully support US politics in the Balkan Peninsula and so did not strive for the accession of Kosovo. They claim that Albanians will be united once they are under a European flag.

The electoral system does not seem to be the main variable but plays a certain role in talking about the National Front (*Balli Kombëtar*, BK)'s gains – even though the party scored better under the electoral system with a majoritarian component than under the proportional system. The majoritarian component prevented a better standing in the elections during the 1990s and also the overall design of the 2009 electoral system, with a high real electoral threshold definitely playing a role in BK's loss. The electoral system in Croatia is also unfavourable to smaller parties, since all electoral designs favoured either the victors of the elections or strong entities, while the electoral law in Montenegro seems to play a supporting role because of the absence of a majoritarian component. The Croatian electoral system also has one important component – a special electoral district for the Croatian diaspora. However, BiH Croats keep on voting HDZ, seeing the party as the one that promotes their interests, not the Far Right HSP. Another reason is that the HDZ has a sister party in BiH – the Croatian Democratic Union of BiH (*Hrvatska Demokratska Zajednica Bosne i Hercegovine,* HDZ BiH) which has been among the strongest Croatian political parties in BiH, and until 2006, HDZ candidates had always won in the elections for the Croatian member of the presidency.

Unemployment might be described as playing a role as a negative case – the unemployment rate in all three countries is among the lowest in the region, and all three states experienced a large decrease in the unemployment rate.

But this argument does not really hold up to examination, since the data is far from accurate and the official unemployment rate differs greatly from the actual numbers.

Countries where Far Right parties are almost non-existent: Macedonia

Political, social and economic variables in Macedonia

Macedonia presents a great opportunity for Far Right parties because of the presence of ethnic minorities and high transformation costs. Despite this, a Far Right has failed to emerge and Macedonia is *the odd man out in the sample.* The transition from a command to a market economy has been very painful and resulted in high unemployment rates[37] and increasing poverty. The economic decline, a non-export-oriented economy, a low level of foreign direct investment, a large informal economy, inefficient labour market policies, rigid labour legislation and weak law enforcement have contributed to a further rise in the unemployment rate (Kjosev 2007:153–154).

Politics in Macedonia are divided along ethnic lines because of the existence of an ethnically Macedonian party system along with the Albanian one. The Left of the Macedonian party system is represented by the communist successor party, the Social Democratic Union of Macedonia (*Socijaldemokratski Sojuz na Makedonija,* SDSM), which ruled the country in the 1992–1998 period and then came back to power from 2002 to 2006. Its counterpart on the Right is the conservative Internal Macedonian Revolutionary Organization–Democratic Party for Macedonian National Unity (*Vnatrešna makedonska revolucionerna organizacija–Demokratska partija za makedonsko nacionalno edinstvoe,* VMRO–DPMNE), which presented itself in the beginning of the 1990s as an anti-Albanian nationalist party. Since then, the rhetoric has been toned down and the party presents itself as Christian-Democratic. In addition to these two parties, there are some political parties which attract large blocks. The Albanian scene is represented by the nationalist Democratic Union for Integration (*Demokratska Unija za Integracija/Bashkimi Demokratik për Integrim,* DUI/BDI) and more moderate Democratic Party of the Albanians (*Demokratska Partija na Albancite/Partia Demokratike Shqiptarëve,* DPA/PDSh). Green parties in Macedonia are not relevant.

The Macedonian electoral system has been changed many times: in 1990 and 1994, Macedonia used a plurality electoral system and in 1998 a parallel mixed system (eighty-five seats elected in a two-round system with run-off, 35 in Conservative Party (*Partidul Conservator*, PR) system in a single electoral district and a 5% threshold). Since 2002, a PR system with no minimum threshold has been used, and the D'Hondt method is used to calculate the distribution of seats (Šedo in Stojarová and Emerson 2010:168). However, the real threshold (somewhere around 3.6%) and the D'Hondt method mean that

the system favours stronger parties, while subjects with minimal representation are strongly underrepresented; no relevant parties on the edge of the
political spectrum emerged and the centrifugal nature of the competition
prevailed (Šedo 2007:163, 256,).

Ethno-cultural variables of Macedonia

Macedonian ethno-cultural variables may be grouped along four main issue
dimensions. These are the Macedonian identity as regards language, geography,
the Orthodox Church and a civic vs. national concept of state. The language
issue noted above represents the chief problem in bilateral relations with
Bulgaria. Geographic and toponymical issues are a stumbling block with
Greece, religion with the Macedonian and Serbian Orthodox Churches and
the state concept with the Albanian national minority.[38]

The Republic of Macedonia is only part of the historical and geographical
region called Macedonia which is at present divided into several states: Pirin
Macedonia in Bulgaria, Vardar Macedonia in Macedonia, Aegean Macedonia
in Greece,[39] the south-eastern portion of Albania, southern Serbia and Kosovo.
The concept of a United Macedonia was promoted by the VMRO, which operated in the late nineteenth and early twentieth centuries. Even though one of the
chief political players in contemporary Macedonia, VMRO–DPMNE, claims a
direct line of descent from VMRO, it does not seek a United Macedonia.

The dispute with Greece has many dimensions. The Greeks feared the
newly emerged state would aspire to control the region called Macedonia in
Greece. They also feared the Macedonians would steal their history, since
Alexander the Great Macedonian would then be claimed by the newly emerged
state.[40] The Greek representation had also reservations about the Macedonian
constitution, in which express support is given for Macedonians abroad – this
was interpreted as encouraging separatism in the Macedonian diaspora. The
Greeks then proposed changing the name of the new state to Vardar Republic,
Republic of Skopje or Former Republic Macedonia of Former Yugoslavia.
Both sides came under intense diplomatic pressure during the war in Croatia
and BiH, and a provisional temporary solution was found – the appellation the
Former Yugoslav Republic of Macedonia (FYROM) was to be used until the
dispute was resolved for the purpose of the UN being not binding for other
parties. The label FYROM is now used for many international occasions;
Republic of Macedonia is used in bilateral relations, once a state recognizes
the constitutional name. The provisional solution was met with internal opposition as protest rallies were held in several cities and the VMRO–DPMNE
called for not accepting the agreement (Šesták et al. 1998:657). Greece
blocked the invitation of Macedonia to NATO and has been threatening to
veto Macedonian integration into the EU as well. A survey by the Center for
Research and Policy Making showed that the vast majority of Macedonians

are against changing their country's name to become a member of NATO – 82.5% of respondents reject Greece's condition for supporting Macedonia's accession to NATO.[41]

International variables in Macedonia

Surprisingly, Macedonia does not have such poor relations with Bulgaria – Bulgaria was among the first countries to recognize its independence and supported Macedonia on its path to integration into NATO. The entry into NATO is backed by the vast majority of Macedonians – a survey showed that 85.2% of respondents support integration of the country into NATO.[42] There is a great difference in attitudes towards the EU between the ethnic groups: Albanians are very supportive of the EU and 84% would approve joining the EU, while only 57% of Macedonians support integration into the EU. The same survey showed that 30% fear certain or probable armed conflict in the region in the next five years and that 84% of Macedonian respondents were convinced that EU accession is needed for peaceful development in the region (Gallup Balkan Monitor 2009).

Interim conclusion: context of the negative case

Why, then, is the Far Right so weak in Macedonia, when the context is so favourable for the rise of such formations? The country experienced high unemployment rates and increased poverty, there is an enormous Albanian national minority in the country and it also has its share of its own nationals abroad. The only characteristic which would hinder the success of Far Right parties is the existence of strong mainstream parties. The VMRO–DPMNE and SDSM actively seek to accommodate relations between ethnic Macedonians and ethnic Albanians and do not skirt the issue. Both parties have a strong electoral base. Another explanation might be found in the electoral system, which favours stronger parties, while smaller parties are strongly underrepresented.

Interim conclusion: how much do external variables matter?

The triumph of Far Right parties very often starts at the local or regional level (Germany, France) but sometimes follows a top-down logic, as was the case for the Vlaams Blok in the electoral breakthrough of 1988. In the Serbian case, the success of Serbian Radical Party (*Srpska Radikalna Stranka*, SRS) came about on the local and regional and state levels simultaneously, while in the Bulgarian case, the ascent of the National Union Attack (*Natsionalen Sayuz Ataka*, Ataka) followed a top-down logic – Ataka was set up right before the parliamentary elections. The inclusion of nationalist formations did not present a problem in Romania and in Serbia where both the Greater Romania

Party (*Partidul România Mare*, PRM) and the SRS had already become part of coalition governments in the 1990s.

The level of trust by citizens in political institutions and party politics remains generally on a very low level in Central and Eastern Europe (CEE), while the church and army enjoy the highest ranking. The scepticism is caused by the conjunction of several factors: citizens' dissatisfaction with the current economic situation, their expectations for its improvement and their satisfaction with the degree of democratic freedom compared with that of the previous nondemocratic era (Rose and Munro 2003). Research has shown that distrust in politics is not only endemic in the CEE but in the Balkans as well. Distrust in politics is usually reflected in the tendency of voters to vote for a new alternative which could come in the form of a Far Right party. Is this true for the Balkans as well? Our analysis showed the only relevant Far Right parties to be the SRS, the PRM and Ataka; the rest of the Far Right political spectrum in the Balkans remains mostly irrelevant. Why, then, is this so and how much do external variables matter? Our main conclusions are as follows:

1. **The position, tactics and strategy of mainstream (whether Left or Right) political parties matter. A proximate party might play a role in certain cases. Convergence of the main players has not led to the emergence of a strong Far Right party in the Balkans.**
   Eatwell claims that when Right and Left occupy the centre, there is space for radical formations (Eatwell 2003). The Balkans show a party system of this nature need not necessarily lead to the rise of Far Right formations (see Table 7.1). In Croatia, the two largest parties (HDZ, SDP) both have very much the same programme. There is consensus in society about the direction of the country and the Far Right remains marginal. In Serbia, there is great polarization concerning the country's direction; the radical Right (SRS) and Left (Socialist Party of Serbia (*Socialistička partija Srbije*, SPS)) meet in their nationalism, xenophobia and traditionalism. The political variables show that convergence of the political parties was not a determinant for the emergence of Far Right political parties – the polarized Bulgarian and Serbian system produced strong representatives of this party family. The discredited Right played a significant role in the case of Bulgaria (Democratic Forces (*Sayuz na Demokratichnite Sili*, SDS), National Movement of Simeon II (*Nacionalno Dviženie Simeon II*, NDSV)) and Romania (Democratic Party (*Partidul Democrat*, PD), Christian-Democratic National Peasants' Party (*Partidul Național Țărănesc Creștin Democrat*, PNȚCD)). There is a vacuum on the Right but a strong Left mainstream party (DPS) in Montenegro, and Far Right parties are almost non-existent. Proximate parties also might play role in certain cases as in the case of PRM and

Table 7.1 The chief political players impacting the Far Right's fortunes in the Balkans

	Extremist Right	Radical Right	Other populist Right/Left	Ethno-regional	National conservative or mainstream Right	Mainstream Left
Serbia	SRS	SNS?	SNS?	Union of Vojvodina Hungarians (*Savez vojvođanskih Mađara*, SVM), Bosniak Democratic Party of Sandžak (*Bošnjačka demokratska stranka Sandžaka*, BDSS), Democratic Union of Croats in Vojvodina (*Demokratski Savez Hrvata u Vojvodini*, DSHV), Party for Democratic Action (*Partia për bashkimin demokratik ië shqiptareve*, PBDSh)	Democratic Party of Serbia (*Demokratska Stranka Srbije*, DSS), Democratic Party (*Demokratska Stranka*, DS), G17+, New Serbia (*Nova Srbija*, NS), Liberal Democratic Party (*Liberalno demokratska partija*, LDP)	SPS, Social Democratic Party of Serbia (*Socijaldemokratska partija Srbije*, SDPS)
Croatia	HSP (1990s and since 2009)	HSP (first decade of new millennium)		Independent Democratic Serbian Party (*Samostalna demokratska Srpska stranka*, SDSS), IDS	HDZ	SDP

(continued)

Table 7.1 (Continued)

	Extremist Right	Radical Right	Other populist Right/Left	Ethno-regional	National conservative or mainstream Right	Mainstream Left
Montenegro	Serbian Radical Party of Dr. Vojislav Šešelj (SRS CG)			SNS, New Serbian Democracy (*Nova Srpska Demokratija*, NSD)		DPS
Macedonia	BK	VMRO–NP		DPA, DUI	VMRO	SDSM
Albania				PBDNJ	PDSh	PSSh
Bulgaria	VMRO	Ataka	GERB	DPS	SDS, NDSV	Bulgarian Socialist Party (BSP)
Romania	PRM, PNG–CD			Democratic Union of Hungarians in Romania (*Uniunea Democrată Maghiară din România*, UDMR)	PD, PNŢCD	Social Democratic Party (*Partidul Social Demokrat*, PSD)

the Party of Romanian National Unity (*Partidul Unității Naționale a Românilor*, PUNR) in the 1990s and presently with the New Generation Party–Christian Democratic (*Partidul Noua Generație–Creştin Demo-crat*, PNG–CD) and also in the Serbian case of SRS and Serbian National Party (*Srpska narodna stranka*, SNS).

In all three successful cases, the party system was highly inclusive, a proportional electoral system was used, and the Right of the party system was either fragmented or vacant – the voters for Far Right parties in the case of Bulgaria and Romania were voters for the former Right party, which had discredited itself before the voters rather than refusing to address the emotional topics preferred by the voters. Voters for the SRS are those who previously supported the SPS.

In addition to showing the mainstream parties matter, the table also makes clear that party position is fluid over time – HSP is a clear example of a party moving from an extreme position during the 1990s to a radical position in the new millennium and then once again back to an extreme position with new leadership. The position of the SNS is also unclear. It was provisionally assigned to the radical Right because of its links with the SRS, but this could change over time, particularly if the party succeeds in future elections and ends up playing an important role in setting up the government. In addition, the party profiles itself more on social populism than on national issues. As regards party ideology, therefore, it would likely fall into a category other than populist parties alongside the Citizens for the European Development of Bulgaria (*Grazhdani za evropeysko razvitie na Balgariya*, GERB). Further developments regarding EU accession will also have great impact on the further position of the party within the party system.

2. **Electoral design matters only in some cases. Single-member districts in the electoral system or a high real threshold might hinder Far Right parties.**

The emergence of a Far Right party in the majoritarian electoral system is almost impossible (one example would be the change to the predominantly majoritarian electoral system in Romania in 2008 and no constituencies won by the PRM or the 2009 elections in Bulgaria and no mandates for Ataka in single-member districts); the proportional system (once established) plays a supporting role. Green parties and the New Left are not significant (if existent at all) in the Balkan countries. The electoral threshold plays some role in the above noted cases. The threshold is 3% in Albania but there has been no minimum threshold in Macedonia since 2002. These are supportive variables for the entrance of new smaller entities (which was not really the case in Macedonia), whereas the high real electoral threshold in Albania in the latest elections was a hindrance to small parties. On the other hand, the high electoral threshold present in Serbia, Romania and Bulgaria was exceeded by Far Right parties.

3. **States in which ethnic borders do not align with national frontiers create the best breeding ground for Far Right parties. This claim is mainly valid for established 'strong (mother) states'; in newly independent states, the national card is played by the main political player – this party usually leaves no space for Far Right formations.**

The ethnic kin abroad variable correlates with the emergence of the Far Right only in the case of Serbia – it is not used by any other successful party and the case of Croatia demonstrates that the diaspora itself does not help much if the nationalist agenda is taken by the mainstream party and accompanied by the lack of charismatic leadership – this can lead to the fragmented spectrum of many Far Right parties, as is the case in Croatia. It must, however, be stressed that having one's 'own nationals abroad' must be tied to a 'strong (mother) state'. This is not valid for newly born states in which ethnic borders do not align with national frontiers. Examples would be BiH or Montenegro, where the bearers of nationalism are the main political players, leaving no space for Far Right formations to arise. It must also be borne in mind that it is the mother state, not neighbours possessing a diaspora from the mother country, that creates the perfect breeding ground for nationalism: Croatia (with a diaspora in BiH), Serbia (diaspora in Croatia and BiH), Romania (Moldova), Bulgaria (Macedonia) and Albania (Kosovo, Macedonia). But this is not the only factor. Others also play a significant role. The Far Right in Croatia is therefore not strong because of the reasons noted above. The Moldovan card was not played by the PRM nor was the Macedonian card played by Ataka. It was the international factor (EU integration) which brought success for Ataka and the failure of BK (US Balkan policy).

Religion as a cultural variable could be supportive in strengthening nationalist feelings – in the three cases featuring strong political parties, it is the Orthodox Church which is tied to the nation and therefore could strengthen nationalist feelings. Nevertheless, it should be mentioned that the Catholic Church in Croatia has also had a great impact in promoting nationalism, while the Orthodox tradition did not automatically mean the success of Far Right in Montenegro as the nationalism was presented by DPS which left no space for Far Right formations.

4. **An ethnic minority with strong political representation is a very supportive factor for the rise of the Far Right.**

A large national minority with strong political representation, then, seems to be among the most important variables for Serbia (Albanians in Kosovo, Hungarians in Vojvodina), Bulgaria (Turks) and Romania (Hungarians). When the presence of a large national minority is accompanied by the frequent use of hate speech in the media, no journalistic ethics and a low level of professionalism among journalists, the Far Right has the perfect nationalist breeding ground.

5. **International variable matters – humiliation of the country or complicated EU integration means higher support for Far Right formations.**

   The international variable was important in Serbia, where state humiliation brought popularity for the SRS. It was also a factor in Albania, where US pressure hindered the promotion of nationalism and a Greater Albania, and in Bulgaria, where Ataka became popular due to the long, complicated EU accession procedure and the issue of Turkey's membership in the EU.

6. **Other political and economic variables (political culture, strong voting for new politics, unemployment) play a supporting role. The post-material dimension plays no role in the Balkans.**

   The success of Far Right parties correlates with rising unemployment and poverty only in the Romanian case; in Bulgaria, unemployment was decreasing, while in Serbia, it was fairly stable. Nevertheless, it must be noted that all cases show high rates of unemployment for long periods. Serbia, especially, was isolated for a long while, and the challenging economic situation lasted for more than two decades, prompting scepticism for the future. Significant voting for new politics definitely played a certain role in Bulgaria, while this cannot be shown for other cases. Immigration is almost non-existent and plays no role in the emergence of nationalist tendencies – the refugees are usually ethnic kin from other states not seen as an alien element by the local population. In addition, causality is reversed: refugees in, for example, Serbia have voting rights and often vote for the SRS.

7. **Last but not least, every country is unique – it is always a set of variables where ethno-cultural variables are sometimes contributory to the success of Far Right parties (Romania, Serbia, Bulgaria), while in other cases (Albania, Serbia), international factors may be a determinant for the (lack of) success of the Far Right party.**

   Despite the fact that Macedonia is a case of great opportunity, its membership in the sample is idiosyncratic. There is a large national minority, transformation costs were quite painful and the country has a great number of nationals abroad. The only explanation is the existence of strong mainstream parties on both the Right and the Left of the political spectrum addressing interethnic relations in the country – this is the only variable which is different from those common for Serbia, Bulgaria and

Table 7.2 Party and organizational strength of the Far Right and contextual factors in selected Balkan countries since 2000

		Croatia	Serbia	Montenegro	Macedonia	Albania	Bulgaria	Romania
Political and social	A1	1	0	–	0	0	0	1
	A2	0	0	0	0	0	1	0
	A3	1	1	1	1	1	1	1
	A4	1	1	1	1	1	1*	1**
	A5	0	1	1	0	0	1	1
	A6	0	0	0	0	0	0	0
	A7	1	1	1	1	1	1	1
Ethno-cultural	B1	1	1	1	1	1	1	1
	B2	0	1	0	0	0	0	0
	B3	1	1	0	0	1	1	1
	B4	1	1	1	1	0***	1	1
	B5	0	1	1	1	0	1	1
Economic	C1	0	–	0	1	0	0	1
	C2	0	1	0	1	1	0	1
International	D1	0	1	0	0	0	0	0
Actor	**Party**	**0**	**1**	**0**	**0**	**0**	**1**	**1**

A1 Party system: convergence 1, polarization 0.

A2 Cleavages: strong new politics voting 1, weak 0.

A3 Political opportunity structures: state and party latitude 1, exclusion/repression 0.

A4 Political opportunity structures: PR electoral system 1, majority 0.

A5 Political spectrum: vacuum or weak (fragmented) Right 1, Right occupied by strong party 0.

A6 Emergence of Green parties and New Left movements: present 1, non-present 0.

A7 Political culture: poor 1, mature 0.

B1 Nation type: ethno-cultural nation 1, political nation 0.

B2 Share of foreign-born population: high 1 (over 5% of the total population), low 0.

B3 Share of ethnic kin abroad: high 1 (over 10% in nationalist self-perception tradition), low 0.

B4 Dominant religious tradition: Orthodox 1, Christian Catholic or Islam, secular 0.

B5 Share of national minorities: high 1 (over 5% of the total population), low 0.

C1 Unemployment and poverty: on rise 1, decreasing 0.

C2 Perception of living standard: bad 1, good 0.

D1 International: state humiliation or exclusion 1, inclusion 0.

Party: strong 1, weak 0.

*Till 2009.

**Albania is taken as a secular country, despite the fact that around 70% of the population claims to be Muslim.

***Until 2008.

Bold print is used when the attribute is true for all three successful cases.

Romania. Cases from the Balkans have shown that every political space is unique and some factors which might play a significant role in one case need not have importance for another. This is probably the most important point; Table 7.2 shows quite clearly that the variables differ from case to case, as follows:

- Serbia: political (strategy of mainstream party), international (state humiliation) and ethno-cultural (ethnic kin abroad, national minority with strong representation)
- Bulgaria: political (strategy of mainstream player and electoral system), ethno-cultural (strong national minority) and international (EU accession)
- Romania: political (strategy of mainstream player and electoral system) and ethno-cultural (strong national minority)
- Croatia: political (strategy of mainstream player, electoral system)
- Montenegro: political (strategy of mainstream player, electoral system)
- Albania: international (US policy in the Balkans) and political (electoral system)
- Macedonia: political (strategy of mainstream player)

One factor was present in most cases: the strategy of the mainstream player. In Bulgaria and Romania, it was the discredited Right which opened space for Far Right formations. In Serbia, it was instead former SPS voters who decided to switch to the SRS. In Croatia and Montenegro, the main political players were the standard bearers for nationalism, while in Macedonia, they were addressing interethnic relations and thus left no room for a Far Right party. Further research into these points would be worthwhile in other European countries. For example, is the Far Right weak in the Czech Republic and Poland because of the position, strategy and tactics of the Civic Democratic Party (*Občanská demokratická strana*, ODS) and Law and Justice (*Prawo i Sprawiedliwość*, PiS), both of which promote soft Euroscepticism? Why is Jobbik so strong when both sides of the political spectrum are occupied?

Also apparent was the impact of Europeanization on the Balkan political space. The possibility arose that Far Right formations might be divided into two groupings: 'hard' (extreme, primordial and old) and 'soft' (radical, modern, new) parties. Hard parties are promoters of nationalism in terms of external exclusivity. They seek the creation of their 'greater' states. These parties include the PRM, SRS, HSP, VMRO and BK. The soft parties, by contrast, are those which focus on nationalism in terms of internal homogenization. They rationally accept the status quo and membership of their countries in the EU but promote national values within the EU. These parties include Ataka, VMRO–People's Party (*Vnatrešna Makedonska Revolucionerna Organizacija–Narodna Partija*, VMRO–NP) and the SNS.

Notes

1 The Croatian Bloc, which was present in the parliament in 2002–2003, could be depicted as being more extreme than the HSP (Buljan and Duka 2003:54).

2 According to a Eurobarometer survey, 74% of Croatians were in favour of joining the EU in autumn 2005 (Eurobarometer 2005:8).

3 Đukanović resigned in the same month Montenegro achieved EU candidate status, and he commented his resignation as follows: 'This decision of mine is not sudden or rash, and was not reached, as certain irresponsible individuals claim for reasons known only to themselves, under anyone's pressure, either from the inside or from the outsider. Today, when Montenegro is a stable country, when it is out of the recession, when it has become a candidate for EU membership, when it is in NATO's front room…conditions have become ripe for my withdrawal from the executive authority' (*Montenegro Prime Ministr Đukanović Resigns*. BBC, 21.10.2010. www.bbc.co.uk/news/world-europe-12051667).

4 Even though the PDSh is traditionally a northern party, it achieved good results in the 2003 local elections, even in some southern municipalities. The north is also a region of royalist and nationalist voters.

5 The only change is that the number of seats reserved for national minorities has been raised from 5 to 8, accompanied by a change in the national structure of national minorities in 2003.

6 In Kukës, 78,031 inhabitants were to vote four seats, which de facto moves the electoral threshold to 25%; in Gjirokastër, 103,406 inhabitants voted for five man-dates, which puts the threshold de facto at 20%.

7 For example, his son Miroslav was chief of the Office for National Security, the Croatian Secret Service. A number of allegations of corruption by senior govern-ment or ex-government officials were investigated in the post-Tuđman era, for example, his daughter Nevenka Tuđman was investigated for corruption.

8 Miranda Vickers claims that every ministry was loaded with PD loyalists, and no one could anticipate the scale of nepotism in the Berisha administration (Vickers and Pettifer 1997:244). Sali Berisha's nephew, Dritan Berisha, was employed in the Interior Ministry. The son and daughter of Prime Minister Shkelzen Berisha and Argita Berisha earn the most money on the issuing of licences and on public tenders. www.albania.de/alb/index.php?s=besnik; http://balkanweb.com/gazetav5/newsadmin/preview.php?id=60582.

9 Đukanović faces a different set of allegations ranging from corruption to nepotism. Criticism relates in particular to privatization deals, the business of Milo Đukanović's brother Aco Đukanović and the origin of the capital that Milo Đukanović has invested in *Prva Crnogorska Banka*. www.esiweb.org/index.php?lang=en&id=270.

10 All three countries enjoyed a significant decrease in unemployment: in 2003, there were 21.7% unemployed in Croatia, 17% unemployed in Albania and 27.7% in Montenegro (data from 2006). See www.indexmundi.com/.

11 For example, the Environmental-Agrarian Party in Albania gained four mandates in 2005.

12 According to the 1991 census, it was 17.4%. Cf. www.fzs.ba/Dem/Popis/NacStanB. htm, www.cia.gov/library/publications/the-world-factbook/geos/bk.html. Besides BiH, there is also a small Croatian minority in Slovenia – 35,642 people according to the 2002 census. Statistical Office of Slovenia. Census 2002. www.stat.si/ popis2002/en/rezultati/rezultati_red.asp?ter=SLO&st=7.

13 One of the closest collaborators of Croatian president Hrvoje Šarinić described the plans: 'Preservation of BiH is against Croatian interests. We must reinstate the borders of the 1939 Serbo-Croatian agreement' (Hudelist 2005:700).

14 Mandates for HDZ were also secured due to the inequality in the elections law. In 1995, HDZ required 8084 votes for a single mandate in the diaspora but 26,033 votes for a single seat in remaining proportional mandates. If the votes for HDZ from diaspora were counted for the state electoral district, the HDZ would gain 49 mandates (instead of 42 from Croatia and 12 from the diaspora) (Kasapović 1996: 271–272).

15 Kasapović, M. *Bosnian Croats Chose the Government of Croatia*. Bosnia Report, January 2005, No. 43–44. Available online at www.bosnia.org.uk/bosrep/report_ format.cfm?articleid=2957&reportid=167.

16 Montenegro had one seat reserved for its delegate at the Paris Peace Conference. The seat remained vacant due to the ongoing conflict between the supporters of the former ruling dynasty and those backing unification with Serbia.

17 These opinions stem from nineteenth- and early twentieth-century books. Dimitrije Sokolović wrote in 1890 fourth-grade geography textbook that Serbian lands encompass Montenegro, Bosnia, Herzegovina, Old Serbia, Macedonia, Dalmatia, Istria, Croatia, Slavonia, Srem, Bačka and Banat (Jelavich 1983). Another example is saying: We are two sides of one log where the log is from the ethnic perception Serbian but the nationality Montenegrin (Samardžić *et al.* 1998).

18 The name is derived from the colour of the voting cards in the Montenegrin Assembly – green voting cards were used by the supporters of Montenegrin identity (*Zelenaši*, Greens), while white cards were used by those who promoted unification with Serbia (*Bjelaši*, Whites).

19 94.1% of voters in the referendum voted to stay in the same state with Serbia. Referendum turnout reached 66.04% (Bieber 2003:21).

20 Serbs were only declared to be a national minority, something which was met with resistance by Serbian representatives.

21 Republic of Macedonia. State Statistical Office. *Census of Population, Households and Dwellings in the Republic of Macedonia 2002*. www.stat.gov.mk/pdf/ kniga_13.pdf.

22 For example, the idea was promoted by the spokesman of the Kosovo parliament, Jakup Krasniqi. *Krasnici: Jug Srbije za Sever Kosova*. 10 February 2010. www. emg.rs/vesti/srbija/113183.html.

23 Chams are ethnic Albanians, predominantly Muslims stemming from northwestern Greece expelled from Greece after the Balkan Wars 1912–1913 and after ratification of the Greek–Turkish agreement in 1923 and at the end of the Second World War. Their representatives demand that Greece admit responsibility for killing 4,000 Chams and taking the property rights of 150,000 others (Vickers 2002).

24 The aim of this formation is to control the region and create Greater Albania in cooperation with other liberation armies. This faction of the Albanian national army has no support from the inhabitants and cooperation with Albanian National Army is also negligible. The UÇÇ seems instead to create cover for local Albanian organized crime (OC) groups.

25 The key identification is 'Albanian', to identify with Gegs or Tosks is secondary, local and as such these terms cannot be taken as denoting distinctive nations or ethnicities.

26 58,758 people registered themselves as ethnic Greeks in the 1989 census, but this number is not accurate; the Greeks say 300,000–400,000 Greeks live in Albania. Real estimates stemming from the counts of the votes for the PBDN in 1992 state 100,000–120,000 (cf. Clewing 1995:418, Pettifer 2001:6).

27 *Albania: Greek Mayor Sentenced to Prison.* 21 April 2009. www.balkaninsight. com/en/main/news/18326/.

28 UNHCR. World Directory of Minorities and Indigenous Peoples – Croatia: Roma. www.unhcr.org/cgi-bin/texis/vtx/refworld/rwmain?page=country&docid=49 749d3544&skip=0&coi=HRV&rid=4562d8b62&querysi=ro ma&searchin=title&display=10&sort=date.

29 Croatia is no exception for the region – for example, neighbouring Slovenia also has reserved seats only for the Italian and Hungarian minority despite a significant Roma minority.

30 See UNHCR figures. www.unhcr.org/cgi-bin/texis/vtx/page?page=49e48d986.

31 Grdešic, I. *Zagreb: Croatian Support for EU Entry Slumps to Record Low.* Autumn 2008. www.europesworld.org/NewEnglish/Home_old/Article/tabid/191/ ArticleType/ArticleView/ArticleID/21223/ZAGREBCroatiansuppor tforEUentryslumpstorecordlow.aspx.

32 One of the populist slogans of the Slovenian democratic party was 'They have taken Carinthia, Trieste and Gorizia – they will not take the sea!' Another slogan cited Tito's post-war Yugoslavia: 'We don't want anything from foreigners, we are not giving anything away.' Cain, P. *Slovenia, Croatia Fights Over a Bit of Sea*, 5 June 2010. www.globalpost.com/dispatch/european-union/100604/slovenia-croatia-eu-bid. The media also played a role in the campaign – two groups emerged on Facebook: one for the international ruling and one against. The hysteria on both sides of the borders is behind the growing number of Eurosceptics among Croatian youth. A July 2010 survey showed that 50% of those questioned were in favour of integration with the EU, 49% against and 1% remained undecided. *Mladi na Hrvaškem Vecji Euroskeptiki Kot Njihovi Starši.* 30 July 2010. www.dnevnik.si/ novice/eu/1042377463.

33 *Referendum o zakonu o arbitražnem sporazumu.* www.dvk.gov.si/AS2010/ AS2010i/index3.html.

34 Support for NATO accession in Croatia was at a similar level as in Slovenia. A May 2007 poll showed that 52% of respondents backed NATO accession in Croatia, while in Slovenia, 56% of respondents backed the entry of the country into the Pact in 1999. Cf. *Croatia: Poll Shows Public Support for NATO Member-ship Growing in Croatia.* www.seeurope.net/?q=node/9134; *Comparative Data*

Related to Slovenian Public Opinion on NATO (1999 and 2001). http://nato.gov. si/eng/public-opinion/public-opinion-data/.

35 Wood, N. *Montenegro Bridles as a Russian Invasion.* 28 October 2006. www. nytimes.com/2006/11/28/world/europe/28iht-montenegro.3701457. html?pagewanted=1&_r=1.

36 NATO and EU are also the most trusted institutions in Albania: 32% trust NATO, 31% trust the EU, while only 9% trust in the government or 12% trust in the fairness of the elections (Gallup Balkan Monitor 2009:5).

37 In 1991, the unemployment rate was about 24%, while in the early 2000s, it was among the highest in CEE, reaching 37.3% in 2005 (Kjosev 2007:153–155).

38 See Cultural variables of Serbia, Bulgaria and Albania.

39 Note that the term Aegean Macedonia is found insulting by Greeks who call it simply Northern Greece.

40 These fears were not idle as, for example, the airport in Skopje is named after Alexander the Great. The flag adopted by the new state placed in its centre the Sun of Vergina – the symbol of Philip II of Macedonia and his son, Alexander the Great. The flag was changed to appease the demands of Greece.

41 *Macedonians Won't Give up Name for NATO.* 13 March 2008. www.angus-reid. com/polls/view/30120.

42 *Macedonians Hugely Opposed to Name Change for NATO Entry– Poll.* 18 September 2008. http://english.capital.gr/news.asp?id=578168&catid=&subcat=& spcatid=&djcatid=90.

8

Voters of the Far Right and legislative implementation in practice

This chapter offers a comparison drawn between the typical Far Right voter living in the Balkans and his counterpart in Western Europe. The second part of the chapter examines hate speech laws (their integration into the legal system and enforcement), activities which promote and incite racial discrimination and other legal issues affecting Far Right parties in the region.

Voters of the Far Right

Voters in the third wave of Right-wing radicalism in post-war democracies are commonly characterized as being younger males with no college education who work blue-collar jobs in the private sector and live in an urban environment. Blue-collar workers are overrepresented, while high-status employees are underrepresented. Medium and lower educational levels are also more common than those with no formal education whatsoever. It is employed people who are afraid of unemployment rather than the actual unemployed who vote for the radical Right. These voters tend to be more pessimistic about their future than the average member of the population, are more afraid of crime and often feel that they are on the wrong side of social change. Feelings of social isolation reinforce the correlation between ethnic nationalism and the preference for these parties – voters for these parties are less integrated in terms of family, friends, neighbours, associations, unions and social agencies (cf. Klönne und Siller in Kowalsky and Schroeder 1994:129–143, 143–159, Betz and Immerfall 1998:251–253, Arzheimer and Carter 2006:438–439, Hainsworth 2008:91–110).

Conclusions from research into the social picture of Far Right voters are similar in nature. Lubbers and colleagues, for example, concluded that in Western European countries, unemployed people in particular were more likely to vote for an extreme Right-wing party, something which also holds true for less well-educated, nonreligious people, younger voters and men. The effect of unemployment may also be negative, since in more prosperous countries, people are more likely to support extreme Right-wing parties

(Lubbers *et al.* 2002). Hendrik Schanovsky examined the electoral base of the German Republican Party and found that the party's voters fell into one of the following groups: adapted Neo-Nazis, conservative–liberal coalition voters frustrated by promised change in 1982–1983,[1] stratum intermedium voters who feared losing their status, disaffected provincial voters, young authoritarian workers and victims of the two-thirds society (Schanovsky 1997:22).

In looking at the Croatian electorate, we must also keep in mind the unfinished transition as well as a couple of other specific features. When the Croatian political scientist, Ivan Šiber, analysed electoral behaviour by voters in Croatia after 1989, he concluded that it is not yet possible to bind the social structure with the political orientation, due to the process of transition, institutionalizing the new sovereign and independent state, and the war.[2] Family roots played a role in the elections – families with partisan ancestors gave their votes mostly to parties on the Left, while families with Ustasha ancestors voted for parties on the Right. As Šiber concludes, voters for the parties on the Right (Croatian Democratic Union (*Hrvatska demokratska zajednica*, HDZ), Croatian Party of the Right (*Hrvatska Stranka Prava*, HSP) and Croatian Christian Democratic Union (HKDU)) are religious and conservative, with authoritarian tendencies. Voters for the HSP are mainly young, between the ages of 18 and 28. The older the voter, the less likely he or she is to vote for HSP (Šiber 2007:152–184). As Šiber notes, the Croatian Right-wing electorate, with its significant state-conservative factors, is more active in the elections than are Leftists and other voters. This state-conservative factor, typical for the most active voters, takes in the support of Croats in Bosnia and Herzegovina (BiH), protecting the dignity of the Patriotic War and strengthening military power and state security, spiritual renewal and demographic growth (Čular 2005:31).

Research undertaken in 1995 also showed greater social distance from the Serbian population in Croatia on the part of voters for radical Right parties than was true for voters for other parties in the sample. The research also shows radical Right voters incline to limit the rights of individuals and groups, to use force in resolving conflicts (40%) and to limit some social rights like the right to hold demonstrations. They also prefer strong leaders to solve problems (42%) rather than leaving them to the democratic process (15%). Twenty-three per cent of respondents choosing the radical Right also believe that political parties are not necessary in Croatia's political system, with only 4% of sample stating they are necessary. The voters of the radical Right also endorse traditional lifestyle values and urge a return to the basic values of the nation, are in favour of national exclusivity and self-reliance and promote the notion of a *pure* nation-state, that is, the idea that each nation should live alone in its own state (34%) (Grdešić in Ramet 1999:181–182).

Other research implies HDZ and HSP voters have authoritarian tendencies. Dissatisfaction with democracy is continually rising among HSP voters, while

HDZ voters began to be dissatisfied with the state of democracy after the 2003 elections (Čular 2005:151–153). In terms of formal education received, 55% have high school diplomas, but overall, they have been in school less than the average voter. The variable that strongly differentiates Far Right voters from others is level of religiosity: 47% are strong believers, with only 2% not religious. Fifty-three per cent of the radical Right constituency agrees with the notion of separating church and state, with remaining respondents partly agreeing (29%) or believing there should be no separation between church and state (17%).

The Serbian Radical Party (*Srpska Radikalna Stranka*, SRS) voters are mainly peasants (30%), workers (19%) and lower class (26%), as opposed to middle class (25%) and white-collar workers who identify with the Democratic Party (*Demokratska Stranka*, DS) (Stojiljković 2006:184). Quite interestingly, the party is usually lumped together with the Socialist Party of Serbia to create the third pole of the Serbian party system, sharing such themes as '*criminal usurpation of the country*', '*anarchy*', the return of '*national-patriotic politics*' and a '*system of law, work and responsibility*' (Komšić 2006:175). The voters of this red–black pole, in contrast with DS voters, identify themselves much more with the nation, do not like Americans, tend towards authority and are traditional, patriarchal, passive, anti-Western, against privatization, against giving rights to minorities and against the membership of Serbia in the European Union (EU) (Mihailović in Lutovac 2006:158). The SRS programme focuses on voters frustrated by the economy, corruption and privatization scandals. In 2004, before the local elections, Nikolić noted that the SRS is a party of '*poor people*' (Djurković 2006:12). Branko Milanović claims that it is not the salary but rather general standard of living which impacts voters; his further conclusions correspond with those of other researchers – less educated males tend to vote for radicals to a greater extent. In addition, radicals have a larger electoral base in Vojvodina, while they receive fewer votes in Belgrade. The electoral base is also recruited from among Croatian and Roma refugees (Milanović 2004).[3]

In Bulgaria, there are no sociological data for the sociological membership profile, though it appears to be predominantly male, educated and relatively young, with a strong sample of historians, lawyers and army and former security service officers (Ivanov-Ilieva in Mudde 2005:5). Savkova notes that the profile of the National Union Attack (*Natsionalen Sayuz Ataka*, Ataka)'s voters is extremely difficult to define: they come from all age groups and regions in Bulgaria, although there is a tendency for voters to be uneducated and ethnically Bulgarian (Savkova 2007:9). Stefanova points out that 'the radical right political agency affects the distribution of electoral preferences whereby voters pertaining to certain sociological and attitudinal categories – blue-collar workers, older voters, and medium-education cohorts in the large cities, voters sharing centrist ideology, lower levels of political trust, and ethnocentrism – are more likely than other groups to vote radical right as an expression of protest against the incumbents, despite the lack of proximity with extreme right ideologies' (Stefanova 2007). Many researchers have stated that quite a lot of support came from protest votes and losers in the state-orchestrated transformation to a market economy. More than 30% of Ataka's electorate consists of people who voted for the National Movement of Simeon II (*Nacionalno Dviženie Simeon II*, NDSV) in the previous election. Quite surprisingly, exit polls put the number of those identifying as Roma who indicated they had voted for Ataka at 12,000. This number may point to bought votes (Tavanier 2005).

The Greater Romania Party (*Partidul România Mare*, PRM)'s electoral base is composed of old people nostalgic for the socioeconomic stability offered by the old communist regime as well as younger educated people not able to deal with the market economy and not ready to emigrate to find jobs corresponding to their university education. Gallagher notes that the support- ers of PRM were those who felt deceived by the new economic conditions in the country: 'either elderly people nostalgic for the strict hierarchy of the communist regime and for stable and predictable economic benefits; youth confused by the cruel competition of "heartless" labour market as well as the clash between what the Romanian education system can offer and what the labour market demands' (Nine O' Clock, cited from Gallagher 2003:13). Voters had attained either a primary or secondary school education (Lachauer 2005:87). The PRM voter base does not show regional discrepancies – in all counties, PRM had its most successful elections in 2000, with one to three mandates. The only difference is the result in Bucharest, where they scored seven out of twenty-nine mandates (24%) for Chamber of Deputies and three out of thirteen (23%) for Senate, and no mandates in the Transylvanian coun- ties mostly inhabited by ethnic Hungarians (Harghita, Covasna).[4]

In general, we find out very little about the voter profile for the different Far Right parties, despite the availability of data in countries where these parties are relevant, such as Croatia, Bulgaria, Romania and Serbia. Data for Albania is difficult to obtain, the National Front (*Balli Kombëtar*, BK) is a very small party, and the Sociological Institutes do not collect data concerning BK voters. Generally, the younger generation initially voted for Right-wing parties, the older generation for the Socialist Party of Albania (*Partia Socialiste e Shqipërisë*, PSSh). However, the change in the leadership and style of PSSh and emergence of the Socialist Movement for Integration (*Lëvizja Socialiste për Intigrim*, LSI) motivated young people to begin voting for the Left. Besides the above-noted information, there are no data available about BK voters. There are no data available for Macedonia. The party is so marginal that the Sociological Institute does not collect data about its voters.

Do social attitudes and values conform to the general description of Far Right constituencies in Western Europe and in the Balkans? Their similarity seems to lie in the fact that most are male and young; the only difference is in Romania, where a portion of the PRM electorate is composed of those longing for the old regime. Unlike in Western Europe, the Far Right electorate in the Balkans is religious – the high level of religiosity is nevertheless typical for these countries. Most of the Balkan Far Right electorate is comprised of peasants and blue-collar workers; this is again motivated by regional particulars. Last but not least, the lack of a university education is characteristic of Far Right voters in both Western Europe and the Balkans.

Far Right parties and legislative implementation in practice

Legislative implementation is based on the international conventions governments have signed at the supranational level, such as the UN International Convention on the Elimination of All Forms of Racial Discrimination (1965), which explicitly states in Article 4b that all signatories 'shall declare illegal and prohibit organisations, and also organized and all other propaganda activities, which promote and incite racial discrimination, and shall recognize participation in such organisations or activities as an offence punishable by law'. The UN Committee on the Elimination of Racial Discrimination is then responsible for monitoring whether the signatories fulfil their obligations under the Convention. In the past, the critique has been aimed at Australia, Norway or Denmark. The controlling mechanism on the supranational level is, then, performed by the EU as well, which gained notoriety for imposing sanctions against Austria when the Freedom Party of Austria (*Freiheitliche Partei Österreichs*, FPÖ) was included in the coalition government (Mudde in Eatwell and Mudde 2004:204–205).

Only in a few cases has the party been banned – most recently the case of the Workers Party (*Dělnická Strana*) in the Czech Republic, which was banned for inciting racism and xenophobia in 2010. Nevertheless, this case (similarly as with the case of the Vlaams Blok) shows that the ban does not resolve the issue, since the leader, Tomáš Vandas, set up a new political party called the Workers Party of Social Justice (*Dělnická Strana Sociální Spravedlnosti*) immediately after the court decision. Pressure is quite often applied by the media as in, for example, the case of the Slovak National Party (*Slovenská národná strana*, SNS), which, during its pre-election campaign in 2010, placed a large Roma man with a gold chain and large tattoo (the picture was adjusted in order to fit the stereotype image of Romanies) on its billboards, with the slogan 'so we don't have to feed those who don't want to work' (*Abysme nekrmili tých, čo nechcú pracovat*). The public's sharp response forced the SNS to contact the man and give him work.[5]

Political parties in the Balkan countries under discussion may be banned on the following grounds not compatible with democracy: anti-democratic policies held by the party and a desired change in state territorial integrity (most countries), breach of the Code of Conduct (Albania, Croatia), failure to respect the electoral laws (Albania), hate speech or inciteful activities (Albania, Macedonia, Romania, Bulgaria), the formation of military units and war propaganda (Macedonia) and the propagation of racism or totalitarianism (Macedonia) (Stojarová *et al.* 2007:25).

In Bulgaria, the Constitution prohibits the formation of political parties on ethnic, racial or religious grounds (Article 11) and organizations inciting to racial, national, ethnic or religious enmity (Article 44). It bans the use of freedom of speech to incite enmity (Article 39). The Constitutional Court then further clarified the provision that the law should relate only to those parties which ban people of other ethnic, racial or religious groups from their membership. Criminal law also prohibits racially motivated violence and incitement to racial discrimination, or to national, ethnic, racial or religious hatred, and Fascist propaganda, as well as the formation of, or membership in, organizations to commit such crimes (Christo-Ilieva in Mudde 2005:16). Since its establishment, the Movement for Rights and Freedoms Party, whose membership and electorate is predominantly Turkish, has been charged with being unconstitutional by ultranationalists and supporters of Ataka, despite a ruling by the Constitutional Court affirming the party's constitutionality at the start of the 1990s. Something similar took place in Albania, where ethnic Greeks were about to found a political party but Albanian law prohibited the founding of a political party on ethnic grounds. Consequently, a political party was set up which was de iure open to all inhabitants of Albania but whose membership and electorate was predominantly Greek and represented the interests of Greeks in Albania. In both cases, obviously, the issue presented a great source of foment for nationalist and populist politicians. The Albanian ban on ethnic parties was lifted in the early 2000s.

Anti-discrimination legislation is probably enforced in Bulgaria more than in the other countries under analysis; the charismatic leader of Ataka, Siderov, has frequently been charged with making discriminatory remarks. For example, Siderov was accused by *Citizens Against Hate* of declaring 'Bulgarians will have the lowest representation in the government and parliament and the next parliament will only be populated by poofs, Gypsies, Turks, Foreigners, Jews and others where there should be only Bulgarians'.[6] The Claim was based on the Law on Protection against Discrimination, International Convention of Elimination of All Forms of Racial Discrimination, International Covenant on Civil and Political Rights and the Constitution of the Republic of Bulgaria. The gathered NGOs gave other examples of Siderov expressions such as 'the international Jewish elite' or 'terrorist Gypsy ghettos'. Siderov's immunity did not help in this case, and the Court of First Instance decided that Siderov must refrain in the future from similar statements, though the request for a public apology was rejected.

Romania has adopted a diversified approach, and not only the Constitution but a special set of laws prohibit discriminatory acts. Article 37.2 of the Romanian Constitution bans 'political parties and organisations which by their aims or activity militate against political pluralism, the principles of a state governed by the rule of law'. In the 2000–2006 period, a diversified legal framework was adopted to prevent and sanction all forms of discrimination and the incitement of hate; the establishment of a Fascist, racist or xenophobic organization is punishable by three to fifteen years (Chiriţă – Săndescu in Salat 2008:62–66). The anti-discrimination law was used against Vadim Tudor, who, in a speech on a public radio station, stated that, during the 1993 pogrom, the Romanians were just defending their *'honour'* against the *'gypsy rapists and thieves'* who wanted to *'slaughter'* them and called on the state authorities to protect the *'peaceful villagers'* against *'the bloody anger of a few brutes'*. The National Council for Combating Discrimination held that Tudor's utterances constituted discriminatory acts and that the use of derogatory terms in relation to persons of Roma ethnicity was in breach of their human dignity and created a humiliating atmosphere towards a group of persons or a community, based on their membership in the Romani ethnicity. Tudor, having parliamentary immunity, was shielded from any sanctions.[7]

Article 49 of the Serbian Constitution prohibits inciting racial ethnic, religious or other inequality or hatred (Art. 49). An anti-discriminatory law was adopted in Serbia only in 2009 and in Macedonia in 2010. While the former included provisions regarding acts of discrimination on the basis of sexual orientation, the latter excluded these for other reasons. Hate speech is clearly defined in the Serbian Public Information Act, which prohibits the publication of 'ideas, information and opinions which incite to discrimination, hatred or violence against an individual or a group of individuals for reasons of their belonging or not belonging to a race, religion, nation, ethnic group, gender or for their sexual orientation, regardless of whether the act of publication constitutes a crime'. Nevertheless, as the publication activity of SRS shows, the law did not gain endorsement for a long period. The first ruling based on hate speech was handed down in September 2008 by the First Municipal Court in Belgrade and then upheld by the Belgrade District Court in April 2009 which rendered it final and not subject to appeal.[8] For a long period of time, Croatian law also poorly addressed praise for nationalism. Pressure from the EU eventually functioned to persuade the Račan coalition government, on 11 July 2003, to pass amendments to the Penal Code outlawing hate speech in a new section entitled *Praising Fascist, Nazi and Other Totalitarian States and Ideologies or Promotion of Racism and Xenophobia*. Despite the approved legislation in both states, the media and various cultural figures (e.g. singer Marko Petrović and his band Thompson in Croatia promoting Croatian nationalism, Croatian and Serbian guslari or Baja Mali Knindža) remain very nationalist, and it is impossible to envision an indictment (or ruling) banning a political party on the basis of nationalist behaviour which is not compatible with democracy. Hate speech is also still present in the Macedonian, Montenegrin and Albanian media.[9] The Montenegrin constitution quite broadly bans 'any direct or indirect act of discrimination for any reason' (Art. 8) and also states that 'incitement of hatred for any reason is prohibited' (Art. 7). Anti-discriminatory legislation was adopted by the Montenegrin government in 2005 but not approved by the parliament; the new law was drawn up under the guidance of Organisation for Security and Cooperation in Europe (OSCE) and finally passed by the parliament in July 2010 – Montenegro was the last country in the Western Balkans to adopt a comprehensive anti-discriminatory law,[10] since Albania had adopted a broadly inclusive anti-discrimination law in February 2010 (the Albanian constitution has also anti-discriminatory provisions in Art. 18: 'No one may be unjustly discriminated against for reasons such as gender, race, religion, ethnicity, language, political, religious or philosophical beliefs, economic condition, education, social status, or ancestry').

It is not only the domestic use of any legal framework but also international covenants and courts which could play a role in anti-discriminatory measures. Vojislav Šešelj is probably the most famous case related to the Far Right party who was indicted by the International Criminal Tribunal for the former Yugoslavia (ICTY) for, among other things, persecution on political, racial or religious grounds, deportation, inhumane acts, crimes against humanity and violations of the laws or customs of war.[11] Ante Gotovina, Ivan Čermak and Mladen Markač, all affiliated to the Ministries of Interior and Defence during Croatian war, were then indicted on similar grounds.

The enforcement of hate speech and anti-discriminatory legislation is carried out at the highest level in Romania and Bulgaria, where even members of the political parties have ended up in front of the courts on more than one occasion. The practice in other countries remains notably poor, despite certain improvements in the adoption of new laws.

Notes

1 Helmut Kohl brought the conservatives back to power.
2 Therefore, workers and craftsmen supported the Right in the first elections in 1990 (HDZ, HSP, HKDU), something which changed in the elections in 2000. Young voters gave their support to the Right-wing parties in 1992 and 1995, then switched to the Left in 2000 and, in 2003, voted once again for the Right. The same goes for unemployed people. The police and army gave their votes in the first elections in

1990 to the parties of the Left. When HDZ came to power, they did a complete about-face and since 1992 have supported Right-wing parties (Šiber 2007:152–176).

3 One of the interpretations could be that Roma vote for Radicals because of their bad economic situation. Other interpretations include purchase of votes or support for SRS in Roma population due to their programme. For analysis of impact of refugees on the SRS success see Grujić 2006, for regional analysis see Mihić (2005).

4 National Statistical Office www.insse.ro/cms/rw/pages/index.ro.do.

5 *Slovenská vládní SNS láká voliče rasismem na Romech.* 5 May 2010. http://zahranicni.eurozpravy.cz/eu/8428-slovenska-vladni-sns-laka-volice-rasismem-na-romech/.

6 *86 organizaciji davat Volen Siderov na sud.* www.segabg.com/online/article.asp?issueid=2036&sectionid=16&id=0000101.

7 ERRC. *Romanian Equality Watchdog Rules Anti-Romani Speech by Romanian politician is discrimina*tory. 14 February 2006. www.errc.org/cikk.php?cikk=2513.

8 For more on the case, see YIHR Newsletter 2009. *The first ruling for hate speech in Serbia.* www.rbf.org/usr_doc/YIHR_Newsletter_-_Initiative_against_hate_speech_in_Serbia.pdf. For hate speech related to the arrest of Radovan Karadžić and the Belgrade demonstration in 2008, see Hatespeech in Serbia by YUCOM. www.yucom.org.rs/upload/vestgalerija_61_18/1231854903_GS0_Hate-Speech-Newsletter-No-3-eng-1389-12-01-09.pdf.

9 See *Is there hate speech in Macedonian media?* www.oneworldsee.org/node/6203; *There is still hatespeech in Montenegro RTV programmes.* http://oneworldsee.org/node/7900; *Serbia and Montenegro: Compliance with obligations and commitments and implementation of the post-accession co-operation programme.* Document presented by the Secretary General. Eighth report (March 2005 – June 2005). https://wcd.coe.int/ViewDoc.jsp?id=879091&BackColorInternet=9999CC&BackColorIntranet=FFBB55&BackColorLogged=FFAC75; Lenkova 1998.

10 *Montenegro fulfills EU membership requirements and protects LGBT people from discrimination.* July 28, 2010. http://eurout.org/2010/07/28/montenegro-fulfils-eu-membership-requirement-and-protects-lgbt-people-discrimination.

11 www.icty.org/x/cases/seselj/cis/en/cis_seselj_en.pdf.

9

Internal supply side: strategy, organization, role of paramilitaries and international cooperation

This chapter briefly outlines internal party factors – first, the strategies and tactics used by Far Right parties. The role of the mass media, demonstrations and language is explored to make a comparison with the situation in Western Europe (WE). The next section focuses on party organizational structure and its relationship to the way parties perform at the polls, the existence of paramilitary organizations tied to the parties and local and pan-European cooperation by Far Right parties.

Strategy and tactics

The strategy and tactics of parties on the Far Right in WE are born of public discontent, either with the socioeconomic standard or with the political representation of the country. As Eatwell notes, a focus on attacking parties in the political spectrum, usually accompanied by a lack of consistent ideology and dissatisfaction with the established parties on the part of voters, is mirrored in the rise of the Far Right and high volatility (Eatwell 2003:51). Parties usually present themselves in a softer light to achieve social acceptability, since voters are looking for limited, rather than extreme, change (Eatwell 2003:65). Alexandre Dézé uses the example of the Italian Social Movement, French National Front, Freedom Party of Austria (*Freiheitliche Partei Österreichs*, FPÖ) and Flemish Bloc to show all these parties have chosen to adapt to the system 'and it is precisely this choice which has forced them to play constantly with various strategic styles' (Dézé in Eatwell and Mudde 2004:35). In WE, there are strong leaders capable of exploiting national and local symbols, leaders conscious of the language they use and capable of communicating with ordinary citizens, who may be said to be truly 'populist' in style as regards public image. The professionalization of media advocacy has been adopted by many of the more successful neo-populist parties. Examples might be Haider and Le Pen, who were most capable media managers (Mazzoleni *et al.* 2003:228–229).

The leaders of Far Right parties in WE have quite often been brought before their national courts for disseminating anti-Semitic or racist ideas or have been accused of doing so by (inter-)national human rights organizations.

A clear example is the leader of the National Front, Jean-Marie Le Pen, who has been convicted several times and paid out thousands of euros in fines for his remarks. The leader of Austrian Freedom Party, Jörg Haider, became known for his statement that the Nazi government had produced a 'proper employment policy' and for describing the concentration camps of the Second World War as 'punishment camps'. The leader of the Liberal Democratic Party of Russia (*Liberalno-Demokraticheskaye Partiya Rossii*, LDPR), Vladimir Zhirinovsky, gained popularity not only by virtue of hate speech and anti-Semitism but also for acting violently and pointing rifles at his political opponents. Probably the most famous quote of Ján Slota, the leader of the Slovak National Party (*Slovenská národná strana*, SNS), is 'let's get into tanks and move against Budapest'. He also refers to 'ugly Hungarian people, of Mongoloid type, with crooked legs and even more disgusting horses'. Most leaders nevertheless get off with criticism or a fine – not many actually end up behind bars.

The role of the mass media, internal party documents and publications
Some political parties publish their own newspapers and magazines. The Serbian Radical Party (*Srpska Radikalna Stranka*, SRS) has its Great Serbia (*Velika Srbija*); the Greater Romania Party (*Partidul România Mare*, PRM) has its Great Romania (*România Mare*)[1] as well as Tricolour (*Tricolorul*). The National Union Attack (*Natsionalen Sayuz Ataka*, Ataka) publishes the journals *Ataka* and *Desant*; the Internal Macedonian Revolutionary Organization (*Vnatrešna makedonska revolucionerna organizacija*, VMRO) publishes *Macedonia* biweekly and the monthly magazine We (*Nie*), which focuses on historical and political analysis, along with a newspaper targeting teenagers, Bread and Salt (*Hljab I Sol*). Most of the journals mentioned are available on the Internet. All are kept updated with recent news, and those belonging to SRS, in particular, are full of photomontages of the party's 'enemies' and those of its voters. Ataka, in addition to written publications, also has close relations with Skat Television, which operates primarily in the Burgas Province and broadcasts programmes which support the party. Skat Television has come under investigation in the past after the Helsinki Committee complained about the racism and nationalism promoted by the station. But the Council for Electronic Media then published a report indicating that TV Skat had been formed by staffers at TV Den after the latter was shut down for similar offences. The Council concluded that the measure was ineffective, also classifying it as censorship.[2] Volen Siderov was a TV personality and thus was skilled in employing the television medium – he made extensive use of television compared to figures in other political parties, using catch phrases such as 'Stop the Gypsy Terror over Bulgarians', 'Drop Turkish Language News Programs from State Television' and 'Give Bulgaria Back to Bulgarians', which became slogans for the coalition (Tavanier 2005).

Skilful orators are an important asset to popular parties. Leaders of two of the parties noted stand out in terms of attracting voters by the ardency of their speech-making. Vojislav Šešelj is well known for the defence he leads at the International Criminal Tribunal for the former Yugoslavia (ICTY) in Hague where he demonizes his opponents – ICTY, North Atlantic Treaty Organization (NATO), the USA and others. The same may be said of Vadim Tudor, who is very skilful in long speeches and uses shock tactics and quips. This is true not only in his newspaper articles but also in his appearances on television. 'His demonisation of opponents, his insistence that only he could defend core Romanian values, and his identification of multiple threats that endangered the very existence of Romania repelled not a few Romanians but far more were mesmerised by his performance' (Gallagher 2005:255).[3]

The SRS is probably most active in book publishing. The SRS compiles the speeches of its leader, Šešelj, and publishes dozens of other books by the leader, who also writes while in ICTY detention. The party also cooperates closely with the self-declared Government of Republika Srpska Krajina (RSK), which regularly sends out open letters dealing with the RSK issue. The Albanian National Front also decided in March of 2009 to produce a series of publications entitled National Front Publications, with the aim of putting out articles, studies and books on national personalities. Similarly, VMRO owns a publishing house specializing in historical books – Macedonia Press. Volen Siderov is also a famous author of several books with titles such as The Boomerang of Evil, which places the burden of responsibility for all the world's ills on the Jews, or Bulgarophobia, where Siderov imputes treasonous motives to anyone who defends the human rights of Romas, gays and other marginalized groups in Bulgaria.

In addition to their Internet websites (only Ataka also has an English-language website), parties have begun to take part in social networking websites, as well, and have all started Facebook pages. Ataka even offers the download of Ataka ringtones for mobile phones and computer wallpapers.

Rallies, protests, violence and football hooliganism

All parties use demonstrations and rallies as part of their campaigns and daily activities. Ataka's 2005 campaign was based upon hastily organized, racially targeted demonstrations and rallies which bordered on Fascist and the opportunity to view the evening 'Ataka' bulletin from the comfort of one's own home on the TV satellite station Skat (Savkova 2005:10). Ataka is well known for protests in front of the Turkish Embassy which demanded an official apology for the killing of Bulgarians during the time of the Ottomans, as well as money the party claims the Turks owe for land taken by force from Bulgarian owners in 1913, and commemorations of the anniversary of the hanging of Bulgaria's national hero, Vasil Levski.[4] VMRO activists have engaged in aggression against nontraditional religious groups, holding protest demonstrations at their activities and interrupting their meetings. Although the party leadership has condemned such acts, some leaders have made numerous explicit extremist statements about religion (Ivanov-Ilieva in Mudde 2005:4).

In speaking of the Serbian Far Right, one must not forget Red Star Belgrade's Ultra fans, the nationalist football hooligans who have engaged in criminal gang activities involving the Arkan gang and from which the paramilitary units of the Serbian Volunteer Guard called the Arkan's Tigers were recruited. These created the electoral basis of the Party of Serbian National Unity and the SRS. Quite close to football is also the Romanian PRM, whose deputy Dumitru Dragomir (2004–2008)[5] is the President of the Romanian 'Professional Football League' and was President of various football clubs.

Some leaders also take part in violence or face trials which give them the reputation of strong party leaders. In 1990, Šešelj attacked one man with a baseball bat. In 1992, he pointed a pistol at demonstrating students; the same year he knocked a Serbian Renewal Movement (*Srpski pokret obnove*, SPO) MP unconscious in the parliament. Two times during 1993, the SRS got in fights with parliamentary security. In 1997, his bodyguards beat up the human rights lawyer Nikola Barović in a TV studio and then got popular for throwing water over Nataša Mičić during a broadcast session and disrupting parliamentary sessions (ICG 2004:5). Parliament even took away Šešelj's immunity, allowing the party leader to be sentenced to 30 days for the incident which took place in the federal parliament.

The leader of the Romanian New Generation Party–Christian Democratic (*Partidul Noua Generaţie–Creştin Democrat*, PNG–CD), Gigi Becali, an independent MP in the European Parliament (EP) elected on the PRM list, was put under a travel ban for the duration of the investigation by police, barring him from taking his seat in the EP. Becali has been sued many times in the Romanian courts for using violence and inflammatory and discriminatory language. In 2002, Becali cursed and threatened well-known journalist Cristian Tudor Popescu. In 2005, he cursed, spat and spilled wine on TV star Şerban Huidu. In 2006, after a football match involving the Steaua football club to which he is attached, his bodyguards attacked a reporter for Realitatea TV. One of the biggest controversies was set off when Becali insulted MP Lavinia Sandru, stating that she should 'go and become a candidate for the beltway, not for the European Parliament' and adding that a woman 'has no further value after she has given a birth to a child'. This was the reason why a group of women reported Becali at the National Council for Combating Discrimination; the Council then ruled that Becali's comments were discriminatory and affected the dignity of women and fined him 500 lei (ca. 120 euros).[6] In 2009, Becali was arrested for holding three people he suspected of stealing his car against their will. Becali was taken into custody before the Easter holiday and compared himself for public benefit to Jesus Christ, saying he, too, had been arrested just before the chief Christian holiday. Becali receives media attention for many controversies related to his inciteful language and use of violence and is loved by a mass media which enjoys serving scandals to its readers.

Language, emotions, fear and conspiracy series

All of the parties create enemies – either nations or ethnicities – whom they characterize by negative propaganda (the *Serbian occupiers, Croatian Ustashas, stinking Gypsies, Turkish enemies, Jewish conspirators, Terror of the Gypsies, bloodthirsty American Spies*) or political parties in power in the state and situation concerned (*government quislings, corrupt politicians tied to organized crime, nepotist leaders, traitors, thieves or even idiots*), etc.[7] The verbiage used is designed to create fear among the people that someone might take their jobs, their homes, the national wealth or the national identity. The language used by SRS is among the most creative, attempting to create the feeling that enemies, as embodied in bloodthirsty Croats, Turks, Albanians, Americans, the international community at large, the European Union (EU) or NATO, have always been against the Serbs and have pushed the Serbian people into poverty and misery. A typical example is a speech by the SRS leader in 1993 in which he stated on live TV that 'the Muslims will be slaughtered with rusty spoons' (ICG 2004:5). Quite innovative in a sense is Vadim Tudor, who attacked his opponents by tossing around language such as 'a cross-breed between a badger and a turkey', 'a shameless dummy', 'drinks like a pig and beats his wife and children until blood flows', 'the biggest bandit known to 20th century Romania is the Hungarian Jew, who steals and lies in a way that comes naturally to him', 'with the ulcerated brain of a hereditary syphilitic' and 'it was the Jews who arrived on the tanks of Red Army, who brought bolshevism to Romania, who contributed to the massacre of Romanian patriots' (Gallagher 2005:286–288). It is a language full of injustices, focused on the historic mission of the nation, and it is used to allow the speaker to gain control over the public and make of themselves messiahs chosen to save the nation from ruin.

Some happenings and gestures may have a cynical meaning, such as when Vadim Tudor uncovered a statue of Israeli Prime Minister Yitzhak Rabin in Brasov, while his speeches made constant anti-Semitic references and denied the Holocaust.[8] In 2004, Tudor applied a new strategy and decided to publicly apologize to everyone he has been insulting for the past 14 years – Jewish people attacked in his pamphlets, the government, the President of the country and all political opponents. Many people saw this action as a means of creating a credible perception for the party and securing it a place as a partner in government (Popa in Karasimeonov 2004:94).

Some parties are keen to project an image of generosity and closeness, such as when Vadim Tudor provides regular hot meals for the poor – a practice he calls *'The Christian Supper'* or feeds stray dogs in Bucharest (Maegerle 2009). As for *România Mare*, most of the space was given to the Democratic Union of Hungarians in Romania (*Uniunea Democrată Maghiară din România, UDMR*) and its perceived attempt to break up the Romanian state, then to Romanian politicians across the political spectrum, or denouncing King Mihai at a time when it was felt he might emerge as a strong rival to Iliescu. Tudor used to label his political opponents bandits and Kominter agents or call them other innovative names: 'Through the capital wander rabid dogs: Dan Ioan Mirescu and Sorin Rosca Stânescu. Under the influence of their hereditary syphilis, these two gypsy terrorists publish in the filthiest pigsty ever seen in the history of the Romanian press the newspaper "Ziua", a series full of lies and insults directed at Corneliu Vadim Tudor and PRM!' No other party has a newspaper with the influence of România Mare. Tudor has also started to cultivate a cult of personality occasionally comparable to Ceauşescu's (Gallagher 2005:284–296).

Nevertheless, there are other distinctive figures in PRM. A quite famous example is the nationalist mayor of the Transylvanian town Cluj, Gheorghe Funar, who attracted media attention by ordering that city sidewalks be painted in the national colours – red, yellow and blue[9] or when the Cluj City Hall refused to wed a Hungarian couple after they said 'Igen (Yes)' in their language, despite the fact that they qualified for a wedding in their mother tongue.[10] The main square of Cluj was also renamed Unification Square (*Piaţa Unirii*), to commemorate the incorporation of Transylvania into Romania, and the label on the statue of Matthias Corvinus was changed from *Matthias Rex Hungarorum* to simply *Matthias Rex*.

Volen Siderov was also in front of the court for its expressive language regarding ethnic minorities and was charged with discrimination based on sexual orientation related to phrases such as 'poof-lesbian gatherings'. The claims were ruled unproven by the Court of First Instance. The Bulgarian politician also gained popularity when his car was hit on the highway and he accused the drivers of attempting to assassinate him. Siderov is a very typical example of a successful political party leader who attracts voters by his accent on a vast, faceless anger. He usually begins speeches by saying 'we are enraged' or 'we are angry', which gives people space to fill in their own reason for anger – unemployment, poverty, crime, non-transparency, corruption, etc. (Karpat 2006). One Siderov article mentions the 'racial discrimination against Bulgarians' and 'systematic genocide' that was being waged against the ethnic Bulgarian majority. 'All minority groups' on the other hand are 'ever more protected by powerful foreign financial structures that aim to divide Bulgaria' (Tavanier 2005).

The parties are truly populist in terms of political style – they claim to be the only representatives of the people who have been robbed; they may be returned to their formerly dominant position only via the party, which is the only competent force. The party's politics is confrontational in the sphere of the national interest – this is used as a lever to gain wide media attention. The leaders of the parties are usually skilful orators capable of long, ardent speeches – Vojislav Šešelj and Vadim Tudor stand out in this respect. The parties also professionalized their media advocacy efforts, helping them to reach 'ordinary' people. The controversial moves and expressions of party leaders attract the attention of the media and secure heavy news coverage for them.

Internal organization and leadership

The internal party democracy strikes a balance between democracy and centralization, between freedom of action for party members and maintaining a certain level of subordination. Too much freedom of action for party members could allow leeway for some of them to foment internal conflicts. The restriction of democratic rights, on the other hand, may forge authoritarian tendencies, apathy and oligarchic rule. In this sense, there is no ideal state for internal party democracy which may be used as the ideal example (Karasimeonov in Karasimeonov 2005:96–97). Despite these initial limitations, one might search for a level of internal party democracy that takes into consideration the position and power of the party's president, the rights of party members to challenge party policy and the opportunity for internal opposition, as well as the power accorded to lower levels vis-à-vis the national and relations between party MPs and the party itself. It has been argued many times that the parties in post-communist countries enjoy a very low level of internal party democracy (van Biezen 2003:206, Djurković 2006:4). This very low level of internal party democracy is then reflected in the leadership of the parties, which has not changed since the early 1990s – this is not only characteristic of the Far Right parties in the Balkans but is rather common to parties throughout the political spectrum.

Strategy and party leaders are of fundamental importance for parties on the Far Right – party presidents are usually charismatic persons able to attract the attention of voters and also capable of keeping the party united (Eatwell 2003:65). As Carter notes, Right-wing extremist parties with strong, charismatic leaders, centralized organizational structures and efficient mechanisms for enforcing party discipline are likely to perform better at the polls than parties with weaker, uncharismatic leadership, less centralized internal structures and lower levels of party discipline (Carter 2005:6). Lubbers and his colleagues come to essentially the same conclusion: extreme Right-wing parties that have favourable party characteristics (a charismatic leader, a well-organized party and an active cadre) are much more successful in national elections than parties which lack these (Lubbers *et al.* 2002:371). Let us have a look at our cases, then.

Croatia and the case of the Croatian Party of the Right
(Hrvatska Stranka Prava, HSP)

The Croatian Act on Political Parties adopted in 1993 stipulates that in order to register a party, 100 citizens are required to pass a party statute and programme. The law also stipulates that parties must follow democratic principles in electing the leadership.[11] The internal structure of HSP consists of three layers: local organizations, the county level and the national level; the national assembly meets every four years. Party members may be expelled for not following either the party statute or the party programme. HSP seems to be the most centralized relevant party in Croatia, as the local bodies may only propose candidates for local elections, with the final decision being the President's. The leadership may interfere in local autonomy by closing the local branch down, with no right to protest the decision. The central level of decision-making in HSP is basically independent from the local level. HSP has an enormously strong party leader – the cabinet chosen by the president is not confirmed by any other party body and is completely subordinated to the president; the president makes an exclusive recommendation of five members for the main political body, may call a meeting of the national committee or any other executive body at the local level and chair it, has the right to initiate suspension procedures for party members and officials and decides on the party lists for national and local elections. The internal democracy in HSP is below that of the average party in Croatia, and HSP is the least democratic Croatian party by far (Čular in Karasimeonov 2005:66–86).

The party has around 15,000 members (Buljan and Duka 2003:52) and was led by its former vice-chairman, Anto Đapić, from 1996 to 2009[12] when Đapić became honorary chairman and Daniel Srb was elected party chairman. As for the role of women in parties of the Right, if we look at the Croatian Parliament, HSP has a very low percentage of female representatives in contrast to the Social Democratic Party. The lowest percentage of women is also found in the Croatian Peasant Party, with 11.1% (*Žene i muškarci u Hrvatskoj 2007*).

Serbia and the case of SRS

In Serbia, the Law on Political Organizations adopted in 1990 stipulated that 100 signatures are needed to register a party; there are no provisions governing termination or banning of a party. As for the internal organization of SRS, party officials are elected using the majority principle through public vote and a procedure which minimizes the possibility of its membership to influencing the election of the party leadership. The highest party body, the SRS Patriotic Congress, acting upon proposals from the central patriotic administration, will first select members of the election committee. The election committee will then draw up a list of candidates for the party leadership, and then the Patriotic Congress will again take a public vote on the candidates nominated on that list. The candidates must be nominated in writing by 30 congress delegates or one SRS executive committee at least seven days before a Patriotic Congress session – alternative candidates remain second class only (Goati in Karasimeonov 2005:15).

These strict electoral procedures lead to a condition of no alternatives being offered, something reflected in the fact that the current leader, Vojislav Šešelj, has been leading the party from its founding up to the present. Since Šešejl left for the Hague, the deputy party president, Tomislav Nikolić, has acted as de facto party leader, attempted to convert the party into a conservative party and negotiated an agreement with the government to see that the legislation necessary to sign the Stabilisation and Association Agreement (SAA) would go through the parliament. Nevertheless, Vojislav Šešelj intervened from the Hague prison, so Nikolić was forced to step down from the office, subsequently forming, along with other 18 SRS MPs, the new Serbian Progressive Party (*Srpska Napredna Stranka*, SNS).[13]

The party had already been forced to face an internal split when the mayor of Novi Sad, Maja Gojković, also tried to move the party to the centre and thereby create an acceptable coalition partner. Gojković left and created the new People's Party (*Narodna Partija*, NP).

Party members must adhere to the party programme and statute and work to spread its ideas and propaganda. Article 205 of the Statute specifies disciplinary measures. Disciplinary offences are listed as follows: participation in activities contrary to the policy or reputation of the party, violations of the statute, unauthorized removal of party documents from the archives, intentional damage or destruction of party property, destruction of party documents, crimes committed at the expense of the party, interference with the work of decision-making bodies of the party, participation in party activities, being drunk or under the influence of narcotics or bringing explosives to party assemblies (Statut SRS 1996, Art. 205).

The party has branches in Bosnia and Herzegovina (BiH), Macedonia, Kosovo and Montenegro. The number of women in the SRS remains quite low compared to other parties, though there are some important figures on the local level. In the 2007 parliament, 14% (12 out of 81) of SRS MPs were women, in contrast to the liberal party G17+ (which claimed to have introduced special quotas for women), where 36% (7 out of 19) were women. The number of women rose sharply after the 2008 elections and the withdrawal of 18 MPs from the SRS in 2008 – 23% (13 out of 56) of SRS MPs are women, as contrasted to the liberal party G17+, 29% (7 out of 24) of whose members are women.

Macedonia and the case of VMRO–People's Party (Vnatrešna Makedonska Revolucionerna Organizacija–Narodna Partija, VMRO–NP)

VMRO–NP was founded in 2004 by Ljubčo Georgievski,[14] who broke away from VMRO–Democratic Party for Macedonian National Unity (*Vnatrešna makedonska revolucionerna organizacija–Demokratska partija za makedon-sko nacionalno edinstvoe*, VMRO–DPMNE). The party statute allows dual membership in both parties. Vesna Janevska was chosen to be the first president, while Georgievski was considered the informal leader; in 2007, Janevska was replaced by Georgi Trendafilov. There are internal factions in the party which cause subsequent loss of potential and weakening of the party, with one section leaning towards the previous chief, Janevska. The internal crisis resulted in the expulsion of Janevska in 2007 after she began publicly voicing her discontent with the party presidency. The party's statute was not available at the time of writing, but it is expected the party will have a centralized model of organization similar to VMRO–DPMNE, in which the presidency has the largest role in constituting party bodies at all levels as well as in the decision-making process.

Albania and the case of the National Front (Balli Kombëtar, BK)
Blendi Kajsiu remarks that without exception, Albanian political parties are organized in a hierarchical fashion and tend to be quite centralized; opposition from local structures is absent and the party leader has exclusive privileges. It is theoretically possible to complain about internal party democracy and the internal electoral procedures to the Electoral College, though it is not advisable as the judiciary – which is often pressured by whatever party is in power – could determine the leadership of the parties, which would generate some flagrant cases of intervention in internal political affairs (Kajsiu in Karasimeonov 2005:142–155).

The organizational scheme of BK is based on the state administrative division having three layers – local, regional and national. The highest political body of the party is the Congress, which meets once every four years and decides BK's politics, chooses the chairman and president of the party and approves the charter and programme. The party presidency is voted on by secret ballot using majority vote, while other issues are voted on by open ballot. The Deputy Chairman and General Secretary of the party are chosen by the party presidency; both may be dismissed for misconduct by the vote of a simple majority of the National Council. The National Council has a very strong position within the party hierarchy; the members of the presidency are direct members of the National Council. The president is elected by majority vote through one or more candidates who must be members of the National Council and whose name has been put forward by at least forty delegates to the Congress, representing at least five local branches. The president leads the party in accordance with the decisions of Congress and the National Council, appoints and dismisses employees who are not elected by the party forums and appoints members of the administration (BK 1998). The party has clearly put an emphasis on the upper level of the hierarchy, in which the presidency essentially decides most of the issues leaving little room for the lower levels. Similarly, it is almost impossible for the lower levels to challenge the presidency by putting forward their own candidate, since the candidate must be a member of the National Council.

The BK was led from 1996 to 2003 by Abas Ermenji. The death of the president brought about a change in party leadership, and since that time, the party has been led by Adrian Alimadhi. The deputy chair is a woman – Majlinda Toro. Youth and women play an integral part in the party. As in the parties noted above, admission to the party membership is for those over 18, though BK specifically states this is regardless of social status, race, religion or gender while stipulating that those who spread unconstitutional and antinational views, former members of the Albanian Party of Labour or members of racist organisations, communist, Fascist and former agents of the State Secret Service will not be accepted as members. As for opposition within the party ranks, members 'although entitled to express their thoughts, must not take actions which would impede the implementation taken by majority'. The statute then quite vaguely states that a member may be expelled if he/she causes significant harm to the party (BK 1998).

Bulgaria and the case of VMRO and Ataka

The situation regarding internal democracy (at least in terms of status) in the Bulgarian party *VMRO* is a little bit better than with other parties noted. There is room for opposition, all available power is not concentrated in the hands of the presidency alone and power sharing on different levels has evolved. The conditions for terminating membership in VMRO do not seem as strict as in the parties already noted – there is no provision which would allow a member to be ejected for disobedience or disapproval of party policy and giving voice to his or her own opinion.

VMRO is organized in four layers – local, municipal, regional and national. The supreme body of the VMRO is the Congress, which is convened every three years and whose tasks include amending the statute, adopting internal documents and electing the President of the Executive Committee and the President of the National Control Commission. Decisions by Congress are taken by open ballot using simple majority rule. The National Assembly is a governing body between the Congress, which approves the programme, and party candidates for the national and local elections. The National Executive Committee (NEC), as the highest executive body, is composed of twelve members: the president, three vice-presidents, the secretary and seven members. The agenda is prepared by the president and the Committee meets at least once a month. The only significant power the Committee has is to manage and coordinate the activities of regional, municipal and local committees and take the necessary measures to deal with irregularities or violations of the party Charter. This highest executive body may also eject members and terminate the mandate of regional and municipal committees. But despite these powers, the NEC is perceived as a single body and the powers of the president are not made explicit; he does not seem to play the role of *primus inter pares* but rather has a simple representative function. The NEC is also controlled in the context of funding by the National Control Commission, which is supposed to check the expenditures of all party bodies (Ustav na VMRO-Bugarsko nacionalno dvizenje 2007).

Despite the above-noted provisions, the VMRO has been led by Krassimir Karakachanov since 1997, serving as vice-president of the party from 1995 to 1997. The party's organizational structures include both women's and youth organizations. There is not a single woman in the leadership out of twenty-nine regional branches in VMRO.

The supreme governing body of the *Ataka* is the National Assembly, which is convened every three years; one delegate represents twenty members of the municipal organization. The National Assembly amends the statute, adopts other internal documents, elects and dismisses the chairman of the party, decides on the reorganization or termination of the party, issues party programmes and activities, adopts the budget, decides on the membership fee, adopts reports, disposes of property and revokes decisions of other organs of the party which are not in accord with the statute and other internal acts. The main executive body, the Central Committee, is comprised of seven people including the chairman of the party. It decides which policies will be carried out, approves candidates for MP posts and issues regulations for the implementation of the statute. The municipal assembly may propose candidates for national as well as local MPs subject to approval by the central committee and may submit proposals for the formation of national policy.

To become a member of the party, one must be eighteen years old; behaviour incompatible with the statute or other internal acts of the party constitutes reason for ejection. The decision to expel a member is up to the local organization, though an appeal may be made to the central committee, whose decision is final. The organization of the party consists of three layers – local, regional and national. The statute bans local branches from making political statements which would contradict those issued on the national level. The party has been led by Volen Siderov since its founding in 2005. During the 2009 elections, three out of twenty-one MPs (14%) elected for Ataka were women, in contrast to 30% with the Citizens for the European Development of Bulgaria (*Grazhdani za evropeysko razvitie na Balgariya*, GERB).

Romania and the case of PRM

The PRM Congress is convened every four years and has the following powers: it examines the work of the National Council, adopts or amends the party programme, establishes the party strategy, elects the President of the party, elects the National Council, elects the Central Commission for Arbitration, elects the Central Commission for Financial Control, resolves complaints and decides on party dissolution. The executive body of the party is the National Council, which meets once a year and has the following tasks: to convene the Congress, organize the activities of the Congress, elect and remove members of the Executive Board, monitor fulfilment of decisions by the Congress, establish strategy and tactics, designate party candidates for the presidency of Romania, approve the government programme and designate the party candidate for prime minister. The Executive Board is the representative body of PRM and is elected by the National Council from among its members by secret ballot. The Permanent Bureau of the party then leads the party in the interval between meetings of the National Council, and its tasks include establishing a list of candidates for parliamentary elections based on proposals submitted by the Commission and developing rules and guidelines for implementing the decisions of Congress.

As for the procedure for electing the leadership of the party, the Commission draws up the list of candidates, which is then approved by open ballot by Congress and, once completed, subject to approval by secret ballot with a simple majority of delegates present at the Congress. In spite of the statute, the party is basically a one-man show, governed since its founding in 1991 by the controversial politician and current European MP, Vadim Tudor, who gives the party its ultranationalist accent and keeps it on the Far Right end of the spectrum.

The party has both youth and women's organizations within its ranks. PRM members have the following obligations: to respect and promote the statute, programme and decisions taken by governing bodies, be loyal to the PRM and work for the dignity of its members and to maintain party unity, comply with party discipline and democracy, contribute to and promote the democratic framework within the party and respect diversity of opinion. Failure to follow these party provisions and the party programme may result in expulsion.

As we have seen, there is not much room left for democracy in the Balkan Far Right parties (Table 9.1). Space for opposition voices is limited, and all parties except VMRO stipulate in their statutes that members may be expelled for behaviour incompatible with the party policy or programme; SRS is the only party which deals with sanctions for being drunk, under the influence of narcotics or bringing explosives to party sessions. The parties emphasize the upper level of hierarchy where most decisions take place, while the lower levels of the party hierarchy have little say.

Party leaders have exclusive privileges, and all party leaders have remained in power since the party's founding or have been in office since the 1990s; the only exceptions are BK, whose first president died, and HSP, which elected a new chairman and gave the older president an honorary chairmanship.

Table 9.1 Internal organization and leadership of Balkan Far Right parties

	HSP	SRS	VMRO–NP	BK	VMRO	Ataka	PRM
Charismatic leadership	–	X	–	–	–	X	X
Centralized organizational structures	X	X	X	X	–	X	X
Efficient mechanisms for enforcing party discipline	X	X	X	X	–	X	X

The parties' MPs do not enjoy much autonomy in parliament, the most lucid example being SRS, where newly elected MPs must sign an agreement in which they swear that if they leave the party, they will give up their parliamentary post as well. The power of the local organizations remains very limited. The parties also have a low number of female members in their ranks, something which is most visible when looking at members of parliament. The only party with a female representative in a high leadership post is the Albanian National Front. Ataka, HSP and SRS have neither young people nor women's organizations within their structures.

The role of paramilitary organizations

Far Right paramilitary organizations[15] and links with political parties were typical in the Balkan environment in the first half of the 1990s. The most famous formations were the Croatian Defence Forces (*Hrvatske Obrambene Snage,* HOS) (the armed wing of HSP), the Voluntary Guard (the so-called Tigers under the command of Željko Ražnatović Arkan, armed wing of the Party of Serbian Unity (*Stranka Srpskog Jedinstva,* SSJ)), Serbian Chetniks Movement (armed wing of SRS), the Serbian Guard (armed wing of SPO) and the Patriotic League (tied to the Party of Democratic Action (*Stranka Demokratske Akcije,* SDA)). These paramilitary formations lived in closed symbiosis with the state and were responsible for most war crimes in former Yugoslavia from April 1991 until the end of the war in 1995. Our aim is to examine whether the links between Far Right parties and paramilitaries still obtain or whether paramilitaries tied to parties have disappeared from the Balkan Peninsula.

Organizations set up after 1999 are rather blurred and, viewed through a particular lens, could be classified as extreme Right paramilitary formations. The most active have operated in Serbia, Albania, Macedonia, Kosovo, Bulgaria and Romania, while there are no such significant groups in Croatia and Montenegro. The Kosovo question is the reason behind the prevalence of Albanian and Serbian paramilitaries in the Balkan region.

The Albanian National Army (ANA) calls itself a successor formation to the Kosovo Liberation Army (*Ushtria Çlirimtare e Kosovës*, KLA or *UÇK*), National Liberation Army and the National Liberation Army of Preševo, Medveđa and Bujanovac while operating in Serbia, Macedonia, Albania, Kosovo and northern Greece.[16] ANA declares it will fight for the creation of Greater Albania.[17] It is estimated to have 200 activists, and it is not known who is at the helm of the group.[18] Initially, ANA was known rather as an Internet phantom which issued statements using contemporary technology. The first reference dates to 2002 and the most famous to 2005, when it attempted to assassinate the president of Kosovo at that time, Ibrahim Rugova. As the organization of ANA remains vague, with the same true of its aims, it is very hard to classify. It oscillates somewhere between a militia, paramilitary organization and insurgent group using terrorist means linked to the organized crime (OC).

But there are other formations alongside the ANA which have grown up in the region. The Army of the Republic of Ilirida was created in 2002 in Macedonia, fighting for the annexation of western Macedonia to either Kosovo or Albania. The group allegedly has around 200 members, who are said to have sworn loyalty to Leka Zogu.[19] In 2005, the Army for the Independence of Kosovo (UPK) emerged in Kosovo, threatening the international administration and demanding the Kosovo Parliament declare independence. The variety of ethnic Albanian groups can be explained by the rivalry of the groups in OC activities and control of smuggling routes. The declared fight for Greater Albania or Greater Kosovo serves as a cover for OC profit-making activities rather than working for the *liberation* of the Albanian nation[20] (*Jane's World Insurgency and Terrorism* 2004:528). All Albanian formations present a security threat for the region on the local and state level and, most importantly, on the human security level. There are still many weapons in the region, and the import of new weapons is facilitated by links between the groups and OC and border permeability.

The ethnic Albanian formations operate subregionally in Kosovo, southeastern Serbia, Albania and western Macedonia. They communicate with each other and presumably with the political wing of ANA – the National Liberation Front of Albanians (*Komitetit Kombëtar për Clirimin dhe Mbrojtjen e Tokave Shqiptare*, KKCMTSH) – based in Tirana. ANA merged with the Party of National Unity in 2002 (*Parti Unitet Kombëtar*, PUK[21]) to create the Albanian Front of National Unification (*Fronti Për Bashkim Kombëtar Shqiptar*, FBKSH).[22]

In Macedonia, a paramilitary force called the 'Lions' (*Lavovi*) emerged in 2001. It was an unauthorized body of former police and military reservists, unofficially sponsored by Ljube Boskovski (Secretary of State for Interior Affairs).[23] It was not until after the conflict (in autumn 2001) that the paramilitary unit was transformed into an official police unit. The Lions were believed to have about 2,000 armed members and actively threatened ethnic cleansing against ethnic Albanians. There has been much post-conflict controversy around the Lions. The head of the Macedonian Orthodox Church, Archbishop Stefan, gave Medallions of Christ to the paramilitaries. The Lions' commander, Goran Stojkov, was promoted to the grandiose rank of major general. These acts were highly criticized by human rights activists. The Lions were finally disbanded in early 2003 with about half their membership being absorbed into the police.

Another paramilitary unit (often confused with the previous formation) emerged in Macedonia under the name 'Macedonian Lions' (*Makedonski lavovi*). The latter had no links to the police or any state structure. It was the product of radical groups supported by the Macedonian Diaspora around the world. The unit was rather limited as regards personnel – there were less than a hundred people. The group was not known for carrying out any actions during the Macedonian–Albanian conflict. It was much more a media phantom. The short duration of the armed conflict and the fact that neither Macedonian society nor state structures favoured these units meant that the group did not expand. It disappeared after a rather short time. Another smaller paramilitary group active in Macedonia was the 'Red Berets'. They continued to intimidate and harass ethnic Albanian civilians even after the Ohrid peace agreement (Phillips 2004:156–160).

On the Serbian side, a new extreme Right paramilitary unit emerged in Kosovo in May 2007 – the Saint Tsar Lazar Guard (*Garda svetog cara Lazara*), allegedly formed mainly of Yugoslavian war veterans. The leaders stated that the formation had around 5,000 members, while other sources stated no more than several hundred. The guard claims a renewed fight for the liberation of Kosovo. Its radical statements include saying that every Albanian will either be killed or returned to Albania and Serbs who do not agree with their views will also be dealt with.[24] The leaders called on the Serbian Parliament to wage a war with Kosovo and called for demonstrations. The main unrest was expected after the declaration of Kosovo independence; the guard does not seem to be supported by the local public, and its actions were halted by Serbian and United Nations Mission in Kosovo (UNMIK) authorities, preventing it from spreading violence. There are other groups, as well, which appear on the Far Right – for example, *Nacionalni stroj, Obraz, Sveti Justin Filozof, Dveri, Poslednji Obracun* and *Srpska Desnica, NP 1389*[25] (The Stephen Roth Institute 2005). These ideological platforms serve as a meeting point for nationalist groups (some of their members having ties with skinheads from Blood and Honour Serbia) recruiting volunteers for the defence of Kosovo and fall rather under the category of violent non-state affiliated actors or other violent subcultural groups rather than paramilitary organizations.

In Romania, the organization with paramilitary tendencies is the New Right (*Noua Dreaptă, ND*) led by Tudor Ionescu. ND seeks a Greater Romania and, like most similar formations, acts in a racist, anti-Semitic manner. The organization claims to have about 6,000 members.[26] One of the biggest manifestations of ND power were protests during the first Gay Parade ever organized in Bucharest in 2007, featuring the statement that 'saying NO to homosexuality is not a prejudice, but the manifestation of a system of values based on the Holy Scriptures and the traditional values of the Romanian family'.[27] It is assumed that the ND preserves links to the New Generation Party–Christian Democratic (*Partidul Noua Generaţie–Creştin Democrat*, PNG–CD).[28]

In neighbouring Bulgaria, it is the Bulgarian National Union (*Bulgarski natsionalen sujuz,* BNS), created in 2001, which is the carrier of Neo-Nazi elements and anti-Roma sentiments.[29] The BNS has its own uniformed guard and refuses closer relations to Ataka, since 'Volen Siderov has gone through four political parties before declaring himself a patriot. He discredited nationalism and to put it succinctly, you can't build a new brothel with old whores'.[30] BNS stands for nationalism and against internationalism, seeks a strong state to prevent crime and corruption and claims that its main goal is Bulgarokratsia – Power of the Bulgarian National Interest.[31] Next to BNS, there are other marginal groupings in Bulgaria, for example, the Warriors of Tangra Movement (*Dvizhenie Voini na Tangra,* DVT)[32] and the Bulgarian National Front – Emigré (*Bulgarski natsionalen front émigré*, BNFe).[33]

As regards the cooperation of Far Right organizations and their integration into existing formations, one must note the International Third Position (ITP), created by a faction of the British National Front and the Italian neo-Fascists, led by Roberto Fiore, advocating a mix of neo-Fascist, back-to-the-land, anti-Semitic and fundamentalist Catholic views (Ryan 2004:62).[34] ITP changed its name in 2001 to England First and then became a part of the newly emerged European National Front (ENF). The principles the organizations agreed on include the defence of culture, tradition and Christian identity against uncontrolled migration, the entrance of Turkey and Israel into the EU, defence of the economic system based on social justice, the defence of traditional family values and a new world order against Yankee imperialism.[35] Members include the Romanian New Right, German National Democratic German Party (*Nationaldemokratische Partei Deutschlands*), Spanish La Falange, Italian New Force, French Renewal (*Renouveau Français*) and Greek Symmaxia. Other parties, for example, Slovenska Pospolitosť and the BNS from Bulgaria, are closely affiliated with the formation. The Phalangist father, José Antonio Primo de Rivera, and the founder of the Romanian Iron Guard, Corneliu Zelea Codreanu, were proclaimed ideological leaders of ENF.[36]

As we have seen, the Balkan environment has changed completely since the beginning of the 1990s. After the end of the war, no paramilitary formations linked to political parties have been described in the post-Yugoslavian region.

The only such case is seen in Romania, where the New Right is allegedly tied to the PNG–CD of Gigi Becali. The New Right is also the only organization with a membership exceeding 5,000. Other existing paramilitary formations are marginal and have no links to existing Far Right political parties.

International cooperation on the Far Right

Bilateral cooperation by Far Right parties and the Euronat

The closest relationships are between the mother parties and branch parties, such as SRS in BiH, Croatia, Macedonia and Montenegro and HSP in Croatia and BiH. As for partners outside of the Balkan region, Vladimir Zhirinovsky's party, the LDPR and the National Front of Jean-Marie Le Pen seem to be the most popular allies of the Balkan parties. SRS and PRM have developed relationships with these two parties, and their leaders paid frequent mutual visits to each other and kept in touch via frequent correspondence. Zhirinovsky even labelled the SRS the protector of the Slavic world (Thomas 1999:217–218). The PRM leader, Tudor, also established relations with some Arab leaders, including Saddam Hussein. Quite naturally, partners were found in within unionist forces in Moldova, notably the Christian Democrat Popular Front. Tudor became the self-proclaimed leader of the movement for union with Moldova (Andrescu in Mudde 2005:189). VMRO's international connections include the Belgian Flemish Block, the Italian National Alliance (*Alleanza nazionale*, AN), the Austrian Freedom Party as well as Macedonian and Bulgarian émigré organizations and Bulgarian minority organizations outside Bulgaria (Ivanov and Ilieva in Mudde 2005:5).

In 1999, there was an attempt to bring together the nationalist parties of Europe by the French National Front, the Flemish Bloc, Hungarian Justice and Life Party (MIEP) in Hungary, PRM, SRS, the Slovak National Party, Sweden Democrats, National Democracy (*Democracia Nacional,* DN) in Spain, the Hellenic Front in Greece, the New Force (*Forza nuova,* FN) in Italy and the National Alliance (*Movimento de Acção Nacional,* MAN) in Portugal.[37] Nevertheless, Euronat officially came into existence only in 2005, without the participation of Eastern European parties. It only had the participation of the BK, British National Party, New Right from the Netherlands, Swedish National Democrats (*Nationaldemokraterna*), Italian Tricolor Flame (*Fiamma Tricolore*) and Spanish DN.[38] The party's website does not clarify why their Eastern European counterparts have not taken part in the grouping.

Far Right cooperation in the European Parliament

In 2007, when Bulgaria and Romania entered the European Parliament, twenty Members of the European Parliament (MEPs) (or 2.5% of the EP's membership) were needed to form a caucus group in the parliament. The incentives to form such a caucus are financial subsidies and guaranteed seats on EU committees. The entry of the Balkan States allowed Far Right parties to create their own group within the EP, called Identity, Tradition, Sovereignty (ITS), in January 2007.[39] The ITS therefore consisted of twenty-three MEPs from six European states: seven from the National Front (France), five from PRM, one independent MEP from Romania, three from Flemish Interest (Belgium), three from Ataka[40] and three independents from the UK.

This was met with concern that public funds were being used to subsidize a group with nationalist positions and there were attempts to change the rules in the European Parliament to hinder the creation of such a group. Other groups in the EP were only able to prevent members of the ITS group from gaining important positions on parliamentary committees. Bruno Gollnisch[41] and the National Front of France became the engine of the group. The group's policies may be summed up in three 'antis': anti-Turkish membership, anti-immigration and anti-EU Constitution. Disagreements within the group escalated after ten months, when Italian MP Alessandra Mussolini made insulting comments about the Romanians, who had been expelled from Italy. This was challenged by the Romanian delegation. The group ceased to exist due to its internal frictions and the withdrawal of PRM members (which caused its membership to fall below the mandatory limit) in November 2007.

In 2009, the PRM increased its share in the EP and gained three seats in the EP, while Ataka's presence fell to two seats. The election results led to another attempt at putting together a union of populist Right-wing parties in the EP. The new formation, *The Europe of Freedom and Democracy*,[42] consists of 33 MEPs from 9 political parties (the Italian Northern League (*Lega Nord, LN*), UK Independence Party, Greek LAOS, Danish People's Party (*Dansk Folkeparti, DF*), Finnish True Finns (*Perussuomalaiset*), Movement for France (*Mouvement pour la France*), Dutch Reformed Political Party (*Staatkundig Gereformeerde Partij*), Lithuanian Order and Justice (*Partija Tvarka ir teisingumas*) and the SNS). The new group rejects the bureaucratization of Europe and the creation of a single European superstate, opposes further European integration and calls for more democracy and more respect for the will of the people and demands Europe's history, traditions and cultural values be respected and its national differences and interests be taken into account. Although the group was described as Far Right, anti-immigration, xenophobic and racist, its programme specifies the rejection of xenophobia, anti-Semitism and other forms of discrimination while 'still believing strongly that the nations of Europe have the right to protect their borders and strengthen their own historical, traditional and cultural values'.[43] The group consists primarily of Eurosceptic parties favouring anti-immigration policies and the return of power to the sovereign states – some parties designated as Far Right still hesitate (FPÖ) and have been rejected from or themselves reject the notion of taking part in the new formation. MEPs from other parties previously described as Far Right – the British National Party, the Dutch Party for Freedom (*Partij voor de Vrijheid*, PVV), Hungarian Movement for a better Hungary (Jobbik), French National Front, Bulgaria's Ataka and the PRM – were left out and acted independently. It would not appear that they share any common ground on which to form an effective caucus, since they do not really engage in mutual dialogue and do not act constructively.

In looking at the prospective membership of the Balkan countries in the EU, it seems quite unlikely that any kind of Balkan Far Right caucus would be formed. Rather, it is to be expected that current MEPs would attempt to hinder the accession of the Balkan States,[44] and once accession has taken place, collaboration will be rendered impossible by the grave differences and disagreements between them. One could hardly expect any long-term cooperation between the HSP and SRS or the Romanian and Hungarian parties. The difficulty Far Right parties find in cooperating stems from their nature, though cooperation on the Balkan Far Right is more complicated than in West Europe because of key party themes, including claims on territory which often overlap. HSP demands the creation of a Greater Croatia, which, in its extreme version, would encompass the entirety of BiH and, in its softest version, those portions of BiH where ethnic Croats reside. SRS, on the other hand, demands territories where Serbs live – the self-declared RSK (part of Croatia), Republika Srpska in BiH, Montenegro, Kosovo and potentially Macedonia. The most fervent radicals deny even the Croatian nation, charging that Croats are just Roman Catholic Serbs. They demand the entire territory of Croatia. The only cooperation which is thinkable would see BiH divided between Croatia and Serbia, but it is impossible to imagine radical Croats and radical Serbs from both Far Right parties sitting around the same table. Similarly, it is unthinkable that the Albanian National Front would sit at a single table with SRS representatives, keeping in mind the claims of BK on territories inhabited by Albanians – Kosovo, the western part of Macedonia, part of Montenegro, Greece and also a small area in south-eastern Serbia, in the Preševo Valley.

In like manner, cooperation between PRM and Jobbik is excluded – Jobbik campaigns for the right of self-determination of Hungarian communities left outside of the Hungarian state after the Trianon Treaty, while PRM is clearly anti-Hungarian, attacking the Hungarian national minority in day-to-day life. The same issue might possibly arise between the Bulgarian VMRO and the Macedonian Far Right, since the Bulgarian Far Right views Macedonians as Bulgarians and claims that the Treaty of Berlin in 1878 left millions of those behind Bulgarian borders, while VMRO–NP relates its existence to a Macedonian origin and would not support the creation of Greater Bulgaria, thus denying the Macedonian nation.

Notes

1 The journal focuses on two main issues: creation of a Greater Romania and denouncing *anti-Romanian activities* promoted by Hungarians, Gypsies and Jews.
2 Council for Electronic Media to monitor TV shows. 23.8.2005. http://sofiaecho. com/2005/08/23/642631_council-for-electronic-media-to-monitor-tv-shows.
3 The use of the mass media by the Far Right in Romania is notable in the PNG–CD as well – its prominent member Marian Oprea hosts a talk show on the second Romanian TV channel, DDTV, and at the same time owner of political magazine Lumea.
4 *Bulgarian Nationalist from Ataka party protested in front of the Turkish Embassy.* www.ataka.bg/en/index2.php?option=com_content&task=view&id=42&-pop=1&page=0&Itemid=26.
5 Dragomir was indicted for accepting bribes in 2008. *Dumitru Dragomir, trimis în judecată pentru corupţie.* 5 May 2008. www.mediafax.ro/justitie/dumitru-drago-mir-trimis-in-judecata-pentru-coruptie-2611370.
6 *Basescu si Becali, "frati" de discriminare.* http://stiri.rol.ro/Basescu-si-Becali-frati-de-discriminare-80279.html.
7 For the language of Right extremism in WE, see, for example, Schuppener (2008).
8 Dedication of Romanian Statue of Rabin a Ploy. 16.1.2004. www.adl.org/PresRele/ ASInt_13/4442_13.htm.
9 *Mayor paints red – and yellow and blue.* 9.11.2001. http://news.bbc.co.uk/2/hi/ europe/1645077.stm.
10 The law stipulated that minority languages can be used in public affairs wherever the minority comprises at least 20% of the population. According to the 1992 census, 22.7% of the population of Cluj are Hungarians. *Letter from Budapest – Nick Thorpe on the Right to Say "Yes".* 5.3.2002. www.bbc.co.uk/worldservice/ europe/europetoday/letters/020305_nthorpe.shtml.
11 Goran Čular notes that the organizational model in Croatian political parties has several characteristics: a very limited (if any) role for non-members in party affairs; a very limited, direct role for party members in the decision-making process; a lack of party factions; weak influence on the part of functional groups within parties; a lack of affiliated organizations; a hierarchical internal order; simple organizational patterns copied at all levels; indirect election of central party bodies; significant overlapping between the party in the central office and in the public office; limited autonomy of the parliamentary party; most influential public positions are held by party presidents; and selection procedures incorporate only the central bodies with a prominent role in choosing a party president (Čular in Karasimeonov 2005:66).
12 Even though Đapić was accused of cheating in the process of obtaining his post-graduate degree at the University of Split and several times accused of faking injuries in order to appear a war veteran, he did not lose his leading position in the party till 2009.

13 The Law on Election of Members of Parliament of 2000 stipulated that an MP would lose his or her office if his/her membership in the party were terminated. Even though the Constitutional Court declared this provision void, party practice was to sign documents in which new MPs would swear obedience to the party and agree to step down from their MP post upon leaving the party. However, at this point, it was Nikolić who was in control of the documents the MPs signed containing the above-mentioned provision, and the MPs therefore remained in the parliament.

14 Georgievski applied for Bulgarian citizenship in 2006, moved there and began to take part in Bulgarian politics, remaining close to GERB.

15 The word *paramilitary* has been used in various ways although its meaning remains ambiguous. For example, the *Encyclopaedia of Fascism* points to three elements of the Second World War paramilitarism: continuous violent propaganda, the image of the street fighter and the presentation of paramilitary groups as mass organizations (Blamires 2006:506). Nevertheless, the emergence of other violent, non-state affiliated actors (VNSA) complicates the issue. They overlap in most cases or transform from one kind into another. As Williams suggests, paramilitary forces are initially an extension of government forces; they come into existence with the tacit consent and often the active encouragement of government or state military forces (Williams 2008:9–17). Mareš and Stojar suggest an enlarged scope in the definition of paramilitaries: those involved in armed post-communist conflicts and the vigilante paramilitary formations (mostly with racist orientation) of political parties and movements (Mareš and Stojar 2011). Again, a problem arises here when considering formations that are not tied to political parties. This would lead us back to the first definition although it must be kept in mind that skinheads and other violent subcultural groups will not be dealt with.

16 Division Skanderbeg (named after the Second World War SS division) in western Macedonia, the Adam Jashari Division (one of the founding fathers of KLA) in Kosovo, Malesia Division in Montenegro and the Chameria Division for southern Albania and northern Greece.

17 Its aims keep changing. In January 2008, its leaders claimed they were not fighting for pan-Albanian unification, but to protect the territorial integrity of Kosovo if threatened (*Kosovo terror group issues fresh* threats, B92, 21/1/2008, available online at www.b92.net/eng/news/politics-article.php?yyyy=2008&mm=01&dd=21&nav_id=471220).

18 Bolju Dilaver, called Leku, is most often mentioned when dealing with the ANA. Some sources state that the political wing is the National Liberation Front of Albanians led by Valdet Vardari.

19 Leka Zogu is the son of the former Albanian king, Zogu I. He has denied any links to the Army of the Republic of Ilirida.

20 The Macedonian security expert, Biljana Vankovska, claims that conflict in Macedonia in 2001 also began as a war between OC gangs rather than an escalation of the ethnic crisis (Informal conversation with Biljana Vankovska in Ohrid 2004).

21 Idajet Beqiri, the founder of the political party, writes in an article entitled *Albanian Nationalism is the National Reunion* that the party does not wish to change the

borders aggressively and that its politics calls for peaceful solutions, but it fights against changing borders using the law of the jungle. 'The Declaration of Helsinki is against changing borders by war but it was not against changing borders peacefully. How come it didn't prevent the reunion of Germany? Why did it not stop fifteen states from changing the borders of the USSR and uniting two Yemen Arab Republics? Why did not it stop creation of Croatia, Slovenia, Bosnia and the crimes of the Frankenstein state of Macedonia? Or was the Helsinki declaration written only for the Albanians?' The article ends with the proclamation: 'In the era of Napoleon in France, the French were talking about consolidation of national states in the future. Are we Albanians still waiting? Certainly we are for peace in the Balkans and in Europe but not for peace on our back or in the enemy's pocket'. Basically, the article's main argument is that if the Helsinki Declaration had already existed in 1912, Albania would have been complete and united (Beqiri 2002).

22 The pseudonyms of the leaders are Valdet Vardari, Alban Vjosa, Vigan Gradica and Ramadan Verikolli. Valdet Vardari is presumably the former collaborator of Ali Ahmeti (real name Gafur Adili) from Macedonia who was arrested by the Albanian police while illegally passing through the borders from Macedonia and is accused of creating terrorist organizations; Vigan Gradica is a former general of the Albanian army (www.fbksh-aksh.org/; http://akshalb.ifrance.com/statuti.htm; Spiro 2004).

23 Boskovski was in 2005 together with ex-security chief Johan Tarculovski indicted by ICTY in connection with an attack on the village of Ljuboten during 2001 conflict in Macedonia. Both face three counts of murder and cruel treatment for their alleged role in the violence.

24 *Czar Lazar Guard: War is inevitable*. B92, 16/11/2007. Available online at www. b92.net/eng/news/politics-article.php?yyyy=2007&mm=11&dd=16&nav_ id=45450.

25 NP 1389 split into two platforms in 2009: Serbian national movement 1389 (Srpski narodni pokret 1389) and Serbian national movement – OUR 1389 (Srpski narodni pokret NAŠI 1389). Their ideology seems to be very much the same (cf. www.snp1389.rs and www.1389.org.rs).

26 www.nouadreapta.org/obiective.php.

27 www.nouadreapta.org/limbistraine_prezentare.php?idx=24&lmb=eng.

28 Note that the PNG–CD leader Becali owns Bucharest Steaua football club which changed its emblem to resemble the triple cross of the Iron Guard.

29 See the web page of the BNS: http://bg.bgns.net/Za-nas/Borba.html.

30 BNS. *Cesto zadavani vaprosi*. http://bg.bgns.net/Za-nas/FAQ.html.

31 BNS. *Cesto zadavani vaprosi*. http://bg.bgns.net/Za-nas/FAQ.html.

32 See their website www.voininatangra.org/modules/news/.

33 For more details, see Mudde (2005:9–13).

34 See declaration of Third Position in Polish *Deklaracja Trzeciej Pozycji* www.nop. org.pl/?artykul_id=7.

35 www.europeannationalfront.org/?page_id=2.

36 www.europeannationalfront.org/?page_id=7.

37 http://fnj.69.free.fr/euronat.htm.

38 The goals of Euronat are as follows: the establishment of a Europe of free nations, respect for the heritage and identity of Western civilization, freedom of speech, self-determination, social justice, no third-world immigration, family as a core societal value, zero tolerance for violence, a high moral profile and cooperation between party members. www.euronat.org/.

39 Until May 2007 or, more precisely, November 2007 (the Romanian elections were postponed for domestic reasons) when the elections took place, the provisional MPs were appointed by the national parliaments – one for Ataka and five for PRM. In the elections, three MPs from the Ataka were elected and none for PRM.

40 Dimitar Stoyanov (stepchild of the Leader of Ataka Volen Siderov) caused outrage from the first moments of his presence in the EP when he sent an email targeting MEP of Romanian origin with a picture of a Gypsy girl stating 'you can even buy one, around 12–13 years of age, to be your loving wife'. Bulgaria votes 2009. Biography of Dimitar Stoyanov. www.novinite.com/elections2009/candidates_mep. php?id=1.

41 Gollnisch was given probation on a three-month prison sentence in 2007 and held responsible for €55,000 in damages for a charge of verbally contesting the existence of crimes against humanity. Two years later, Gollnisch was ultimately found not guilty by the Court of Cassation. *Contestation de crimes contre l' humanité: Gollnisch blanchi par la Cour de cassation.* 24/06/2009. http://tempsreel.nouvelobs. com/depeches/societe/20090624.FAP0255/contestation_de_crimes_contre_ lhumanite_gollnisch_blanc.html.

42 The group was composed of the groups *Independence/Democracy* and *Union for Europe of the Nations.* See www.efdgroup.eu/.

43 *Far-Right MEPs form group in European Parliament* 1/7/2009. www.euractiv. com/en/eu-elections/far-right-meps-form-group-european-parliament/article-183696.

44 See, for example, speech of Dimitar Stoyanov in the EP on 16 September 2009: 'The Bulgarian minority in Serbia for nearly a century has been absolutely neglected and discriminated against. And since its creation, Macedonia has maintained a constant, consistent anti-Bulgarian policy. Bulgarian society cannot grant concessions to countries that violate the rights of Bulgarian citizens, i.e., citizens of the European Union.' www.europarl.europa.eu/sidesSearch/search.do?type=C RE&language=CS&term=7&author=34254.

10

Concluding remarks

Linz and Stepan concluded as far back as 1996 that 'one of the most dangerous ideas for democracy can be summed up in the maxim that every state should strive to become a nation-state and every nation should become a state' (Linz and Stepan 1996:29–30). This paradigm is very much visible in the Balkans, where the nation- and state-building process was delayed, only reaching its end at the beginning of the twentieth century, whereas other European nations had succeeded in forming their own states more than a hundred years earlier. The Far Right in the Western Balkan region demonstrates features dangerous for democracy – striving after monoethnic countries with expanded borders as well as xenophobia aimed at local ethnicities.

What is the state of the Far Right party family in the Balkans then? Our main findings are as follows:

1. **The ideological core of the Far Right in the Balkans is identical to that of Western Europe (WE).**
   The main core of the ideology of the Far Right Balkan parties is composed of nationalism, xenophobia and law and order, while welfare chauvinism is present fully in some cases and in some cases reaches borderline values. All parties also share a populist ideology. Thus, if we return Cas Mudde's second revised concept for the Far Right, which includes nativism (a combination of nationalism and xenophobia), authoritarianism (a combination of law and order and punitive conventional moralism) and populism (populism as a thin, centred ideology that considers society to be separated ultimately into two homogeneous, antagonistic groups, 'the pure people' vs. 'the corrupt elite'), we must conclude that the revised concept functions better as a minimalist defining criteria for the Far Right party family. However, since populism is present in other party ideologies as well, it is probably wiser to treat it as a purely complementary feature. However, the issue deserves special attention and should be explored in further research. Additional features reveal some differences. First of all, they are not necessarily

anti-European or anti-North Atlantic Treaty Organization (NATO), as is true of some of their counterparts in WE. What is more, some even support the Euro-Atlantic integration of their country. As immigration is not an issue in the Balkans, the countries also do not promote anti-immigration policies. There are also differences in their views on the economy – most support the nationalization of property and more state involvement in the economy, with only the Internal Macedonian Revolutionary Organization (*Vnatrešna Makedonska Revolucionerna Organizacija*, VMRO) partially preferring neoliberal values. However, the economy is not the centre of attention for the parties analysed – as is true for WE Far Right parties.

2. **The most important context variables include the position, tactics and strategy of the mainstream political party, the ethnic diaspora behind the borders of an established, 'strong' state, an ethnic minority with potential political representation, state humiliation and a long, complicated European Union (EU) integration process. Other variables (design of the electoral system, long-term unemployment) have a supporting function. The set of the most important variables is unique for each country.**

The position and strategy of the main Right party in the political spectrum seems to have a great impact on the emergence and success of Far Right parties. When there is a dominant Right party (e.g. Albania), the Far Right has not much chance to flourish. Nevertheless, research shows that proximal mainstream Right parties are not the only actors which shape the fortunes of Far Right parties. The analysis demonstrated the validity of Meguid's claims in the case of Balkans as well – the location on the scale, whether Right or Left, is not pertinent. The tactics of the Leftist mainstream party may also be a determinant for the success or failure of Far Right parties, as shown in the cases of Montenegro and Serbia. This issue is also related to the process of state building – states which fear secession or which at some point in their history had more territory (Serbia, Bulgaria, Romania) have the most successful Far Right parties. In states seeking independence, the main carriers of nationalism are parties not on the fringe of the political spectrum but rather those occupying a dominant position either on the Right or Left (e.g. the Croatian Democratic Union (*Hrvatska demokratska zajednica*, HDZ) in Croatia, Democratic League of Kosovo (*Lidhja Demokratike e Kosovës*, LDK) in Kosovo, Internal Macedonian Revolutionary Organization–Democratic Party for Macedonian National Unity (*Vnatrešna makedonska revolucionerna organizacija–Demokratska partija za makedonsko nacionalno edinstvoe*, VMRO–DPMNE) in Macedonia, Party of Democratic Action (*Stranka Demokratske Akcije*, SDA) in Bosnia and Herzegovina, Democratic Party

of Socialist (*Demokratska Stranka Socijalista*, DPS) in Montenegro) –
there is then no room left for an extremist party.

The design of the electoral system also plays a certain role in the
success of Far Right parties – the case of newly adopted majoritarian
components in the electoral design led to a decrease in electoral gains by
the Far Right in Romania and Bulgaria. The electoral design in Croatia,
Macedonia or Albania is unfavourable to the small parties, that is, Far
Right parties. Other political variables (strong voting for new politics in
Bulgaria, poor political culture) may sometimes play a supportive role;
the post-materialist dimension is non-existent and so plays no role. The
convergence of mainstream political parties has not led in the case of
Balkans to the emergence of strong Far Right formations.

Ethno-cultural variables are very important in the Balkan States.
States whose national minorities have strong political representation, as
well as those with a large diaspora abroad, present high opportunity
cases for the emergence and success of Far Right parties. An (anti-)
immigration cleavage has not emerged, since the countries are still countries of origin rather than countries of destination. Despite the fact that
the Roman Catholic Church is not tied to the state, it has aroused nationalism in the same way as the Orthodox Churches and played the same
supporting role. Economic variables (unemployment and the perceived
living standard) play only a supporting role – the rise of unemployment
does not correlate with the rise of the Far Right. On the other hand, all
the countries analysed have experienced a long period with a level of
official unemployment exceeding 15% or more. The international variable, in the form of state humiliation, was present only in the Serbian
case and played a dominant role in the success of the Serbian Radical
Party (*Srpska Radikalna Stranka*, SRS). EU integration was important
in the case of Bulgaria, when the National Union Attack (*Natsionalen
Sayuz Ataka*, Ataka) gained support by criticizing *unfavourable conditions*
for Bulgaria, claiming that Bulgarians had the status of second-class
citizens within the EU.

3. **Voters for the Far Right in the Balkans are mainly male and young
and have no higher education – these characteristics are shared with
voters in WE. The Romanian case is an exception, with voters mainly
from the old cadres of the previous regime. The difference is that
most Far Right voters in the Balkans are peasants and blue-collar
workers with a high degree of religiosity.**
Voters of the Far Right, just as in WE, are young and male – the only
exception is the Greater Romania Party (*Partidul România Mare*, PRM)
voters, who are old and nostalgic for the Ceauşescu regime – former
cadres. Far Right voters are also highly religious, unlike in WE – a high

level of religiosity is typical for the entire region. The electorate of Far Right parties in the countries under analysis is comprised of peasants and blue-collar workers, unlike in WE, where they are mainly blue-collar workers. Again, this is due to regional specifics. The lack of a university education among Far Right voters is consistent with findings in WE.

4. **The legal framework controlling the banning of parties for reasons to do with hate speech, nationalist propaganda and revisionism is slowly being integrated into the legal systems of the countries analysed. In practice, however, the law is not enforced. The situation is best (in terms of compatibility and use in practice) in the EU countries – Romania and Bulgaria.**

   Laws are only being adopted in most countries and their enforcement is very lax. Nationalism and hate speech are not considered bad things. They are frequently promoted by a local media lacking in professionalism and journalistic ethics. Bulgaria and Romania are the only countries where a member of a political party has been before the court for hate speech. In spite of the laws regarding hate speech and inciteful activities, none of the parties have faced any threat of being banned.

5. **The strategy and tactics of the Far Right in the Balkans resemble those of WE.**

   In some cases, party politics and strategy resemble what one might find in WE parties – initially provocative and hostile and, once in power, with softened rhetoric to make the party more acceptable to the ordinary voter. The parties use demonstrations and rallies to attract attention, publish their newspapers and books, host television programmes and create websites, Facebook profiles, etc. The most successful parties use a confrontational style, provoke, come before the courts and are on the daily TV news. They charge that people are being robbed by politicians and declare themselves the only truthful representatives of the people, working in the people's interest instead of for self-aggrandizement.

6. **The research shows that most parties have centralized organizational structures and efficient mechanisms for enforcing party discipline; those which also possess charismatic leadership have the greatest success.**

   The organizational structure of the parties reveals a low level of democracy, with power given to the upper level of the hierarchy and the lower levels not invited to the decision process. In most cases, the leaders have exclusive positions and privileges and rule autocratically – in almost all cases, the leaders have been in office since the establishment of the party. The most successful parties possess charismatic leadership and strong party organization. Most parties do not have women as party cadres – the only party with women in top leadership posts is the National Front (*Balli Kombëtar*, BK).

7. **Far Right parties no longer have their own paramilitary structures. The only exception is the New Right and an alleged relation to the marginal political party New Generation Party–Christian Democratic (*Partidul Noua Generație–Creștin Democrat*, PNG–CD) in Romania.**
   There are many paramilitary organizations in the Balkan countries – currently, the most active seem to be in Albania, Serbia, Romania and Bulgaria. Nevertheless, none of these have active links with relevant Far Right parties in the countries in question. The only party which allegedly possesses links to such organizations is the PNG–CD of Gigi Becali, which is allegedly tied to the paramilitary organization New Right.

8. **The most significant collaboration is that between the mother party and its branches; any other cooperation between Far Right parties seems to be utopian.**
   The greatest cooperation between parties is visible between the mother parties and their branches abroad. The emergence of trans-Balkan Far Right groups is utopian because of grave differences, disagreements and, above all, a breed of nationalism not compatible with the nationalism of other parties. Far Right parties already in the EU also oppose the accession of Balkan States (and Turkey) to the EU.

   Analysis of the Far Right parties in Croatia, Serbia, Montenegro, Macedonia, Albania, Bulgaria and Romania shows that the main factors important for the success of these parties in these countries are charismatic leadership and strong party organization, the position and strategy of the dominant Right/Left party, the state-building process, a national minority or diaspora abroad and an electoral system; other factors (such as unemployment or new voter strength) play a supporting role. The international variable might also play a strong role in the (lack of) success of Far Right parties.

   The Far Right party family in the Balkans is in every respect a heterogeneous group. The *softer* radical Right variant would encompass the Internal Macedonian Revolutionary Organization–People's Party (*Vnatrešna Makedonska Revolucionerna Organizacija–Narodna Partija*, VMRO–NP), Ataka and possibly Serbian National Party (*Srpska narodna strana*, SNS) – the only parties to display nationalism purely in terms of internal homogenization, as opposed to external exclusivity. The *harder* extreme Right would include the SRS, Croatian Party of the Right (*Hrvatska Stranka Prava*, HSP), Serbian Radical Party of Dr. Vojislav Šešelj (SRS CG), BK, VMRO, PRM and PNG–CD – all parties exhibiting nationalism both in terms of external exclusivity and internal homogenization and so have an anti-system position. However, as has already been noted numerous times, these categorizations remain fluid and time-limited – some parties may be labelled as extremist, but, over time, their ideology, strategy and position may place them in the radical Right group. As research in WE has shown, once the parties are accepted as political partners, they soften and change their political profiles to suit the *ordinary* voter. The discussion as to whether there are actually two distinctive party families or only one is for further debate. The position of SNS remains unclear at present. In view of its membership and links to SRS, it should fall into radical Right category. However, the party profiles itself instead on social populism instead of national issues and has features resembling the Citizens for the European Development of Bulgaria (*Grazhdani za evropeysko razvitie na Balgariya*, GERB) in Bulgaria. The results of elections in Serbia and future developments in the EU accession effort will impact the future positioning of the party in the political party spectrum. SNS, as the new political player, is unpredictable. If successful in the upcoming elections, its presence will shake up the party system and create new configurations. Similarly, the position of HSP will be shaped by Croatia's accession to the EU and the position and strategy of the main political players on the Croatian political scene. If HSP was willing to increase its share of political power, it would have to moderate its views in order to become acceptable to the average voter. If it maintains its extreme positions, it will remain marginalized as a political party or could even disappear from the political scene altogether.

Despite the fact that nationalism prevailed during the 1990s in the Balkans and some countries found themselves at war, Far Right parties are not particularly successful in the region. The bearers of nationalism were the mainstream political parties behind independence in the countries and the transition – these political players left no space for Far Right parties. It was also during the 1990s that Far Right parties participated in coalition governments (SRS, PRM, the Party of Romanian National Unity (*Partidul Unităţii Naţionale a Românilor*, PUNR)); since 2000, no Far Right party has appeared in any government. The Far Right in most countries is non-existent or weak and remains at the fringes of the political spectrum; the only successful parties are the SRS, Ataka and PRM, but it is not clear that PRM will survive in the context of a new electoral system. The PRM would be able to regenerate itself if Romania decided to change its electoral laws, after the 2009 referendum which proposed altering legislative power.[1] Ataka still has a chance even in the modified electoral system – seats from single-member constituencies still make up only a small fraction of the parliamentary total.

Currently, the Far Right appears to be in retreat in the Balkans. However, the long integration process into Euro-Atlantic structures could arouse populism and scepticism (as already observed in Croatia), which could then lead to a radicalization of voters and more votes for Far Right parties. This process would nevertheless likely go hand in hand with the parties softening their views and shifting in the direction of the ideological centre. The research shows that the Far Right party family is a broad group with great inclusiveness and many differences. Further investigation is needed to understand the mechanism and strategies of the Far Right. It is the author's hope that this text will serve as a basic resource for further research.

Note

1 The population was consulted about turning the parliament into unicameral body. Even though most of the voters voted for downsizing the number of chambers from two to one and also downsizing the number of deputies to a maximum of 300 persons, the referendum is not binding.

References

(online documents accessed in the period January 2008–December 2010)

AIIS. (2003) *Albania and European Union: Perceptions and Realities*. Tirana: Albanian Institute for International Studies.

Antić, M. and Gruičić, M. D. (2007) The Parliamentary Election in Croatia, November 2007. *Electoral Studies*, 27(4), 752–755.

Arzheimer, K. and Carter, E. (2006) Political Opportunity Structures and Right-Wing Extremist Party Success. *European Journal of Political Research*, 45/2006, 419–443.

Ataka. (2005) *20 Principles of ATAKA Political Party*. Available online at www.ataka. bg/en/index.php?option=com_content&task=view&id=14&Itemid=27.

Ataka. (2005) *Ustav na politiceska partija Ataka*. Available online at www.ataka.bg/ index.php?option=com_content&task=view&id=3374&Itemid=98.

Backes, U. (2007) Meaning and Forms of Political Extremism in Past and Present. *Central European Political Studies Review*, IX(4), 242–262. Available online at www.cepsr.com/clanek.php?ID=316.

Backes, U. and Jesse, E. (2006) *Gefährdungen der Freiheit. Extremistische Ideologien im Vergleich*. Göttingen: Vandenhoeck & Ruprecht.

Backes, U., Jaskułovski, T. and Polese, A. (eds) (2009) *Totalitarismus und Transformation. Defizite der Demokratiekonsolidierung im Mittel- und Osteuropa*. Dresden: Vandenhoeck & Ruprecht.

Bâdescu, G., Kivu, M. and Robotin, M. (eds) (2005) *Barometer of Ethnic Relations 1994–2002. A Perspective of the Interethnic Climate of Romania*. Cluj: EDRC Publishing House.

Bâdulescu, A. (undated) *Şomajul în România. O analiză retrospectivă (1991–2005)*. Available online at www.ectap.ro/articole/40.pdf.

Barić, N. (2005) *Srpska pobuna u Hrvatskoj 1990–1995*. Zagreb: Golden marketing. Tehnička knjiga.

Barjarba, K. (2004) Migration and Ethnicity in Albania: Synergies and Interdependencies. *Brown Journal of World Affairs*, Summer/Fall 2004, XI(I). Available online at www. watsoninstitute.org/bjwa/archive/11.1/Essays/Barjarba.pdf.

Barzachka, N. (2009) *Mechanisms of Electoral System Choice: Bulgaria 1990, 1991, 2009*. Available online at www.irex.org/programs/iaro/research/08-09/Barzachka. pdf.

Becker, J. (1993) *Neo-Nazism: A New Threat to Europe?* London: Alliance for the Institute for Strategic and Defence Studies.

Beichelt, T. and Minkenberg, M. (2002a) Rechtsradikalismus in Osteuropa: Bilanz einer Debatte. *Osteuropa*, 52 Jg., 8/2002, 1056–1062.

Beichelt, T. and Minkenberg, M. (2002b) Rechtsradikalismus in Transformationsgesellschaften. Enstehungsbedingungen und Erklärungsmodell. *Osteuropa*, 52 Jg., 3/2002, 247–262.

Beqiri, I. (2002) *Nacionalizmi Shqiptar kërkon ribashkim kombëtar*. 1 November 2002, Pasqyra. Available online at www.pasqyra.com/arkivi/2002/01112002/faqe/nacionalizmishqiptarkerkonribashkimkombetar.htm.

Betz, H.-G. (1994) *Radical Right-Wing Populism in Western Europe*. New York: St. Martin Press.

Betz, H.-G. and Immerfall, S. (1998) *The New Politics of the Right. Neo-Populist Parties and Movements in Established Democracies*. New York: St. Martin's Press.

Biberaj, E. (1998) *Albania in Transition. The Rocky Road to Democracy*. Boulder: Westview Press.

Bieber, F. (2003) Montenegrin politics since the disintegration of Yugoslavia. In: Bieber, Florian (ed.), *Montenegro in Transition. Problems of Identity and Statehood*. Baden-Baden: Nomos Verlagsgesellschaft.

van Biezen, I. (2003) *Political Parties in New Democracies: Party Organisation in Southern and East-Central Europe*. London: Palgrave Macmillan.

BK. (1998) *Statuti i Partisë "Balli Kombëtar 1998*. Available online at www.ballikombit.org/Statusi.html.

BK. (2006) *Dekalogu. Programi i Ballit Kombëtar*. BK. Tirana. Available online at www.ballikombit.org/index.php?option=com_content&task=view&id=27&Itemid=39.

BK. (undated) *Platforma politike, ekonomike dhe sociale e partisë 'Balli Kombëtar'*. Available online at www.ballikombit.org/Platforma.html.

BKK. (2001) *Program i partisë Balli Kombëtar Kosovë*. Prishtinë 2001. Electronical version obtained by approaching BK.

Blamires, C. P. (2006) *World Fascism: A Historical Encyclopaedia*. Santa Barbara.

Buljan, I. and Duka, Z. (2003) *Izbori. Duh stranaka i duše političara. Vodič kroz hrvatsku političku scenu*. Zagreb: Profil.

Butterwegge, Ch. (2002) Traditioneller Rechtsextremismus im Osten – modernisierter Rechtsextremismus im Westen. *Osteuropa*, 52 Jg., 7/2002, 914–920.

Camus, J.-Y. (2007) The European Extreme Right and Religious Extremism. *Central European Political Science Review*, IX(4), 263–279.

Canovan, M. (1981) *Populism*. New York: Harcourt Brace Jovanovich.

Canovan, M. (1999) Trust the People! Populism and the Two Faces of Democracy. *Political Studies*, XLVII(2), 2–16.

Carter (2005) *The Extreme Right in Western Europe*. Manchester: Manchester University Press.

CEDIME-SE (2000) *Roma in Albania*. Available online at www.greekhelsinki.gr/pdf/cedime-se-albania-roma.doc.

Clewing, K. (1995) Zwischen Instrumentalisierung und Brückenfunktion. Die griechische Minderheit in Südalbanien als Faktor in der Albanienpolitik Athens. *Südosteuropa*, 44, 6–7/1995, 413–432.

Cohen, P. J. and Riesman, D. (1999) *Serbia's Secret War: Propaganda and the Deceit of History*. Texas University Press.

Čular, G (ur.) (2005) *Izbori i konsolidacija demokracije u Hrvatskoj*. Zagreb: Fakultet političkih znanosti sveučilišta u Zagrebu.

de Raadt, J., Hollanders, D. and Krouwel, A. (2004) *Varieties of Populism: An Analysis of the Programmatic Character of Six European Parties*, Working Papers Political Science, No. 2004/04, Vrije Universiteit Amsterdam.

Djurković, M. (2006) *Political Parties in Serbia. Source of Political Instability*, Swindon, Conflict Studies Research Centre. Available online at www.defac.ac.uk/colleges/csrc/document-listings/balkan/06(10)mj.pdf.

Dočekalová, P. (2006a) *Komparace krajní pravice v zemích západní a východní Evropy*. Dizertační práce Olomouc.

Dočekalová, P. (2006b) Komparace krajní pravice v západní a východní Evropě. In: Němec, J. and Šůstková, M. (eds), *III. Kongres českých politologů*. Praha-Olomouc: Česká společnost pro politologické vědy, pp. 261–275.

Duverger, M. (1972) Factors in a Two-Party and Multiparty System. In: *Party Politics and Pressure Groups*. New York: Thomas Y. Crowell, pp. 23–32.

Eatwell, R. (2003) Ten Theories of the Extreme Right. In: Merkel, P. H. and Weinberg, L. (eds), *Right-Wing Extremism in the Twenty-First Century*. London-Portland: Frank Cass, pp. 47–73.

Eatwell, R. and Mudde, C. (2004) *Western Democracies and the New Extreme Right Challenge*. Oxon: Routledge.

Eurobarometer (2005) *Eurobarometer 64. Nacionalni izveštaj. Hrvatska*. Available online at http://ec.europa.eu/public_opinion/archives/eb/eb64/eb64_hr_exec.pdf.

Fennema, M. (1997) Some Conceptual Issues and Problems in the Comparison of Anti-immigrant Parties in Western Europe. *Party Politics*, III(4), 473–528.

Frölich-Steffen, S. and Rensmann, L. (Hg.) (2005) *Populisten an der Macht. Populistische Regierungspateien in West- und Osteuropa*. Wien: Wilhelm Braumüller.

Frusetta, J. and Glont, A. (2009) Interwar Fascism and the Post-1989 Radical Right: Ideology, Opportunism and Historical Legacy in Bulgaria and Romania. *Communist and Post-Communist Studies,* 42(4), 551–571.

Gallagher, T. (2003) *Romania' s Greater Romania Party: Defying Political Categorisation?* Paper presented on ECPR Conference in Marburg, Germany, 23 September 2003. Available online at www.essex.ac.uk/ecpr/events/generalconference/marburg/papers/10/2/gallagher.pdf.

Gallagher, T. (2005) *Theft of a Nation. Romania since Communism*. London: C. Hurst & Company.

Gallup Balkan Monitor (2009) *Insights and Perceptions: Voices of the Balkan*. Gallup in Partnership with European Fund for the Balkans. Available online at www.balkan-monitor.eu/.

Givens, T. (2005) *Voting Radical Right in Western Europe*. Cambridge: Cambridge University Press.

Goati, V. (2001) *Elections in FRY. From 1990 to 1998. Will of People or Electoral Manipulation?* Beograd: CESID.

Golder, M. (2003) Explaining Variation in the Success of Extreme Right Parties in Western Europe. *Comparative Political Studies*, 36(4), 432–466.

Griffin, R. (2000) Revolution from the Right: Fascism. In: Parker, D. (ed.), *Revolutions and the Revolutionary Tradition in the West 1560–1991*. Oxon: Routledge, pp. 185–201. Available online at http://ah.brookes.ac.uk/resources/griffin/fasrevolution.pdf.

Grujić, J. (2006) *The Refugee Electorate: Past, Present and the Future*. Prague: Multicultural Centre Prague. Available online at http://aa.ecn.cz/img_upload/3bfc4 ddc48d13ae0415c78ceae108bf5/The_Refugee_Electorate_final_version.pdf.

Grün, M. (2002) Rechtsradikale Massenmobilisierung und "radikale Kontinuität" in Rumänien. *Osteuropa*, 52 Jg., 3/2002, 293–304.

Hainsworth, P. (2008) *The Extreme Right in Western Europe*. London: Routledge.

HB. (2006) *Program Hrvatskog bloka*. Hrvatski blok. Zagreb. Available online at http://hrvatski-blok.hr/doc1/program.pdf.

HB and HIP (2003) *Deklaracija izborne koalicije 'Za modernu Hrvatsku'*. Zagreb. Available online at http://hrvatski-blok.hr/doc1/Deklaracija.doc.

HČSP. (2007) Deklaracija opcega sabora starčevićanske mladeži HČSP-a. HČSP. Available online at www.hcsp.hr/priopcenja.php?subaction=showfull&id=1192350 474&archive=&start_from=&ucat=3&.

HČSP. (2007a) *Izborni program*. Available at www.hcsp.hr/priopcenja.php?subaction =showfull&id=1192350129&archive=&start_from=&ucat=3&.

HČSP. (2007b) *Temeljna načela*. Available at www.hcsp.hr/nacela.php.

HDZ 1990 – Programska Deklaracija. HDZ-1990. Mostar 2006. Available at www. hdz1990.org/dokumenti/Programskapercent20deklaracijapercent20HDZpercent 201990.doc.

HDZ. (2002) *Program Hrvatske demokratske zajednice*. Zagreb. Available online at www.hdz.hr/images/site/upload/program.pdf.

HIP (2001a) *Politički profil*. Zagreb. Available online at http://hidra.srce.hr/ arhiva/392/5980/www.hipnet.hr/kategorije.phppercent3fKATEGORIJA_ID percent3d33.html.

HIP (2001b) *Program stranke*. Zagreb. Available online at http://hidra.srce.hr/ arhiva/392/5980/www.hipnet.hr/kategorije.phppercent3fKATEGORIJA_ID percent3d19.html.

HPB (2004) *Programska deklaracija političke stranke Hrvatsko pravaško bratrstvo*. Arbanija 2004. Available online at www.hpb-makarska.com/content/view/6/11/.

HP-HPP. Temeljna načela. Available online at www.hrvatskipravasi.hr/index. php?id=m&lnk=2.

Hradečný, P. and Hladký, L. (2008) *Dějiny Albánie*. Praha: Nakladatelství Lidové noviny.

HSP (1861) *Temeljna načela Hrvatske stranke prava-1861*. Available online at www. hsp1861.hr/1temeljna.htm.

Hudelist, D. (2005) *Tuđman: Biografija*. Zagreb. Profil International.

Human Rights Watch (2003) *Broken Promises: Impediments to Refugee Return to Croatia*. Available online at www.unhcr.org/refworld/country,,HRW,,HRV,,3fe47a375,0.html.

Humoreanu, D. (undated) *His Blood Upon Your Children*. Available online at bu.edu/globalbeat/ROMANIA/romdaniela.html.

ICG. (2004) *Serbia' s U-Turn*. Europe Report N 154. Available online at www. crisisgroup.org/home/index.cfm?id=2552&l=1.

IDEA (1997) *Democracy in Romania*. Available online at www.idea.int/publications/
country/romania.cfm.

IDM (2007) *Albanian Perceptions on NATO Integration*. Tirana: Institute for Democracy
and Mediation.

IDMC (2008) *Croatia: Reforms Come Too Late for Most Remaining Serb IDPs*. Available
online at www.internal-displacement.org/8025708F004CE90B/(httpCountries)/7928
D486A14C897D802570A7004C7215?OpenDocument.

Ignazi, P. (1995) *The Re-Emergence of the Extreme Right in Europe*. Reihe Politikwis-
senschaft, no. 21. Wien: Institut für Höhere Studien. Available at www.ihs.ac.at/
publications/pol/pw_21.pdf.

Ignazi, P. (1996) *New Challenges: Post-Materialism and the Extreme Right*. Estudios
No. 91. Madrid: Instituto Juan March de Estudies e Investigaciones.

Ignazi, P. (2003) *Extreme Right Parties in Western Europe*. Oxford: Oxford University
Press.

Ionescu, G. and Gellner, E. (1970) *Populism. Its Meanings and National Characteristics*.
London: Weidenfeld and Nicolson.

Jackman, R. and Volpert, K. (1996) Conditions Favouring Parties of the Extreme Right
in Western Europe. *British Journal of Political Science*, 26, 501–521.

Jane's World Insurgency and Terrorism (2004) Issue 20. Surrey, UK.

Jano, D. (2008) *On Parties and Party System in Albania: What Implications for
Democr*acy. Central European Case Studies Vol. 2. Karacsony, G. and Smuk, P.
(eds) Gyor: Universitas – Gyor, pp. 85–103. Nonprofit Kft. Available online at
http://papers.ssrn.com/sol3/papers.cfm?abstract_id=1154507.

Jelavich, Ch. (1983) Serbian Textbooks: Toward Greater Serbia or Yugoslavia? *Slavic
Review*, 42(4), 601–619.

Jesuit, D. and Mahler, V. (2004) *Electoral Support for Extreme Right-Wing Parties: A
Subnational Analysis of Western European Elections in the 1990s*. Luxembourg
Income Study Working Paper Series, Working Paper No. 391. Available online at
www.lisproject.org/publications/liswps/391.pdf.

Jovanović, M. (2005) Izborni prag i stranački sistem. In: Z. Lutovac (ed.), *Političke
stranke u Srbiji: Struktura i funkcionisanje*. Beograd: Friedrich Ebert Stiftung/
Institut društvenih nauka.

Karagiannopoulou (2004) *Party System and Cleavages in pre-Communist Albania.
The kaleidoscope of the German and Greek diplomaty*. Genehmigte Dissertation.
Darmstadt.

Karasimeonov, G. (2005) *Political Parties. Development in Bulgaria*. Sofia: Institute
for political and legal studies. Available online at http://ipls.dir.bg/Barpercent2001-
03.2005percent20E.pdf.

Karasimeonov, G. (ed.) (2004) *Political Parties and the Consolidation of Democracy
in South Eastern Europe*. Sofia: Fridrich Ebert Stiftung.

Karasimeonov, G. (ed.) (2005) *Organisational Structures and Internal Party Democracy in South Eastern Europe*. Sofia: Gorex Press.

Karpat, C. (2006) *Presidentil Elections in Bulgaria: Full Details*. 15.10.2006. Axis
Information and Analysis. Global Challenges Research. Available online at www.
axisglobe.com/article.asp?article=1097.

Kasapović, M. (1996) 1995 Parliamentary Elections in Croatia. *Electoral Studies*, XV(2), 269–282.

Kitschelt, H. (1995) *Radical Right in Western Europe. A Comparative Analysis.* Michigan: University of Michigan Press.

Kjosev, S. (2007) Unemployment in the Republic of Macedonia – Specifics and Possible Solutions. *Facta universitatis*, Series: Economics and Organisation, 4(2), 153–160. Available online at http://facta.junis.ni.ac.rs/eao/eao200702/eao200702-07.pdf.

Kneblová, E. (2009) Změna volebního systému v Albánii v roce 2009 a její dopad na parlamentní volby. *European Electoral Studies*, 4(2), 172–182.

Komšić, J. (2006) *Dileme demokratske nacije i autonomije. Ogledi u političkoj tranziciji u Srbiji.* Beograd: Službeni glasnik.

Kopeček, L. (2007) Far Right in Europe. *Central European Political Studies Review*, IX, Part 4, 280–293. Available online at www.cepsr.com/index.php?ID=33.

Kowalsky, W. and Schroeder, W. (1994) *Rechtsextremismus: Einführung und Forschungsbilanz.* Opladen: Westdeutscher Verlag.

Lachauer, Ch. (2005) *Die dunkle Seite Europas. Rechtsextreme auf dem Weg zum politischen Akteur? Netzwerkbildung der Rechten in der Europäischen Union.* Marburg: Tectum Verlag.

Lenkova, M. (ed.) (1998) *"Hatespeech" in the Balkans.* Vienna: The International Helsinki Federation for Human Rights. Available online at www.greekhelsinki.gr/pdf/hatespeech.pdf.

Light, D. and Phinnemore, D. (eds) (2001) *Post-Communist Romania: Coming to Terms with Transition.* Houndmills: Palgrave Macmillan.

Linz, J. J. and Stepan, A. (1996) *Problems of Democratic Consolidation. Southern Europe, South America and Post-Communist Europe.* Baltimore and London: The Johns Hopkins University Press.

Lubbers, M., Gijsberts, M. and Scheepers, P. (2002) Extreme Right-Wing Voting in Western Europe. *European Journal of Political Research*, 41, 345–378.

Lutovac, Z. (ed.) (2006) *Demokratija u političkim strankama Srbije.* Beograd: Institut društvenih nauka.

Maegerle, A. (2009) *Rechts am Rand in Osteuropa. Ein überblick über osteuropäische Rechtsaußenparteien.* Available online at www.bpb.de/themen/94RSX4.html.

Mahoney, J. and Goertz, G. (2004) The Possibility Principle: Choosing Negative Cases in Comparative Perspective. *American Political Science Review*, 98(4), 653–669.

Mammone, A. (2009) *Italian Neo-Fascism from 1943 to the Present Day.* Oxon: Routledge.

Mareš, M. (2001) Moravismus a extremismus. *Středoevropské politické studie*, 4, III, podzim 2001. Available online at www.cepsr.com.

Mareš, M. (2003) *Pravicový extremismus a radikalismus v ČR.* Brno: Barrister & Principal.

Mareš, M. (2009) The Extreme Right in Eastern Europe and Territorial Issues. *Central European Political Science Review*, XI, Part 2–3, 82–106.

Mareš, M. and Stojar, R. (2011) Extreme Right Paramilitary Units in Eastern Europe. In: Mammone, A., Godin, E. and Jenkins, B. (eds), *Mapping the Far Right in Contemporary Europe: Local, National, Comparative, Transnational.* Oxford: Berghahn.

Marginean, I. (2004) *Quality of Life in Romania*. Bucharest: The Expert Publishing House. Available online at www.iccv.ro/oldiccv/romana/articole/quality.pdf.

Maškarinec, P. (2008) Volby do Evropského parlamentu 2007 v Bulharsku. *European Electoral Studies*, 3(1), 113–129. Available online at http://ispo.fss.muni.cz/uploads/EVS/005/EVS_3_1_7.pdf.

Mazzoleni, G., Stewart, J. and Horsfield, B. (2003) *The Media and Neo-Populism. A Contemporary Comparative Analysis*. London: PRaeger.

Meguid, B. M. (2005) Competition Between Unequals: The Role of Mainstream Party Strategy in Niche Party Success. *American Political Science Review*, 99(3), 347–359.

Meguid, B. M. (2010) *Party Competition Between Unequals. Strategies and Electoral Fortunes in Western Europe*. New York: Cambridge University Press.

Merkl, P. H. and Weinberg, L. (1997) *The Revival of Right-Wing Extremism in the Ninetees*. Oxon: Frank Cass and Co. Ltd.

Mihić, V. (2005) Povezanost biračkog opredeljenja i nekih političkih stavova stanovnika Vojvodine. *Psihologija*, 38(2). Available online at www.doiserbia.nb.rs/img/doi/0048-5705/2005/0048-57050502197M.pdf.

Mikić, L. (2006) *Croatia: Challenges for Sustainable Return of Ethnic Serb Refugees*. Vukovar: Center for Peace, Legal Advice and Psychosocial Assistance. Available online at www.minorityrights.org/download.php?id=100.

Milanović, B. (2004) *Ko je glasao za radikale?*, Vol. 1. Beograd: Prizma, pp. 10–18. Available online at www.b92.net/feedback/misljenja/analize/radikali.php.

Milardović, A., Lalić, D. and Malenica, Z. (2007) *Kriza i transformacija političkih stranaka*. Zagreb: Centar za politološka istraživanja.

Minkenberg, M. (2008) *The Radical Right in Europe*. Gütersloh: Bertelsmann Stiftung.

Minkenberg, M., Sucker, D. and Wenniger, A. (2006) *Radikale Rechte und Fremdenfeindlichkeit in Deutschland und Polen. Nationale und europäische Perspektiven*. Bonn: Informationszentrum Sozialwissenschaften.

Miščević, N. (2006) *Ante Starčević – između liberalizma i rasizma. Novi list* (Rijeka 25 February 2006). Available at www.novilist.hr/default.asp?WCI=Pretrazivac&WCU=285A28602863285A2863285A28582858285E28632863286328592860285828 5E285B2858286328632863286328592863E.

Mudde, C. (1995) Right-Wing Extremism Analyzed. A Comparative Analysis of the Ideologies of Three Alleged Right-Wing Extremist Parties (NPD, NDP, CP'86). *European Journal of Political Research*, 27.2, 203–224. Available online at http://works.bepress.com/cas_mudde/19.

Mudde, C. (2000a) Extreme-Right Parties in Eastern Europe. *Patterns of Prejudice*, 34(1), 5–27.

Mudde, C. (2000b) *The Ideology of the Extreme Right*. Manchester: Manchester University Press.

Mudde, C. (2002a) In the Name of the Peasantry, the Proletariat, and the People: Populisms in Eastern Europe. In: Mény, Y. and Surel, Y. (eds), *Democracies and the Populist Challenge*. Oxon: Palgrave.

Mudde, C. (2002b) Warum ist der Rechtsradikalismus in Osteuropa so *schwach*? *Osteuropa*, 52 Jg., 5/2002, 626–630.

Mudde, C. (2004) The Populist Zeitgeist. *Government and Opposition*. Oxford: Blackwell Publishing, pp. 541–563.

Mudde, C. (2007) *Populist Radical Right Parties in Europe*. Cambridge: Cambridge University Press.

Mudde, C. (ed.) (2005) *Racist Extremism in Central and Eastern Europe*. Oxon: Routledge.

Panizza, F. (ed.) (2005) *Populism and the Mirror of Democracy*. London: Verso.

Pavlović, S. (2003) Who Are Montenegrins? Statehood, Identity, and Civic Society. In: Bieber, F. (ed.) *Montenegro in Transition. Problems of Identity and Statehood*. Baden-Baden: Nomos Verlagsgesellschaft.

Payne, S. G. (2001) *A History of Fascism: 1914–1945*. London: Routledge.

Petrovic, R. and Blagojevic, M. (1992) *The Migration of Serbs and the Montenegrins from Kosovo and Metohija: Results of the Survey Conducted in 1985–1986*. Beograd: Serbian Academy of Sciences and Arts. Available online at www.rastko.rs/kosovo/istorija/kosovo_migrations/index.html.

Pettifer, J. (2001) *The Greek Minority in Albania in the Aftermath of Communism*. G97 Conflict Studies Research Center, July 2001. Available online at www.csrc.ac.uk.

Phillips, J. (2004) *Macedonia. Warlords and Rebels in the Balkans*. London: U.B. Tauris.

Pleše, Mladen. (2003) Anto Djapić and Miroslav Tuđman – Together in the Elections. *Nacional*. 10 June. Available at www.nacional.hr/en/articles/view/18225/.

Popis stanovništva, domaćinstava i stanova u 2003 (2004) Podgorica: Republika Crna Gora Zavod za statistiku. Available at www.monstat.cg.yu/engPopis.htm.

PRM. (2008) *National Doctrine 2008*. Available online at www.prm.org.ro/index. php?option=com_content&task=category§ionid=13&id=37&Itemid=211.

PRM. (undated) *Statutul partidului România Mare*. Partidul Romania Mare. Available online at www.prm.org.ro/node/2.

Prtina, S. (2004) Srbsko a parlamentní volby: Výsledek, který nešel změnit. *Mezinárodní politika*, roč. XXVII, č. 3, 2004, 11–12.

Ramet, S. (ed.) (1999) *The Radical Right in Central and Eastern Europe Since 1989*. Pennsylvania: Pennsylvania State University Press.

Roberts, G. K. (1994) Extremism in Germany: Sparrows or Avalanche? *European Journal of Political Research*, 25(4), 461–482.

Rose, R. and Munro, N. (2003) *Elections and Parties in New European Democracies*. Washington, DC: CQ Press.

Ryan, N. (2004) *Into a World of Hate. A Journey Among the Extreme Right*. New York: Routledge.

Salat, L. (ed.) (2008) *Politici de integrare a minorităţilor naţionale din România. Aspecte legale şi instituţionale într-o perspectivă comparată*, Cluj, Edit. CRDE. Available online at www.edrc.ro/publication_details.jsp?publication_id=27.

Samardžić, S., Nakarada, R. and Kovačević, Đ. (1998) *Lavirinti krize. Preduslovi demokratske transformacije SR Jugoslavije*. Beograd: Institut za evropske studije.

Savkova, L. (2005) *Election Briefing No. 21. Europe and the Parliamentary Election in Bulgaria*, 25th June 2005, University of Sussex, Sussex European Institute. Available online at www.sussex.ac.uk/sei/documents/epern-eb-bulgaria_2005.pdf.

Savkova, L. (2007) *European Parliament Election Briefing No. 23. The European Parliament Elections in Bulgaria*, 20 May 2007. University of Sussex, Sussex

European Institute. Available online at www.sussex.ac.uk/sei/documents/epern-ep-bulgaria07.pdf.

Schanovsky, H. (1997) *Rechtsextremismus und neue Rechte. Völkischer Paramilitarismus und rechtsradikale Ästhetik. Mit einer empirischen Untersuchung zum Thema rechte Denk-und Wertmuster bei den Studenten der Johannes-Kepler-Universität Linz.* Dissertation zur Erlangung des Doktorgrades an der Geisteswissenschaftlichen Fakultät der Universität Salzburg. Salzburg.

Schmidt-Neke, M. (2001) Die Normalität als Ereignis: die Parlamentswahlen in Albanien. *Südosteuropa,* 50(7–9), 324–345.

Schuppener, G. (Hrsg.) (2008) *Sprache des Rechtsextremismus. Spezifika der Sprache rechtsextremistischer Publikationen und rechter Musik.* Edition Hamouda Wissenschaftsverlag.

Šedo, J. (2007) *Volební systémy postkomunistických zemí.* Brno: ISPO.

Segert, D. (2002) Viel weniger Rechtsradikalismus, als zu erwarten wäre. Kritische Anmerkungun zu einem interessanten Vergleich. *Osteuropa,* 52 Jg., 5/2002, 621–625.

Šešelj, V. (2000) *Hajka na heretika.* Beograd: Srpska radikalna stranka.

Šešelj, V. (2002) *Ideologija srpskog nacionalizma,* Beograd: Velika Srbija. Available online at (www.srs.org.yu/index.php?list=izda).

Šešelj, V. (2007) *Ili Karlin svedok ili smrt.* Beograd.

Šesták, M., Tejchman, M., Havlíková, L., Hladký, L. and Pelikán, J. (1998) *Dějiny jihoslovanských zemí.* Praha: Nakladatelství Lidové noviny.

Shafir, M. (2008) Rotten Apples, Bitter Pears: And Updated Motivational Typology of Romania's Radical Right's Anti-Semitic Postures in Post-Communism. *Journal for the Study of Religions and Ideologies,* 7 (21 Winter), 149–187.

Šiber, I. (2007) *Političko ponašanje. Istražianja hrvatskog društva.* Zagreb: Politička kultura nakladno-istraživački zavod.

Smilov, D. and Jileva, E. (undated) *The Politics of Bulgarian Citizenship: National Identity, Democracy and Other Uses.* Available online at www.law.ed.ac.uk/cit-modes/files/bulgaria.pdf.

Smrčková, M. (2009) Comparison of Radical Right-Wing Parties in Bulgaria and Romania: The National Movement of Ataka and the Great Romania Party. *Central European Political Science Review,* XI(1), 48–65.

SNSD (not dated). *Program saveza nezavisnih socijalnih demokrata.* Available online at www.snsd.org/lat_program.html.

Spiro, B. (2004) *Pan-Albanianism: How Big a Threat to Balkan Stability?* ICG Europe n. 153, 25 February 2004. Available at www.crisisweb.org.

SRS. (1991) *Program Declaration of SRS from 1991.* Available online at www.helsinki.org.yu/doc/programmepercent20declaration.doc.

SRS. (1996) *Statut Srpske radikalne stranke 1996.* Microsoft Word document obtained at the Central SRS office in Zemun, Belgrade.

SRS. (undated) *Program Srpske radikalne stranke.* (Programme of SRS) Word document from SRS.

SRS. (undated) *Programma Serbskoj radikaljnoj partii.* Available online at www.srs.org.yu/onama/progru.php.

Stefanova, B. (2007) *Testing Theories of Radical Right Voting: Social Structure versus Political Agenda and Electoral Support for the Attack Party in Bulgaria.* Prepared for delivery at the Annual Meeting of the APSA August 2007. Available online at www.allacademic.com//meta/p_mla_apa_research_citation/2/0/9/6/3/pages209637/p209637-1.php.

Stefanova, B. (2008) The 2007 European Elections in Bulgaria and Romania. *Electoral Studies,* 27, 547–577.

Stojar, R. (2006) Vnitřní makedonská revoluční organizace (VMRO). In: Souleimanov, E. (ed.), *Terorismus. Válka proti státu.* Praha: Eurolex Bohemia.

Stojarová, V. and Emerson, P. (2010) *Party Politics in the Western Balkans.* Oxon: Routledge.

Stojarová, V., Šedo, J., Chytilek, R. and Kopeček, L. (2007) *Political Parties in Central and Estern Europe. In Search of Consolidation.* Stockholm: IDEA. Available online at www.idea.int/publications/pp_c_and_e_europe/index.cfm.

Stojiljković, Z. (2006) *Partijski sistem Srbije.* Beograd: JP Službeni glasnik.

Strmiska, M. (2000) Utváření rumunského multipartismu (1990–1999). Pluralita a polarita rumunského systému politických stran. In: *Středoevropské politické studie* 1/II zima 2000. Available online at www.cepsr.com/clanek.php?ID=130.

Strmiska, M. (2001a) Major Poles, "Third Parties" And Bulgarian Multipartism. In: *Středoevropské politické studie,* 1/111/ Winter. Available online at www.cepsr.com/clanek.php?ID=92.

Strmiska, M. (2001b) Parties, Poles, Alliances and Romanian Pluralism, 1990–2000. In: *Středoevropské politické studie,* 2/111/spring 2001. Available online at www.cepsr.com/clanek.php?ID=84.

Sum, P. (2008) *The Radical Right in Romania: Political Party Evolution and the Distancing of Romania from Europe.* Paper prepared for presentation at the 104th Annual Meeting of the American Political Science Association, Boston, August 28–31, 2008. Available online at www.allacademic.com/one/www/www/index.php?click_key=1.

Taggart, P. (2004) Populism and Representative Politics in Contemporary Europe. *Journal of Political Ideologies,* IX(3), 269–288.

Tavanier, Y. B. (2005) Massive Attack. In: *Transitions Online.* 8.7.2005. Available online at www.tol.org/client/article/14263-massive-attack.html.

The Stephen Roth Institute (2005) *Republic of Serbia 2005.* Available online at www.tau.ac.il/Anti-Semitism/asw2005/serbia.htm.

Thieme, T. (2007) Hammer*, Sichel, Hakenkreuz. Parteipolitischer Extremismus in Osteuropa. Entstehungsbedingungen und Erscheinungsformen.* Dissertation. Berlin.

Thomas, R. (1999) *Serbia under Milošević. Politics in the 1990s.* London: C. Hurst & Company.

Trifković, S. (1998) *Ustaša – Croatian Separatism and European Politics 1929–1945.* London: The Lord Byron Foundation for Balkan Studies.

Tulejkov, D. (2001) *Obrečeno rodoljubie VMRO v Pirinsko 1919–1934.* Blagoevgrad: MNI.

UNDP Hrvatska (2007) *Kvaliteta života u Hrvatskoj. Regionalne nejednakosti.* Zagreb: UNDP. Available online at www.undp.hr/upload/file/167/83979/FILENAME/Regionalne_nejednakosti.pdf.

United Nations (UN) (1965) *International Convention on the Elimination of All Forms of Racial Discrimination*. Adopted and opened for signature and ratification by General Assembly Resolution 2106(XX) of 21 December 1965 entry into force 4 January 1969. Available online at www.bayefsky.com/treaties/cerd.php.

Urbat, J. (2007) *Rechtspopulisten an der Macht. Silvio Berlusconis Forza Italia im neuen italienischen Parteiensystem*. Hamburg: Lit Verlag.

Ustav na VMRO-Bugarsko nacionalno dvizenje (2007). Available online at http://vmro.bg/modules.php?name=Ustav.

Van der Brug, W. and Fennema, M. (2007) What Causes People to Vote for a Radical-Right Party? A Review of Recent Work. *International Journal of Public Opinion Research*, 19(4), 474–487.

van der Brug, W., Fennema, M. and Tillie, J. (2005) Why Some Anti-immigrant Parties Fail and Others Succeed. A Two-Step Model of Aggregate Electoral Support. *Comparative Political Studies*, 38, 537–573.

Vejvodová, P. (2008) Autonomní nacionalismus. In: *Rexter* 02/2008. Available online at www.rexter.cz/autonomni-nacionalismus/2008/11/01/.

Vickers, M. (2002) *The Cham Issue Albanian National & Property Claims in Greece*. G109, Conflict Studies Research Center, April 2002. Available online at www.csrc.ac.uk.

Vickers, M. and Pettifer, J. (1997) *Albania: From Anarchy to Balkan Identity*. New York: New York University Press.

VMRO (undated). *Programa VMRO*. Available online at http://vmro.bg/modules.php?name=Programa.

VMRO-NP (2006) *Idnina namesto sudbina. Izborna programa*. Available online at www.vmro-np.org.mk/upload/dokumenti/ip2006vmronp.pdf.

Weichsel, V. (2002) Rechtsradikalismus in Osteuropa – ein Phänomen *sui generis*? *Osteuropa*, 52 Jg., 5/2002, 612–620.

Williams, M. H. (2006) *The Impact of Radical Right-Wing Parties in West European Democracies*. New York: Palgrave Macmillan.

Williams, P. (2008) *Violent Non-State Actors and National and International Security*. International Relations and Security Network. Available online at www.humansecuritygateway.com/documents/ISN_ViolentNon-StateActors.pdf.

Important websites

Croatia

Anarchist journal Ispod pločnika www.ispodplocnika.net/
Anarchist Library http://infoshop-dislexia.blogspot.com/
Anarchist web Što čitaš? www.stocitas.org/
Anarhistički sajam knjiha www.ask-zagreb.org/
Ante Gotovina www.antegotovina.com/
Center for Anarchist Studies http://anarhizam.hr
Croatian Agrarian Party (Hrvatska seljačka stranka, HSS) www.hss.hr/onama_prog.php?id=1
Croatian Bloc (Hrvatski blok, HB) http://hrvatski-blok.hr/

Croatian Democratic Union (Hrvatska demokratska zajednica, HDZ) www.hdz.hr/
Croatian Elections (Hrvatski izborni podaci) www.fpzg.hr/hip/
Croatian Party of the Right (Hrvatska stranka prava, HSP) www.hsp.hr/
Croatian Party of the Right (in Bavaria) www.hsp-bavarska.de/hsp/index.php
Croatian Party of the Right 1861 (Hrvatska stranka prava-1861) www.hsp1861.hr/
Croatian Party of the Right dr. Ante Starčević www.hsp-ante-starcevic.hr/
Croatian Pure Party of the Right (Hrvatska čista stranka prava, HSČP) www.hcsp.hr/
Croatian Right-Wing Brotherhood (Hrvatsko pravaško bratstvo, HPB) www.hpb-makarska.com/
Croatian Right-Wing Movement (Hrvatski pravaši – Hrvatski pravaški pokret, HP-HPP) www.hrvatskipravasi.hr/
Croatian Statistical Office (Državni zavod za statistiku) www.dzs.hr/
Croatian True Revival (Hrvatski istinski preporod, HIP) http://hidra.srce.hr/arhiva/392/5980/www.hipnet.hr/
Hrvatska kulturna zakladna www.hkz.hr/
Mreža anarhosindikalista i anarchosindikalistkinja www.masa-hr.org/
Party of Croatian Right http://shp.bizhat.com/onama.html
Simply Croatian (Jedino Hrvatska) www.jedinohrvatska.hr/
Sociological Institute www.instituti-sociologjise.org/files/INDEX.HTML

Serbia

Antiglobalizam www.antiglobalizam.com/
Blood and Honour Serbia (Krv i čast Srbija) www.bhserbia.org/
Delije www.oaza.rs/sport/delije/
Freedom fight (Pokret za slobodu) http://freedomfight.net
Serbian national movement 1389 (Srpski narodni pokret 1389) www.1389.org.rs
Serbian national movement us 1389 (Srpski narodni pokret naši 1389 www.snp1389.rs
Serbian Progressive Party (Srpska napredna stranka, SNS) www.sns.org.rs
Serbian Radical Party (Srpska radikalna stranka, SRS) www.srs.org.yu/index.php
Serbian Statistical Office (Republički zavod za statistiku) http://webrzs.statserb.sr.gov.yu/axd/index.php
Vojislav Šešelj www.vojislavŠešelj.org.yu/

Kosovo

AKSh http://akshalb.ifrance.com/
Army for the Independence of Kosovo (Ushtria për Pavarësinë ě Kosovës UPK) http://sweb.cz/messin/upk.htm
Serbianna www.serbianna.com/

Montenegro

Montenegrin Statistical Office (Zavod za statistiku Crne Gore) www.monstat.cg.yu/
Republika Crna Gora Zavod za statistiku (2004) *Popis stanovništva, domačinstava i stanova u 2003*. Podgorica 2004. www.monstat.cg.yu/engPopis.htm
Serbian National Party (Srpska Narodna stranka, SNS) www.sns.cg.yu

Serbian Radical Party (Stranka srpskih radikala, SRS) www.srpskaradikalnastranka. org.rs

Albania

Abas Ermenji www.ermenji.org/
AKSh http://akshalb.ifrance.com/statuti.htm
Albanian Electoral Commision (Komisioni Qendror i Zgjedhjeve) www.cec.org.al/
Albanian Statistical Office (Instituti i Statistikës. Republika ë Shqipërisë) www.instat. gov.al/
Balli i Kombit http://ballikombit.albanet.org/
FBKSh www.fbksh-aksh.org/
Institute of Sociology www.instituti-sociologjise.org/files/INDEX.HTML
Political Party G99 www.g99.org/

Macedonia

Democratic Albanian Party (Partija Demokratik Shqiptare, PDSh) www.pdsh.org/; www.gurra-pdsh.org/
VMRO – National party (VMRO-Narodna partija) www.vmro-np.org.mk/#

Bulgaria

Anarchist Federation in Bulgaria http://anarchy.bg/istoria.html
Anarcho-biblioteka http://lib.a-bg.net/
Ataka Journal www.vestnikataka.com/
Ataka www.ataka.bg/
Bulgarski nacionalni sajuz http://bg.bgns.net/
Dvizenie vojni na Tangra www.voininatangra.org/modules/news/
Electoral Commission Bulgaria 2005 elections http://2005izbori.org/results/index.html
Free education http://freeeducation-orm.blogspot.com/
GERB www.gerb.bg/
Indimedya Bulgaria http://bulgaria.indymedia.org/
National Statistical Insitute www.nsi.bg/index.php
Parliament www.parliament.bg/
Slobodna misl http://sm.a-bg.net/
TV SKAT www.tvskat.net/
VMRO http://vmro.bg/

Romania

Census 2002 http://recensamant.referinte.transindex.ro/
Electoral Results 1990–2004 http://alegeri.referinte.transindex.ro/
George Becali Personal Webpage www.georgebecali.ro/blog/
Institut for Public Policies www.ipp.ro/pagini/index.php
Metro Media Transylvania www.mmt.ro/en/main.html
National Statistical Office www.insse.ro/cms/rw/pages/index.ro.do
PNG-CD www.png.ro/

PRM www.prm.org.ro/
Resource Centre for Etnocultural Diversities www.edrc.ro/
România Mare www.romare.ro/
Romanian Social Data Archive www.roda.ro/en/en11.htm
Tricolorur www.ziarultricolorul.ro/

Others

Adam Carr Archive http://psephos.adam-carr.net/
Anarchist Balkan Bookfair http://balkanbookfair.blogspot.com/
Anarcho-syndikalist web www.inicijativa.org/
Anarkismo www.anarkismo.net/about_us
Eurobarometer http://ec.europa.eu/public_opinion/index_en.htm
Euronat www.euronat.org/
Europe of Freedom and Democracy www.efdgroup.eu/
European National Front www.europeannationalfront.org/
Eurostat http://epp.eurostat.ec.europa.eu/portal/page/portal/eurostat/home/
Flemish Interest www.vlaamsbelang.org/
Gallup International www.gallup-bbss.com/index.php?id=127903188050&
IPU Database www.ipu.org/
Merriam-Webster's Online Dictionary www.meriam-webster.com/dictionary
MIPT Terrprism Knowledge Base. www.tkb.org/Incident.jsp?incID=35446
Stand Up to Hate http://standuptohate.blogspot.com/
Stormfront www.stormfront.org/forum/
Venice commission www.venice.coe.int
Women in Leadership www.guide2womenleaders.com/index.html

Index

EU authorised representative for GPSR:
Easy Access System Europe, Mustamäe tee 50,
10621 Tallinn, Estonia
gpsr.requests@easproject.com

www.ingramcontent.com/pod-product-compliance
Lightning Source LLC
Chambersburg PA
CBHW052008270326
41929CB00015B/2832